American Cooking: The Great West

Foods of the World

American Cooking: The Great West

by
Jonathan Norton Leonard
and the Editors of
TIME-LIFE BOOKS
Photography by
Mark Kauffman, Richard Meek
and Ted Streshinsky

TIME-LIFE BOOKS, NEW YORK

THE AUTHOR: Jonathan Norton Leonard *(far left),* for 20 years Science Editor of TIME magazine, now freelances at his home in Hastings-on-Hudson, New York. He has written 15 books, including *Latin-American Cooking* and *American Cooking: New England* in the FOODS OF THE WORLD library, *Planets* in the LIFE SCIENCE LIBRARY and *Ancient America* in the TIME-LIFE BOOKS' GREAT AGES OF MAN series. Leonard's research for *American Cooking: The Great West* took him on gastronomic tours totaling some 5,000 miles.

THE CONSULTANT: James Beard, the leading authority on regional American foods, served as special consultant for this book. He has written *Delights and Prejudices* and *The James Beard Cook Book,* among many others.

THE PHOTOGRAPHERS: Mark Kauffman *(far left),* a former LIFE staff photographer, took the studio pictures for *American Cooking: The Great West.* His other books in the FOODS OF THE WORLD library include *The Cooking of Provincial France, American Cooking, Classic French Cooking* and *American Cooking: Southern Style.* Richard Meek *(center)* was a field photographer for this book. His work also appeared in three previous volumes of the FOODS OF THE WORLD library: *The Cooking of Scandinavia, The Cooking of the Caribbean Islands* and *American Cooking: The Northwest.* Ted Streshinsky *(right)* also took field pictures. A widely traveled freelance photographer, he has done work for TIME, LIFE, FORTUNE and SPORTS ILLUSTRATED.

THE CONSULTING EDITOR: The late Michael Field, who supervised the recipe writing, was one of America's best-known culinary experts. His books include *Michael Field's Cooking School* and *All Manner of Food.*

THE COVER: A typical dinner of the Great West features charcoal-broiled steak and baked potatoes—in this case, a two-inch-thick T-bone and stuffed potatoes topped with melted Cheddar cheese *(Recipe Index).* The tile evokes the region's Spanish-Mexican background.

TIME-LIFE BOOKS

EDITOR: Jerry Korn
Executive Editor: A. B. C. Whipple
Planning Director: Oliver E. Allen
Text Director: Martin Mann
Art Director: Sheldon Cotler
Chief of Research: Beatrice T. Dobie
Director of Photography: Robert G. Mason
Associate Planning Director: Byron Dobell
Assistant Text Directors: Ogden Tanner, Diana Hirsh
Assistant Art Director: Arnold C. Holeywell
Assistant Chief of Research: Martha T. Goolrick
Assistant Director of Photography: Melvin L. Scott

PUBLISHER: Joan D. Manley
General Manager: John D. McSweeney
Business Manager: John Steven Maxwell
Sales Director: Carl G. Jaeger
Promotion Director: Beatrice K. Tolleris
Public Relations Director: Nicholas Benton

FOODS OF THE WORLD

SERIES EDITOR: Richard L. Williams
EDITORIAL STAFF FOR AMERICAN COOKING: THE GREAT WEST:
Associate Editor: William Frankel
Text Editor: L. Robert Tschirky
Picture Editor: Grace Brynolson
Designers: William Rose, Albert Sherman
Staff Writers: Gerry Schremp, Gerald Simons
Chief Researcher: Sarah B. Brash
Researchers: Patricia Mohs, Wendy Rieder, Lyn Stallworth, Toby Solovioff, Barbara Ensrud, Clara Nicolai
Test Kitchen Chef: John W. Clancy
Test Kitchen Staff: Tina Cassell, Leola Spencer
Design Assistant: Anne B. Landry

EDITORIAL PRODUCTION
Production Editor: Douglas B. Graham
Quality Director: Robert L. Young
Assistant: James J. Cox
Copy Staff: Florence Keith
Picture Department: Dolores A. Littles, Joan Lynch, Barbara S. Simon
Studio: Gloria duBouchet

The text for this book was written by Jonathan Norton Leonard, the recipes by Michael Field and Gerry Schremp, and other material by the staff. Valuable assistance was given by these individuals and departments of Time Inc.: Editorial Production, Robert W. Boyd Jr., Margaret T. Fischer; Editorial Reference, Peter Draz; Picture Collection, Doris O'Neil; Photographic Laboratory, George Karas; TIME-LIFE News Service, Murray J. Gart; Correspondents Helena L'Hommedieu (Albuquerque); Guy Shipler Jr. (Carson City); Patsy Swank (Dallas); Blanche Hardin (Denver); Leo Janos, Rose Blatch (Houston); Chris Chrystal (Las Vegas); Don Neff, Marti Haymaker, Barbara Wilkins (Los Angeles); Dexter Duggan, Ed McDowell, Sterling Ridge (Phoenix); Tom Arden (Sacramento); Roy Gibson (Salt Lake City); Fern Chick (San Antonio); Edward Deverill (San Diego); Jesse Birnbaum, Chris Andersen, Martha Green (San Francisco); William Hale Jr. (Tucson).

Contents

The Recipe Booklet that accompanies this volume has been designed for use in the kitchen. It contains more than 130 recipes, including all of those printed here. It also has a wipe-clean cover and a spiral binding so that it can either stand up or lie flat when open.

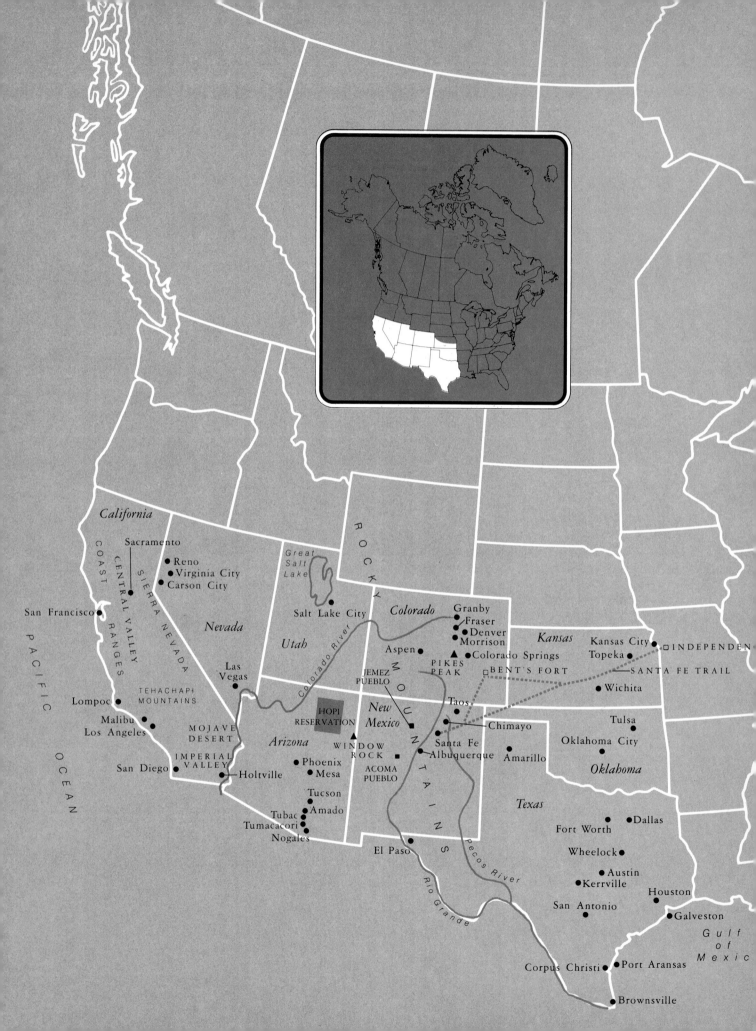

Growing Up to a Composite Cuisine

The cuisine of America's Great West combines the hardiest traditions of pioneer appetites from a dozen cultures: Indian, Mexican and Spanish, French, German, Yankee, Japanese and Chinese, and even a few others. It uses all the fruits of the Great West's soils and waters, from cactus to crabs. It combines them in a free and easy way that is, as far as I know, the most thoroughly relaxed cooking of good regional food anywhere and the least tainted with ethnic prejudices. Westerners of every known racial group eat of their traditional enemies' "soul food" with guileless pleasure, both in public and in the privacy of their patios, grand or simple.

This receptivity to new culinary experiences is, I think, unique. The difference between cooking and eating one's own food in, say, Southern France on the one hand and in Northern California on the other is that around Marseilles there is no deep appetite for anything but the native cuisine. In San Francisco it is natural to shift in one day or even in one meal from traditional French dishes to Korean, from New England style to Creole to Mexican. The Great West culture, kitchen and otherwise, is very new, and it is based on an agreeable tolerance of all that is good. I grew up in California, and from an early age began to experience gastronomic concepts that were formed long before the first settlers brought them into our young country. My personal culinary history may serve as a characteristic record of the Western cuisine.

At home near Los Angeles, after the family moved from Iowa via Michigan, we ate predominantly Midwestern dishes, but they had been shaped by immigrants from Ireland, Sweden and Germany. Away from our own dining room and kitchen there were adventures like the weekly encounter with the tortilla man, who for a nickel would peel off one limp tortilla from a steamy pile and roll it for a quick dip into his little pot of red sauce. (It was doubly hot and delicious on the tongue because it was frowned on by Grandmother as exotic and therefore un-Christian.) Or I would collect a pocketful of dried litchi nuts from the Chinese grocery on the Plaza in Los Angeles, or a cheekful of its deceptively sweet ginger root, whose juices seeped down my throat like heavenly hell-fire.

On Sunday nights in the "R" months we would eat a majestically innocent stew of oysters or clams dug clandestinely by my father and his footloose cronies along the coast. Or, if we were at the beach, there would be mussels, steamed over fresh kelp the way the Japanese did them. Now and then we nibbled on tiny bones of quail brought in from the edge of the desert, or feasted on a hunter's pot of venison and wild mushrooms. Early in this pattern, which was always a kind of counterpoint to the staid rhythm of our three meals a day of plain, nourishing middle-class provender, we would eat pronghorn antelope . . . until my father rebelled at the way the tender little beasts were being slaughtered by hunters in the newly opening valleys of the state. (By now the animals have been wiped out there, as far as I know, and I prefer not to remember the taste of their flesh, but imagine it to be delicate and helpless—like milk-fed veal, or perhaps domestic rabbit or fowl.)

In the first decade of my life in California, in the little town of Whittier, we did not eat meals in the open air, except of course for picnics, which were festivals of joy for the family fledglings and an obvious effort for the late-Victorian ladies of the family, unused to sprawling against eucalyptus trees and brushing voracious wasps from the sandwiches. Then we moved to the country, comparatively speaking, and more and more we ate under a giant privet tree in what was called the *side* yard. We never had what is currently called a patio, and we never used a portable barbecue, electric or otherwise, but we ate out of doors as often as was decently possible. We thought it was fun, which indeed it mostly is. We had gone free, at least a little.

There have always been good restaurants in the West, and my parents used them as escape hatches from the decorum required of a non-Quaker newspaper editor and his wife in a small town founded by and for members of the Society of Friends. In and near Los Angeles were "French" and "Italian" eating places ranging from top-notch classical to family style, and a handful of German taverns, and our own table was slowly influenced by all the dishes and wines my father and mother enjoyed in them. Later on we learned to buy supplies from the little Mexican stores and tortilla factories around the Plaza and Olvera Street, so that we could dine on an occasional meal not dictated by the inherited strictures of Iowa and County Tyrone. Thus, willy-nilly, one family adjusted to what is by now one of the most diffuse and at the same time most clearly regional styles of eating on this planet.

—*M. F. K. Fisher,*
author of The Cooking of Provincial France

I

Where Western Food Begins and Ends

An array of breadstuffs reflects many culinary influences on the Great West. Clockwise from center right are a square of Mormon johnnycake, cowboy soda biscuits fried in a skillet, and Mexican tortillas, one of the most common "breads" of the region. At bottom left is a ring of potato-enriched monkey bread from California; above it are Navajo fry breads, cooked in lard, and deep-fried New Mexican *sopaipillas*. At top left are round and cylindrical loaves of San Francisco sourdough bread, and a rich loaf of sheepherders' rye bread. (For details, see Recipe Index.)

When I was a small boy in Massachusetts a favorite book of mine in my father's library was an atlas published in England in the early 1800s. Its map of North America showed a large empty area labeled simply "Great American Desert." As best I can remember, the desert extended from what is now central Texas all the way to the California coast. I thought of it as a nearer Sahara, complete with Arabs and camels.

When I was a larger boy the family moved to Arizona, where my father was to teach in a ranch school. By then I had learned that the Great West was not wholly a desert. It had towns and cities, rivers and mountains, roads and railroads (but no Arabs or camels), and the ranch where we were going to live was surrounded by green alfalfa fields. But when we arrived, I found to my joy that a desert stranger than any in my dreams began on the far side of an irrigation ditch near our house. I could ride for miles on my stocky white horse, which bore a "US" brand (it had belonged to the army), and see nothing but clumps of prickly pear, giant cacti and other improbable vegetation. Sometimes I rode all the way to the sandstone mesas and hills that ringed the thorny plain. Once I got lost in a cactus forest, spent the night under the brilliant stars and at sunrise let the wise old horse carry me home again.

Since that romantic year of my boyhood I have visited the West over and over and learned to love the country and its friendly, hospitable people. The towns and cities have grown; the farms and irrigated oases have spread and multiplied. Horses are scarce now, automobiles are many—but there are still vast reaches of sunny, open, silent space. I believe it is this

spaciousness that gives Western people a buoyancy that is rare in more crowded places. They are confident of their future and proud of their country. They even have kindliness left over to lavish on the stranger.

I also have come to love and eagerly anticipate Western food in all its vigorous variety. I shall never forget, for example, one marvelous mid-day meal on an oil-well platform off the Texas coast—a lonely speck in the blue water, first stop for shrimp boats coming in from the Gulf of Mexico. The cook had lowered buckets into one of the boats and pulled them up brimming with freshly caught shrimp. Within the hour, those shrimp appeared on the long table as golden-fried mounds, two feet high, flanked by hot biscuits, fresh corn on the cob (flown in by heli-copter), beans with red-hot Mexican sauce, sweet-potato-and-pecan pie, and great pitchers of iced tea with lemon halves afloat in it. For the extra-hungry oil workers or the few who did not care for shrimp (and there are such melancholy people), there were also steaks pounded thin, dipped in a batter of egg and flour mixed with cornmeal, and fried crisp. I had heard of this Texan delicacy, the famous "chicken-fried steak," and had deplored it in advance—but those steaks were delicious. And at the end of the meal the boss of the rig explained that if the company did not dish out "pretty good grub," his crew would take off and go someplace else.

I remember, too, a gorgeous dinner in a restaurant on the Arizona side of the Mexican border. The proprietor undertook to demonstrate the dif-ference between Chihuahuan and Sonoran cooking—two schools of Mex-ican cuisine, named after the states in which they evolved. Dish after dish marched past me, all bright-colored, hot and fragrant. I rose slowly from the feast of *venado a la serrana* (venison mountain style), *lomo relleno* (stuffed fillet of beef), *menudo estilo Sonora* (tripe Sonoran style) and *carne mochoma* (shredded dried beef with chilies) with a feeling of pleasant repletion and a cozy fire of chili burning in my innards.

I had a very different sort of meal outside a California winery, whose owner apologized because he had no kitchen to prepare a hot meal for his guests. Instead he offered me a box lunch. It was in a box, all right, a large cubical one, but it was unlike any other box lunch I had ever eaten. Its main course was an enormous roast beef sandwich made of paper-thin slices of beef with herb-flavored butter spread between each slice to make up a full inch of flavorsome tenderness. On the side was a potato salad, at least half of which was chopped romaine, onions, endive and green peppers. In a little covered plastic dish was a stuffed egg. It had been sliced in half lengthwise and the seasoned yolks of at least two hard-boiled eggs were spun on the halves in patterns with a cake decorator. For bread there were two croissants, and for dessert a slice of wonderful semisoft Brie cheese produced in nearby Petaluma. All this came with an unlimited supply of one of my host's fine wines, a full-bodied Cabernet Sauvignon. I do not know how the winery obtained such food for an impromptu lunch; it was better than if it had been flown from Paris over the North Pole.

Foods of such splendid diversity could come only from a diverse region, and in fact the Great West is in no way uniform—in geography, climate, products or population. Some of its people, for example, speak Southern

English; some speak Texan, a sort of robust Southern; many speak Spanish, in a variety of dialects. Some towns are as new and gleaming as a dream kitchen in a magazine; others boast some of the oldest houses in the United States. Some regions like central Nevada and California's Death Valley consist of all but uninhabited deserts and alkali flats; elsewhere, as in Colorado and Utah, scattered settlements roost on high plateaus or cling to the slopes of some of America's most rugged mountains. Kansas and Oklahoma suffer bitterly cold winters, while in parts of Texas, New Mexico, Arizona and California the trying season is summer, when for weeks temperatures rise above 100° and everyone who can manage it lives in the artificial cool of air conditioning. The food varies with all these factors and many more.

To appreciate the cooking of any part of this region it helps to know its history, which in most cases is as vivid as the sky overhead. The story begins with the Indians, as it does in the rest of the United States, but with a difference. Some of the Southwestern Indian tribes dwelt in permanent villages like those of Mexico to the south, growing corn, beans, squash and other native crops, often with the help of skilled irrigation techniques. The northernmost of these settled peoples were the Pueblo Indians (*pueblo* is Spanish for village) of the upper Rio Grande in what is now New Mexico and Colorado, who lived in well-built adobe apartment houses several stories high. For a thousand years and more they had led their communal lives in almost total isolation, but it was these civilized Indians who made New Mexico so different from other states. They are still around, many living in their ancient pueblos, others scattered nearby. For centuries they have lived in close association with Spanish-speaking New Mexicans, exchanging ideas and customs, and they get along comfortably with the more recently arrived English-speakers, or "Anglos," who are fascinated by their stable way of life and enchanted with their imaginative handiwork in silver, turquoise and pottery. The food of the upper Rio Grande is strongly influenced by the Indians, notably in the use of corn as the staff of life. An attractive example of this ancient food, and one that can still be bought in New Mexican markets, is *chicos*—sun-dried grains of roast sweet corn. *Chicos* keep indefinitely, but when soaked and boiled they taste very much like fresh corn.

After the Indians, the next great influence on the West and on its food was Spanish. The Spaniards under Cortés who conquered the Aztecs in 1521 introduced cattle into Mexico. Slowly but inexorably the wave of settlement moved north. Wherever grass and water were to be found for their herds, Spanish cattlemen established ranches. The Spaniards penetrated only a little way into Texas, which was inhabited by the fiercest Indians of all; only a few made forays into Arizona and California, but the temperate, fertile valley of the upper Rio Grande, in what is now New Mexico, was just what they liked.

The descendants of these venturesome men are still there. They retain many Spanish ways, and their cooking, as we shall see in Chapter 3, still has Spanish elements that distinguish it from the various types of Mexican cooking now popular in the Southwest. The sweet anise-flavored cookies, for instance, that one finds in New Mexico today are baked much the same way they were made in kitchens of 17th Century Spain for the feast of Christmas.

During the 18th Century, as the power of Spain declined, other peoples began to encroach on its overextended American holdings. Anglos were advancing westward from the English colonies on the Atlantic Coast, and in the mid-1700s the Russians began to move down toward California from Alaska. To ward off the intruders from the East, the Spanish Crown sent armed expeditions to establish strong posts in southern Texas around San Antonio and some much feebler ones on the East Texas coast. To thwart the intruders from Alaska, it established a long chain of missions and forts stretching from Tucson all the way up the California coast to what is now San Francisco.

During their heyday these missions were thriving establishments. The friars who ran them must have eaten well in the style of Spain, to judge by their elaborate kitchens, some of which have survived, and by their fruitful fields and orchards. The small towns and scattered ranches that succeeded the missions did not do as well. According to early accounts their food was mostly meat, beans and crude bread made of grain pounded in a mortar. "Jerky," dried beef, was an indispensable part of the diet. The best California dish of the period that I know of consisted of dried beef stirred in a frying pan with boiled potato, onion, lard, tomato and hot chili. Comforting, yes; inspiring, no.

The Spanish settlers in California built up enormous herds of cattle and maintained an archaic style of life, out of touch with the times. Their small population increased slowly, but by the mid-1800s it was too late. Across the Rockies came the English-speaking frontiersmen, well armed, well organized and as tough as any men on earth. Other invaders swept across the plains of Texas. The Spanish-speakers, poorly supported by Mexico, which had fallen into confusion after it won its independence from Spain in 1821, were overwhelmed.

In the early 19th Century, some of the newcomers to East Texas were wealthy planters who brought slaves with them and set up frontier copies of the cotton-growing estates of Mississippi and Alabama. Other pioneers were poorer families from Tennessee or Kentucky who rarely owned slaves but wanted land to cultivate with their own hands. Kansas and Colorado were settled mostly by Northerners. In Utah the pioneers were Mormons; from their stronghold at Salt Lake City they sent wagon trains of colonists out into Arizona and Nevada. Then English-speaking settlers began to filter through the passes in the Sierra Nevada and settle in the fertile Central Valley of California. These two cultures of California —Spanish and Anglo—might have blended peacefully if it had not been for the discovery of gold at Sutter's Mill near Sacramento in 1848. As soon as the news reached the outside world, floods of hardy adventurers converged on California. Most were Americans from the Northeast or Middle West, but many came from Europe, from Latin America, even from China. Ever since the Gold Rush, California has had an extremely heterogeneous population, with strong flavors of Europe and Asia.

Nowhere in the West, however, was the Spanish influence entirely suppressed. Even in parts of Texas where few or no Spaniards or Mexicans

   Continued on page 16

Sand and sagebrush stretch across the floor of New Mexico's Santa Cruz Valley to the snow-capped Jemez Mountains.

The Great West: A Region of Vast Spaces and Hard-won Wealth

The 16th Century Spanish explorers who fought their way into the Great West were seeking seven legendary cities filled with silver and gold free for the taking. What they found was a land that seemed rich only in size and in diversity: scorching deserts and prodigious green valleys; forested uplands and mountains topped by snow. There were silver and gold in the hills, and fortunes to be made in ranches and oil wells, in farming and fishing, but the big land yielded its resources only to a special breed of settler—the kind of man who wanted plenty of elbowroom, and would endure long journeys and lonely labor to get it. The wealth of the West has helped to create a way of life that is full of everything from fine food to ferocious traffic jams, yet much of the land has retained its primeval combination of spaciousness and stark beauty.

Some 50 miles west of Albuquerque, New Mexico, a 400-foot-high sandstone mesa rises like a great fortress against the hot sky. Atop the mesa sprawls one of the oldest settlements in North America, the pueblo of Acoma, occupied since 1539 by a tribe of the Keres Indians. Moisture trapped in the sandstone is used by the Indians on the desert floor to irrigate subsistence crops.

Near Lompoc cactus stands guard at the walls of La Purísima Concepción, one of 21 California missions founded during the 18th and early 19th Centuries by Franciscan fathers. The padres raised livestock, grew grain and fruit, built drainage systems and fashioned utensils of all sorts, and they taught their Indian converts these basic skills. Along with such plants as olives, grapes and citrus fruits, and such food animals as cattle and hogs, the Franciscans introduced Spanish mules and horses into the region; one writer of the time told of how the Indians "blessed the beasts which relieved them from burden bearing."

Ray Huntington and his cousin Don drive Hereford steers on Ray's ranch at Castle Dale, Utah. Huntingtons have lived in Utah since the first of them arrived as a scout for Brigham Young. "To raise cattle today," says Ray's brother Earl, "you need more land than most people have, more feed than they can afford"—but the family still runs 300 to 400 head of cattle on some 1,500 acres.

The Pacific Ocean, ultimate boundary of the Great West, provides both a major part of the nation's seafood and, for some lucky Californians, a splendid setting for a seafood meal. One such repast is shown here aboard the sloop *Happy Talk* as it sails in San Francisco Bay with the Golden Gate Bridge in the background. *Happy Talk's* owner, gourmet skipper Eunice Pratt *(in white)*, serves crewmen Tracy Giesen and Paul Rogers a luncheon of Dungeness crab, tossed salad with Green Goddess dressing and sourdough bread, washed down with pink and white champagnes.

had ever settled, the new cattlemen learned Mexican techniques of cattle breeding and adapted from the Spanish such words as lariat, from *la reata* (the rope), and buckaroo, from *vaquero* (cowboy). The Spanish-speakers themselves were not eliminated or absorbed. To their rescue came two blessings in disguise: distance and aridity. In much of the West, only irrigated land could produce dependable crops, and these oases were many miles apart, with thinly populated range land or open desert between them. Under such conditions cultural mixing was impossible; even today, some oases are still Spanish in culture, while others are not.

So the Great West is a fascinating patchwork of diverse peoples and ways of life. At its various borders, regions blend into their neighbors to the east and north. East Texas is rather like Louisiana and Arkansas, with a Deep South atmosphere and slightly modified Southern cooking. East Texans love rice, crawfish and duck gumbo. Kansas is the West's boundary with the Midwest, afloat in thick steaks and big coffee cups half full of heavy cream. Colorado has Kansas-like wheat country in its eastern half, but it has a Spanish ambiance in its south, and its west is a mountain wilderness where game is still an important part of the diet. Most of the people of Utah are Mormons, a special breed of Anglo; their food includes such dishes as spiced red cabbage, brought to Utah by German or Scandinavian converts to Mormonism. California, as we shall see, is its own patchwork of terrains, climates and cuisines. As for Nevada, most of its few inhabitants are recent arrivals, supported indirectly by tourism and by the "industry" of gambling. Las Vegas must have had some Spanish influence once; its name means "the meadows" in Spanish. Mexican food is popular, but if there is a typical Nevadan dish it is cheese blintzes with sour cream, tasting just as they do in New York City.

To be sure, the eating habits of the West have elements of sameness. Big highways mean highway food, which is uniformly dull over most of the United States. But beyond the hamburger stands and chain restaurants, the food is wonderfully varied. Local restaurants and private homes make good use of local produce, especially fruits—some unfamiliar to most Americans elsewhere. Extraordinary things are done, for instance, with fresh figs, which come to perfection only when they are permitted to ripen on the tree. You can serve ripe figs with sour cream: fresh-picked and fully ripe, they are just sweet enough to create an ideal counterpoint to the cream's slight acidity. In grocery stores there are such odd items —odd to an outsider, but standard in the Southwestern states—as dried chilies. And there is jerky: although it is no longer a vital staple of the diet, as it was in frontier days, this variety of beef, hard, dried, smoked and sometimes peppered, remains a Western favorite.

Mexican food is everywhere. Anglo restaurants serve Mexican dishes, and Anglo housewives cook them. The ingredients can be bought in most markets. In some cities small tortilla factories, selling both cooked and uncooked tortillas, are actually more common than bakeries. In Texas, Mexican restaurants are especially popular, and the food they serve is, to my taste, better than most of the food to be had in Mexico City.

Of all the areas of the Great West, California is a special case. In any earlier age it would have become an independent nation, walled off from the rest of the continent by deserts and towering mountain ranges. Part of the state is oasis country; the Imperial Valley, which lies in the extreme south and grows fruit and vegetables for shipment to Eastern markets, is a giant oasis supported by irrigation from the Colorado River. But most of California has mild winters, with a good deal of rain, and hot dry summers. It is a climate very nearly identical to that of the countries around the Mediterranean.

Some Californians assert that this Mediterranean climate makes them, like the classical Greeks, culturally superior to their neighbors. However that may be, the California climate—assisted by irrigation—enables the state to grow traditional crops of the Mediterranean world in lavish abundance. The European wine grape, which flourishes nowhere else in the United States, is thoroughly at home in California. So are oranges, lemons, figs, walnuts, almonds, peaches, plums and nectarines—as well as innumerable less-familiar fruits such as loquats, pomegranates, guavas and Kiwis. Although most of the fruit is shipped out of the state, Californians really get the best for themselves, for the most delicious varieties do not travel well. They also eat lots of leafy vegetables, which are always available and cheap. To my knowledge, California is the only place where truck drivers eat fresh salads with their meals without fear of being considered effete. It is also the only state where wine is drunk in something like Southern European quantities and where average Americans blossom into wine connoisseurs. The Grand Central Market of Los Angeles, where local growers offer mountains of colorful produce and many booths cook favorite items for on-the-spot eating, is as spectacular a show as any put on by Hollywood at its height.

All through the state, up the rugged coast and in the vast Central Valley, the parade of wonderful food unfolds. There are mammoth fields of artichokes, borne on giant thistle plants; there are huge tracts planted with walnut trees; and there are grapes growing in enormous corporate vineyards or serried in cherished rows in little nooks in the hills. The culinary culmination of all this staggering abundance is San Francisco, a city of gourmets, where the cooking of all the world can be found, often improved by San Francisco's good taste and proximity to the best of ingredients. The Chinese, for instance, have been firmly established in San Francisco for a century; and though their cooking has remained distinctly Oriental, it has been changed in many ways by the new environment. Likewise Mexican, Italian, Yugoslav, Russian and Japanese cooking—the cornucopia of California has enriched them all.

The Great West is changing fast, as befits so dynamic a region, but not necessarily for the worse. Despite the camper jams in the Yosemite Valley, the terrifying freeways that lace Los Angeles and the yellowish smog that dims the sun over many cities (including such comparatively small ones as Phoenix), there is plenty of brilliant open space left, and effective programs are being mounted to protect it. Best of all, the people still retain the relaxed and friendly attitude that makes them marvelous hosts. They have a zest for experimentation, in food as in most other things. It will be a long time, if ever, before the cooking of the West levels to uniformity or dullness.

Foods for a Western cocktail party fill a table of offbeat culinary treats. A huge wheat tortilla topped in pizza style with cheese and chili strips *(far left)* sets off an intricate platter ringed *(from left, clockwise)* with meat turnovers called *turcos;* caraway twists; *tostaditas,* or deep-fried bits of corn tortilla; and cheese balls. The pot offers *chile con queso,* a cheese dip; the hibachi, Texas-broiled shrimp. At bottom right are bacon-wrapped oysters called *angelenos.* (For details, see the Recipe Index.)

How to Handle Hot Chilies

Hot peppers, or chilies, vary in piquancy—sometimes even on a single plant. The fresh red and green chilies used in recipes in this book are generally hot. (Fresh green chilies are underripe red chilies, and taste almost the same.) Canned green chilies are mildly piquant; canned *jalapeño* chilies are fiery. Though most dried chilies are hot, the *ancho* variety is almost sweet and is used primarily to give sauces a maroon color.

The volatile oils in any of these chilies may burn your skin and make your eyes smart. Wear rubber gloves if you can, and be careful not to touch your face while working with chilies. After handling the hot peppers, wash your hands (and the gloves) thoroughly with soap and water.

Before chopping chilies, rinse them clean and pull out the stems under cold running water. Break or cut the pods in half and brush out the seeds. The chilies may be used at once or soaked in cold salted water for an hour or so to make them less hot.

Small dried chilies should be stemmed, broken open and seeded before they are used. Dried *ancho* chilies should be plumped as well. Place the seeded *ancho* chilies in a bowl, pour in enough boiling water to cover them completely, and let them soak for at least 30 minutes. If you wish to remove the skins, slip them off with your fingers or a small knife, or put the chilies through the finest blade of a food mill.

Canned chilies should always be rinsed in cold water (to remove the brine in which they were preserved) before they are cut and seeded.

To make 2½ to 3 cups

3 medium-sized firm ripe tomatoes or 1 cup chopped drained canned tomatoes
2 tablespoons butter
2 tablespoons flour
1 cup light cream
½ teaspoon finely chopped garlic
½ teaspoon salt
A 4-ounce can green chilies (not the *jalapeño* variety), drained, stemmed, seeded and finely chopped *(caution: see note, above)*
2 cups (½ pound) freshly grated Monterey Jack cheese, or substitute 4 cups freshly grated Münster cheese

Chile con Queso
CHEESE-AND-GREEN-CHILI DIP

If you are using fresh rather than canned tomatoes, drop them into enough boiling water to immerse them completely. After 15 seconds, run the tomatoes under cold water and peel them with a small sharp knife. Then cut out the stems, slice the tomatoes in half crosswise and squeeze the halves gently to remove the seeds and juice. Chop the tomatoes coarsely.

In a heavy 1- to 1½-quart saucepan, melt the butter over moderate heat. When the foam begins to subside, add the flour and mix well. Stirring constantly with a wire whisk, pour in the cream in a slow, thin stream and cook over high heat until the sauce comes to a boil, thickens heavily and is smooth. Reduce the heat to low and simmer for 2 or 3 minutes to remove any taste of raw flour. Set the sauce aside off the heat.

Combine the tomatoes, garlic and salt in a heavy 10- to 12-inch skillet and, stirring frequently, cook briskly, uncovered, until the mixture is thick enough to hold its shape almost solidly in a spoon. Reduce the heat to low and stir in the cream sauce and chilies. Without letting the mixture boil, stir in the grated cheese a handful at a time.

To serve, light the burner under a fondue pot or chafing dish. If you are using a chafing dish, pour hot (not boiling) water into the bottom pan. Ladle the *chile con queso* into the fondue pot or chafing dish and serve at once, accompanied by *tostaditas (Recipe Index)* or crackers.

Chiles Rellenos
BATTER-FRIED CHILIES WITH CHEESE FILLING

If you are using the fresh chilies, preheat the broiler to its highest setting. Spread the chilies on a baking sheet and broil them 3 or 4 inches from the heat for 5 minutes, turning them so that they blister and darken on all sides. Wrap the chilies in a dampened kitchen towel and let them rest for a few minutes. Then rub them with the towels until the skins slip off. With a small sharp knife, cut all around the stem of each chili and pull out the stem and the seeds that cling to it. Discard the stems and seeds and set the chilies aside. If you are using canned chilies, drain and rinse them under cold running water. Cut a slit down the side of each chili. Spread the chilies flat and scrape away any seeds with a small knife.

Combine the cheese sticks and onions in a bowl and turn them about gently with a spoon until well mixed. Stuff the cheese-and-onion mixture into the fresh chilies through the stem openings, dividing the mixture evenly among them. To stuff the canned chilies, place equal portions of the cheese-and-onion mixture in the center of each chili. Fold the ends over the mixture and roll the chili around it. In either case, arrange the stuffed chilies on a plate or baking sheet and refrigerate them for about 1 hour before cooking.

Pour oil into a deep fryer or large heavy saucepan to a depth of about 3 inches and heat the oil until it reaches a temperature of 360° on a deep-frying thermometer. Preheat the oven to its lowest setting. Line a shallow baking pan with a double thickness of paper towels, and place the pan in the middle of the oven.

Prepare the batter coating for the chilies in the following manner: With a wire whisk or a rotary or electric beater, beat the egg whites until they are stiff enough to stand in unwavering peaks on the whisk or beater when it is lifted from the bowl. Combine the flour, baking powder and salt, and sift them together into a small bowl.

In a separate bowl with the same beater unwashed, beat the egg yolks for 2 or 3 minutes. When the yolks are thick, add the flour mixture and beat well. With a rubber spatula, scoop the egg whites over the yolks and fold them together gently but thoroughly.

Immerse one chili in the egg batter to coat it evenly, place the chili on a saucer, and slide it carefully into the hot oil. Deep-fry two chilies at a time, turning them with a slotted spoon for 3 to 4 minutes, or until the batter puffs up and is golden brown. As they brown, transfer the chilies to the paper-lined pan and keep them warm in the oven.

Arrange the *chiles rellenos* attractively on a heated platter and serve at once while they are still hot.

10 large fresh green *poblano* or *ancho* chilies or 10 canned green chilies (not the *jalapeño* variety)
½ pound sharp Cheddar cheese, sliced ¼ inch thick and cut into sticks 3 inches long and ¼ inch wide
⅓ cup finely chopped onions
Vegetable oil for deep frying
4 egg whites
¼ cup unsifted flour
¾ teaspoon double-acting baking powder
¼ teaspoon salt
4 egg yolks

Salsa Cruda
UNCOOKED VEGETABLE SAUCE

Combine the tomatoes, chilies, onions, vinegar and sugar in a bowl and stir until well mixed. Taste for seasoning. Let the *salsa cruda* rest at room temperature for about 30 minutes before serving. *Salsa cruda* is a traditional accompaniment to all-day beans *(Recipe Index)* and may also be served with tacos or enchiladas.

To make about 2 cups

A 1-pound can tomatoes, drained and finely chopped
A 4-ounce can Mexican green chilies (not the *jalapeño* variety), stemmed, seeded and finely chopped
½ cup finely chopped onions
1 tablespoon distilled white vinegar
1 teaspoon sugar

Burritos and Chimichangos
ROLLED WHEAT TORTILLAS WITH BEAN-AND-POTATO FILLING

Drop the potatoes into enough boiling water to cover them completely and cook briskly, uncovered, until a potato quarter can be mashed against the side of the pan with the back of a fork. Drain the potatoes, then force them through a ricer or food mill set over a bowl. In a small skillet, bring the beans and water to a boil over moderate heat. Drain off the liquid and set it aside. With a fork, mash the beans to a coarse purée, beating in the reserved liquid by the spoonful if the beans seem dry. Add the beans to the potatoes, stir in the chilies, and taste for seasoning. Cover the bowl with foil to keep the filling mixture warm while you prepare the tortillas.

Place one tortilla in a heavy 10-inch skillet set over moderate heat, and turn it frequently with tongs for 30 seconds, or until it is soft. Spread ⅓ cup of the filling in a band 4 inches long and 1 inch wide across the center of the tortilla; then turn up the ends, fold one long side over the filling, and roll the tortilla into a cylinder. Repeat until all the tortillas are softened, filled and rolled. At this stage the tortillas are called *burritos*. Serve them warm, accompanied if you like with red taco sauce *(Recipe Index)*.

To make *chimichangos,* pour vegetable oil into a heavy 12-inch skillet to a depth of 1 inch, and heat the oil until it is very hot but not smoking. Fry the rolled tortillas two or three at a time, turning them with a slotted spoon, for about 2 minutes, until they are crisp and golden brown on all sides. As they brown, transfer the *chimichangos* to paper towels to drain.

Arrange the *chimichangos* on a heated platter and serve them hot, accompanied if you like by red taco or *ancho* sauce *(Recipe Index)*.

All-Day Beans

Wash the beans in a colander set under cold running water and discard any blemished beans. In a heavy 3- to 4-quart saucepan, bring the water to a boil over high heat. Drop in the beans and cook briskly, uncovered, for 2 minutes. Then turn off the heat and let the beans soak for 1 hour.

Add the salt pork, chilies and onion slices, and bring the mixture to a boil over high heat. Reduce the heat to its lowest setting and simmer tightly covered for 5½ hours. Stir in the salt and simmer for 30 minutes longer, or until a bean can be easily mashed against the side of the pan with the back of a spoon. (Stir the beans from time to time. If the water seems to be cooking away, add more boiling water by the ¼ cup. When fully cooked, however, the beans should have absorbed most of the liquid.)

Ladle the all-day beans into individual heated bowls and mound a teaspoon of *salsa cruda* on top of each portion. Spoon the remaining *salsa cruda* into a separate bowl and serve it at once with the beans.

To make 8 rolled tortillas

BURRITOS
2 medium-sized boiling potatoes, peeled and quartered
2 cups freshly cooked or drained canned pinto, pink or kidney beans, rinsed in a sieve under cold running water if canned
½ cup water
2 canned green chilies (not the *jalapeño* variety), drained, halved, seeded and finely chopped
8 seven-inch wheat tortillas *(Recipe Booklet)*

ADDED INGREDIENT FOR CHIMICHANGOS
Vegetable oil for deep frying

To serve 4 to 6

2 cups (1 pound) dried pinto beans
6 cups water
A 2-ounce piece of lean salt pork, with the rind removed
4 dried hot red chilies, each about 1 inch long, stemmed, seeded if desired, and pulverized in a blender or with a mortar and pestle *(caution: see note, page 20)*
1 medium-sized onion, peeled and thinly sliced
1 teaspoon salt
1 recipe *salsa cruda (page 21)*

Mexican-inspired foods abound throughout the West. Favorites include, from the top left, clockwise: *enchiladas de Jocoque* (chicken-filled tortillas with sour cream), "all-day" beans, *chiles rellenos* (batter-fried, cheese-stuffed chilies), stacked cheese enchiladas, red tomato taco sauce and *salsa cruda* (uncooked sauce). On the center platter, from the top, clockwise: beef tacos with *ancho* sauce, *chorizo flautas* (sausage-filled tortillas), chicken *tostadas* with avocado "poor man's butter," and *chimichangos* (deep-fried tortillas with bean and potato filling). For all recipes, see the Recipe Index.

To serve 4 to 6

½ cup vegetable oil
3 cups coarsely chopped onions
1 tablespoon finely chopped garlic
A 1-pound can tomatoes, drained
    and coarsely chopped with the
    liquid reserved
1 cup canned tomato purée
¼ cup coarsely chopped fresh hot
    red chilies including the seeds
    (caution: see note, page 20)
2 tablespoons dry mustard
2 tablespoons sugar
1 tablespoon distilled white vinegar
1½ teaspoons salt
4 pounds spareribs, in 4 pieces,
    trimmed of excess fat

Barbecued Spareribs with Red Sauce

First prepare the red sauce in the following manner: In a heavy 10- to 12-inch skillet, heat the vegetable oil over moderate heat. Add the onions and garlic and, stirring frequently, cook for about 5 minutes, or until they are soft and translucent but not brown. Stir in the tomatoes and their liquid, the tomato purée, chilies, mustard, sugar, vinegar and salt, and bring to a boil over high heat. Cook briskly, uncovered, until the sauce is thick enough to hold its shape almost solidly in the spoon. Remove the pan from the heat and taste the red sauce for seasoning. Set it aside.

To barbecue the ribs, light a 2-inch-thick layer of charcoal briquettes in a charcoal grill equipped with a rotating spit. Let the coals burn until white ash appears on the surface.

Thread the spareribs on the spit, running the spit through the meat over and under alternate pairs of ribs. Then secure them at both ends with the sliding prongs. Fit the spit into place about 6 inches above the surface of the coals and barbecue the ribs for 45 minutes, or until they are lightly and evenly browned. Watch carefully for any sign of burning and regulate the height of the spit accordingly.

With a pastry brush, spread the red sauce evenly on both sides of the spareribs. Basting the ribs every 5 minutes or so, continue to barbecue them for about 30 minutes longer, or until they are richly colored and glazed with sauce.

To serve, remove the spit from the grill, unscrew the prongs and slide the spareribs off the spit onto a heated platter. Before serving, insert skewers into each section of ribs if you like.

To serve 4

GREEN-CHILI SAUCE
2 tablespoons lard
½ cup finely chopped onions
An 8½-ounce can tomatitos
    (Mexican green tomatoes),
    drained and coarsely chopped
2 four-ounce cans green chilies
    (not the jalapeño variety),
    drained and finely chopped
    (about 1 cup)
½ cup light cream
1 teaspoon salt

ENCHILADAS
Vegetable oil
Twelve 5- to 6-inch corn tortillas
    (Recipe Booklet), thoroughly
    defrosted if frozen
4 cups (1 pound) freshly grated
    Monterey Jack or Cheddar cheese

Stacked Cheese Enchiladas, New Mexico Style

First prepare the green-chili sauce in the following manner: In a heavy 8- to 10-inch skillet, melt the lard over moderate heat. Add the onions and stir frequently for about 5 minutes, or until they are soft and translucent but not brown. Add the tomatitos and mash them with the back of the spoon. Stir in the chilies, then add the cream. Stirring constantly, cook briskly until the sauce is thick enough to hold its shape almost solidly in the spoon. Add the salt and taste for seasoning. Remove the skillet from the heat. (There will be about 2 cups of sauce.)

Preheat the broiler to its highest setting. Pour vegetable oil into a heavy 10-inch skillet to a depth of about 1 inch and heat the oil until it is very hot but not smoking. Pick up one tortilla at a time with kitchen tongs, immerse it in the oil for a few seconds to heat and soften it, and immediately transfer it to paper towels to drain.

To assemble each enchilada, place a hot tortilla on an ovenproof serving plate and spread 2 tablespoons of the chili sauce over it. Scatter about ¼ cup of cheese on top, add a second tortilla and cover it with chili sauce and cheese in the same fashion. Set a third tortilla on top, spread it with ¼ cup of chili sauce and scatter about ½ cup of cheese over it.

When all the enchiladas are assembled, slide them under the broiler for 30 seconds or so, to melt the cheese topping. Serve at once.

Charcoal-barbecued spareribs (above) are basted with a chili-seasoned Texas-style red sauce for a special tang and a toothsome crunch.

II

Texas: Too Big for Just One Cuisine

A Texas barbecue for 900 guests —the 300 employees of the Houston Club and their families—is prepared by Roland Bisset *(left)* and Jeff McNeill of the Lenox Barbecue and Catering Company. In preparation for the feast, 130 eight-pound chunks of beef brisket were hickory-smoked for 18 hours. Spareribs, chicken halves and sausages were added before the "Chow time!" bell was finally rung.

Texas is big enough to contain several countries' worth of climates and customs, and has food enough to go with each of them. East Texas is comparatively humid, with piny woods and steady, slow-flowing rivers. Much of West Texas is semidesert; the plants on its arid plains have thorns or prickly leaves, the better to survive drought, and most of its streams flow only now and then. North Texas, the Panhandle, is freezing in winter, while the area at the southern end of the state, around Browns-ville at the mouth of the Rio Grande, is profusely tropical, gay with bou-gainvillea and crape myrtle.

The people of Texas are just as diverse. East Texans are like South-erners, easygoing and courtly. In southern Texas many of the people are of Mexican ancestry. Central and West Texas are (or were) the cowboy paradise of song and story, where men wore big felt hats and high-heeled riding boots and carried guns, as in the movies. Few carry guns now, and high-heeled boots, though sometimes worn, are not much use in a country that has more cars and trucks than horses. The big hats, though, are still common, and as flattering as ever to masculine looks.

But however diverse Texas may be in climate and style, it still has a feel-ing of identity that few other states can match. The people speak of them-selves proudly as Texans, even when they are recent immigrants from Minnesota or New Jersey, and they have special Texas traits. One of these is a devotion to large and lavish barbecues, which a true Texan will gladly drive 200 miles (at 90 miles an hour) to attend. Generally given in honor of a public figure or to commemorate a historical event, such as the founding of a city, these big barbecues are authentic folk festivals. They offer a genial opportunity to renew old friendships and meet new people, and the food served on these occasions is not, you may be sure, the rubbery chicken passed out so lackadaisically at outdoor eating events in many parts of the United States. It is unbelievably varied, plentiful and lovingly prepared.

My first gastronomic encounter with Texas took place at one such barbecue. Years ago, when I was science editor of TIME magazine, I wrote an article about new techniques of oil-well drilling. As a part of this assignment, I attended a barbecue that must have been one of the high points in the history of corporate hospitality. The sponsors were several major oil companies with fields in West Texas, and the occasion was the dedication of a pipeline to carry crude oil to the Gulf Coast.

The guests were invited to come to Dallas and check in at the railroad station in the late afternoon. There we were met by a small army of smiling greeters in big hats who gave us name cards and sets of instructions. Presently a train of sleeping cars pulled into the station. The greeters explained happily that this was the longest train of sleeping cars ever assembled anywhere on earth; the cars came from all over the country, and a special crew had been hired to man them. (Every fifth car, incidentally, was a well-stocked bar.) Three engines pulled the train in front, and two more pushed at the rear.

I climbed on board, put my bag in my berth and repaired to the nearest bar car, where the oilmen and their guests held a merry party that lasted most of the night. Food was served, as well as drinks, but nothing more than sandwiches and such minor matters. "We've got to save up for the barbecue," I was told.

All night the train lumbered westward, cheers ringing into the darkness from every fifth car. In the early morning it stopped at a tiny railroad station on a limitless, scrub-covered plain. A few small houses and stores stood in a straggling row. "Nobody lives around here," said an oilman, "except jack rabbits and oil wells." A high-school band from somewhere played a medley of tunes as the guests left the train and found their seats in a fleet of buses with license plates that showed they had been brought in from as far away as Idaho.

Marshaled into a roaring procession, the buses set off across the plain, on which I saw neither jack rabbits nor oil wells. Eventually we reached a place where thick steel pipes, bright with fresh aluminum paint, sprouted out of the ground and converged on a group of enormous valves. This was the point in the new pipeline at which individual oil fields made their contributions. It was also the site of the dedicatory barbecue. A temporary grandstand was already erected around a speakers' stand. The speakers were ready too. They had come ahead in Cadillacs and were waiting for the buses to arrive with their audience.

There was no sign of food as yet, but a convoy of monster trailer trucks was approaching across the plain. They had driven all night from Dallas, and their crews were fresh, eager and efficient. Some of the trucks disgorged a tremendous circus tent that began to take shape with a good deal of shouting before my awestruck eyes. From others came smaller

Sausage, spareribs, brisket of beef and chicken—the succulent products of the barbecue pit shown on page 26—are served up with coleslaw, potato salad, barbecue beans, *jalapeño* chilies, onion rings and dill pickle slices. Sourdough bread, soft drinks and beer accompanied the meal; and a powerful barbecue sauce enriched by 11 condiments and by the smoky drippings from the meat was available for diners with preconditioned palates.

tents, tables, benches, cooking apparatus, cartons of plastic plates, cylinders of liquefied gas. Other trucks were refrigerators packed with food. One was a rolling treasury of hard and soft drinks.

While I watched, the great tent was erected and delicious smells of food began to drift out from it. At the same time, the guests on the grandstand began to turn away from the speakers. Most of them had had no breakfast, and little supper the night before. They were ravenous. In twos and threes, then in sixes and sevens they sneaked toward the tent. Finally, when the last of a long list of speakers sat down, someone shouted, "Go get it!" and the stampede was on.

Inside the tent were benches and long tables covered with oilcloth. On other tables was an array of food that could have fed three times the number of guests. The eatables were divided into two classes, American style and Mexican style, and both seemed equally popular. On the American side there were broiled steak, ham, fried chicken, fried shrimp, potatoes, macaroni, fresh-baked biscuits and a great assortment of pies and ice creams. On the Mexican side were barbecued lamb and tender *cabrito* (young goat), along with fiery stews and a host of other equally fiery things that I could not identify. The hot sun, the long semifast and the empty landscape stimulated eating, and if any Eastern guests brought ulcers or balky stomachs to that gargantuan feast, I saw no sign of it. Everyone ate and ate and showed no distress.

About the time that my own eating slowed down, I learned that the wonderful crew of truckborne caterers had brought along a meteorologist to warn them against dust storms. I found this expert set up with a two-way radio, listening to reports from weather stations and neighboring oil fields. A moderate dust storm was indeed headed our way, but by the time it arrived the crew had erected a sloping windshield of canvas between the storm and the tent. The feasters within never knew that a great billow of dust had been deflected high over their heads.

Most Texas barbecues are not as flamboyant as that one, though many are even larger. Small private barbecues are popular, too, and Texans do a much better job of their outdoor cooking than those suburbanites elsewhere who char hot dogs or hamburgers over smoking briquettes on little backyard grills. There is a long and strong tradition behind Texas barbecuing, and every detail of the operation is taken seriously.

The word barbecue comes from the Spanish *barbacoa,* which in turn came from an Indian word for a framework of green wood on which meat or fish could be broiled. The most ancient method of barbecuing, which under various names was used by Indians from New England to Chile, was to cook the meat over hot coals or stones set in a hole in the ground. It is still practiced by traditionalists who are willing to go to a lot of trouble, and it produces marvelous results.

For one traditional Texas version of a *barbacoa,* the cook starts by digging a hole in hard ground about three feet deep and two feet wide. If the nature of the soil permits it, the hole should have a narrow mouth and a side vent leading to the surface from two thirds of the way down. (The vent supplies air and speeds the burning, but is not absolutely necessary.) Fuel, in the form of brush, small sticks of wood and even entire logs, is fed into the hole, where it burns down to form a layer of glowing coals; additional wood can be burned outside the hole and the coals it produces shoveled in as needed. In Mexico the meat to be barbecued is often wrapped in maguey (century plant) leaves, beaten to make them flexible; most of Texas lacks maguey, and wet gunny sacks are generally used instead. The meat, rubbed with salt and wrapped in a clean cloth and the wet sacks, is placed on top, and the hole is covered with earth and left to itself for at least eight hours, sometimes overnight. Even the toughest meat comes out wonderfully tender, with a distinctive and delightful flavor. Sometimes an earthern pot of beans or garbanzos (chick-peas) and water is put in the hole along with the meat to mature slowly.

Any kind of meat can be cooked in this ancient way, but the most truly traditional offering is the head of a steer or calf. (Among the Indians and the early settlers of Texas, a buffalo head was sometimes used instead.) The horns are cut off and the head is skinned and thoroughly washed. Sometimes hot chilies are put in the mouth. Not many hosts are hardy enough (or have sufficiently hardy guests) to set the head on the table whole. It is more esthetic to separate the cooked meat, including the tongue and brains, and spirit the skull away.

Nowadays, as an alternative to the traditional methods and foods, barbecuing is often done on a grid of iron bars or heavy wire supported on a box of stones two or three feet high. A layer of glowing coals is spread on the bottom of the box and renewed when necessary from a bonfire smoldering nearby. The meat cooked in this way is generally lamb or *cabrito*, cut into chops and similar smallish pieces. The distance between meat and coals makes the cooking slow and gentle; equally important, the flames produced by dripping fat do not give the meat a sooty flavor.

The best barbecue of this kind I ever ate was *cabrito* cooked near Kerrville, about 50 miles from San Antonio, by Felix Real, a cattle rancher who devoted a long afternoon to the ceremony. He made his own barbecue sauce in a bucket, using two quarts of cooking oil, two quarts of vinegar, the juice of six lemons, six chopped onions, a small bottle of Worcestershire sauce and a quarter of a bottle of A.1. sauce. He rubbed the meat with salt and pepper and allowed it to sit for an hour before putting it on the fire. Then, for three hours at 15-minute intervals, he brushed each piece with the sauce, using a small paint brush, and turned it over. Felix did this with long-handled tongs; a fork might have punctured the crust and allowed juice to escape. An hour before the meat was to be served, he let the fire burn very low and added half a pound of butter and two bottles of ketchup to the sauce. He could not do this sooner, he explained, because butter and ketchup are fine for forming a crust but leave a burnt flavor when exposed to high heat. The result was beautiful, both to look at and to eat. The delicate *cabrito* meat, enclosed in its zesty crust of baked-on sauce, was at once crisp and juicy.

This sort of barbecuing is for festive occasions, of course; it would be much too much trouble for everyday eating. But Texans have no lack of good, practical daily food. They are the heirs to at least three excellent culinary traditions: cooking that was brought from the Old South; cooking that was originally developed in the East and the Middle West; and

Tex-Mex at Its Best:
A Cabrito Asado Barbecue

Roast kid, or *cabrito asado,* the preferred meat at a traditional Mexican barbecue, has been happily absorbed into the composite cuisine called Tex-Mex. It is frequently served to guests at the Treasure Hunt Ranch, Carson and Adrienne Pryor's 1,300-acre spread near Wheelock, Texas. According to Carson Pryor, a year-old kid weighing from 10 to 15 pounds makes the best eating. To season the meat Pryor applies both a dry barbecue mix and a basting sauce, a procedure he recommends for use in barbecuing deer or suckling lamb as well as goat. The dry mix, applied before cooking, consists of 3 ounces of chili powder; 1 tablespoon each of paprika, black pepper and salt; and 1 teaspoon each of cayenne, cumin, sage, sugar, celery seed, garlic powder and oregano. The sauce consists of a chopped and seasoned onion, ½ pound of butter and 3 cups of white wine. After 3 to 4 hours of roasting over a mesquite fire the *cabrito* emerges as a Tex-Mex triumph.

Carson Pryor sprinkles dry barbecue mix on a *cabrito* rubbed with lemon juice and oil. The kid will rest for at least an hour before being set over the fire.

Pryor lashes the *cabrito* to a Mexican-style barbecue spit with two crosspieces. The cast-iron framework was handcrafted for him by a local blacksmith.

Cushioned on bales of hay, the guests enjoy *cabrito* with traditional barbecue trimmings: black beans, coleslaw and cornbread.

Cabritos are turned every half hour for three hours, then, for another hour, basted every 10 minutes with sauce from the pot.

—most exotic of all—Mexican cooking derived from the rich and varied traditions south of the border.

Some of the best Southern-style cooking in the nation is done in eastern Texas. I have long shared the Southern love of hot biscuits, but a home in Houston is the only place where I ever saw them arrive at the dining table at five-minute intervals, fresh from the oven and almost too hot to touch. When I dabbed butter on them, the butter almost vaporized. As a native New Englander with a stubborn streak of frugality I wanted to ask the hostess what happened to the many biscuits taken away uneaten, but I did not think it seemly. I had enjoyed my own share too much.

When Mrs. Mary Faulk Koock of Austin, great authority and connoisseur of Texas cooking, surveyed the East Texas cuisine, she noted that most of the distinctive dishes she admired had something of the Old South about them. Rice dishes are common in East Texas, as they are in most of the South (rice is, of course, an East Texas crop), and so are dishes with crawfish or okra. There is a general difference, however: Texas-Southern dishes tend to be richer than their Old South originals. As befits the famous affluence of East Texas, they go heavier on the more expensive ingredients, such as mushrooms and almonds.

Other parts of the state are equally affluent, but belong to another tradition. Many of the early settlers, especially in central and southern Texas, were Daniel Boone-like characters who came, not from the Old South, but from the less aristocratic border states, and they eventually turned not to farming but to cattle breeding. Theirs was a hard and dangerous life, punctuated by periods of bitter warfare with the Comanche and other Indians who roamed Texas; but it was a romantic life, too, and still retains a powerful emotional appeal. Many present-day Texans who can well afford to live in citified luxury buy and operate ranches in remote places. Many more cling to some of the customs of the ranching era—customs that prevailed before Texas began to float on petroleum.

According to Texans with long memories, the old-time ranchers lived largely on hot breads, on the mottled kidney beans called pinto beans and on "chicken-fried" steak. Since Texas cattle in those days were fed solely on grass (or, in times of drought, on cacti with the thorns burned off), their meat was usually tough. It was therefore cut in steaks half an inch thick and beaten with a mallet. Then the meat was dredged with flour and fried in lots of hot fat. This brutal treatment is a good way to take the fight out of tough beef, but it is really no longer necessary, for most of the cattle consumed in Texas are now fattened and tenderized on feeds made with locally grown cottonseed, corn and sorghum. Many Texans, however, still insist upon chicken-fried steak and profess to be horrified by rare meat. One standard story tells of a rancher who draws his gun at the dinner table, thinking that an especially rare roast may still be alive. Another Texas reaction to rare meat is to remark, mildly: "Why, I've seen critters hurt worse than that get up and walk away." Besides disliking rare meat, many conservative Texans refuse to eat most vegetables and any "fancy, fixed-up" dishes.

This attitude is changing; rather, it has already changed. Though modern Texans revere their cattle-ranching tradition, they have become far more broadminded in the matter of food. Many of them do, in fact, enjoy rare or medium-rare beef, and they delight in chicken, which old-time cattlemen tended to despise. One excellent dish—and one that shows the influence of the East and the Middle West—is chicken with dumplings. It is a wonderfully easy dish to prepare. Just cut up a large, fat, full-grown hen (not a watery broiler or a frying chicken), season it and simmer it until the meat is tender and can be removed from the bones in large pieces. Make a dumpling dough, and drop very small spoonfuls of it into the simmering broth and cook for 10 minutes. Then return the chicken pieces to the broth and cook for 10 more minutes. A more unusual Texas dish is "German fried" liver. Calf's liver is sliced thin, dipped in seasoned cornmeal, fried in bacon drippings and arranged on a platter along with strips of crisp bacon. Then—this is the unexpected Texas touch—three quarters of a cup of strong coffee is added to the frying pan and allowed to simmer gently until it combines with the bacon and liver drippings to make a lively sauce, which may be poured either over the liver or on hot biscuits.

Perhaps the pleasantest characteristic of all Texas-American cooking is the lavish use of rich, fresh ingredients. The varied climates and soils of Texas grow almost everything—pink grapefruit from the lower Rio Grande Valley that are to my mind the best in the world; cantaloupes with flesh so thick that hardly any space is left for seeds; peaches so enormous that they are hard to believe, but are still excellently flavored. One of the

A pedigreed bull draws high bids at an auction at the Nine-Bar Ranch, 35 miles northwest of Houston. The animals sold here, representing the Santa Gertrudis breed developed by the mammoth King Ranch of Texas, are among the heaviest and hardiest of all beef cattle. Every year a thousand or more buyers attend the auction in search of bulls and heifers to improve their herds. Favored customers are invited to a pre-auction cocktail party (*overleaf*), and all spectators are welcome to a barbecue at the ranch.

A Texas-style buffet at Houston's plush Petroleum Club provides a lavish overture to the Nine-Bar cattle auction *(preceding page)*. For some 550 guests, ranch owners Gus Wortham and Sterling Evans offer a cornucopia of canapés and hors d'oeuvre, including shrimp with sauces, marinated raw snapper, water chestnuts wrapped in bacon, and assorted Mexican tidbits. For heartier eaters there are oysters Rockefeller, roast beef, ham and turkey—and for everyone there is a bottomless supply of hard liquor.

best pies I ever ate (and I am a New England-born pie-fancier) was served on a Texas cattle ranch. It had flaky bottom crust, then half an inch of slightly sweetened homemade cream cheese, and then a layer of fresh peaches topped off with lots of whipped cream. The pie teemed with calories and cholesterol, but it was also utterly delicious. And my hostess said that it would have been better if I had come earlier and picked some fresh figs for the filling.

Such fresh vegetables as cucumbers, tomatoes and peppers are available from some part of Texas nearly all the year round, and since they do not have to travel far, they reach market almost before the dew of innocence is off them. As I have suggested, not all Texans take advantage of their state's bounty of fresh vegetables; some of them, like too many other Americans, think that vegetables come only canned or frozen or built into TV dinners. But enough are appreciative to make vegetable side dishes a frequent and outstanding part of the meal.

No one can do much eating in Texas without becoming warmly conscious of the Mexican-influenced sector of Texas food, which many visitors consider the best and which is certainly the most unusual. The taste for it is not limited to people of Mexican ancestry. Texans who are no more Mexican than Sam Houston eat it delightedly. In many Texas cities the best and most popular restaurants serve food prepared in the Mexican style, and the ubiquitous taco stands compete vigorously with hot-dog and hamburger vendors for the quick-snack trade.

Though Mexican influence on Texas food has had an explosive increase in recent years, it is by no means a recent arrival from south of the border. Its central characteristic, the use of chilies (hot peppers), is older

As a fanciful centerpiece for the Nine-Bar buffet, a Texas buckaroo carved in suet rides a cold boiled Maine lobster. The canapés ranged around the steed and rider include red and black caviar, deviled eggs, and swirls of Roquefort mousse and purée of foie gras on toast. For a final fantastic note of color, the tray is garnished with sparkling pools of diced aspic, tinted a light pink.

than the first Americans in Texas, older even than the first Spaniards. Long before white men first arrived in the region, the Indians used as spice a red tomatolike berry called *chiletepín* that still grows wild in much of Texas—and this fiery spice may well be one of the ancestors of the cultivated chilies of Mexico. Besides putting *chiletepín* in their food (no doubt with due caution) the Indians of Texas ground it up and dusted the powder on buffalo meat before drying the meat in the sun, perhaps in the hope that the strong spice covering would discourage flies and wild animals from attacking the meat. When the Indians came to eat the buffalo jerky, they washed off most of the potent powder and enjoyed the "burn" of the rest.

Chiletepín is still picked wild to form the basis of an intensely hot sauce. It is also cultivated, and can be bought as a pickled or dried spice in many markets, but it is not the most popular kind of chili today. In its place, many other kinds are offered in fresh, dried and canned forms. The most common are probably *jalapeños,* which are fairly hot chilies, sharp-pointed and two or three inches long. They are usually picked green but may be allowed to ripen and turn bright red.

The use of chilies is not confined to Mexican-style food. It has worked its way into such typically "Anglo" dishes as cornbread and potato salad. Red-hot sausages are popular, beans and spaghetti are apt to have chilies in them, and so is any kind of stew. A Texas specialty is a chili jelly *(Recipe Index)* served with meat and made of chopped hot chilies, mild chilies, vinegar and sugar, with pectin to make it jell. I have encountered innocent-looking salads with decorative green slivers that turned out to be some of the hottest kinds of chili.

There is a mystique about chilies that is not associated with other hot spices such as black pepper or mustard. Some people, including my own wife, cannot abide chilies. Others cannot get enough of them, and compulsively search for hotter and hotter kinds. They claim that they still feel the burn—a burn so fiery it would incapacitate an untempered mouth —but that they taste behind the burn a wonderful flavor that the uninitiated can never appreciate. Not only does the chili itself have flavor; it makes other flavors taste better and does not drown them out. I myself am a chili lover. I cannot as yet eat the smallest, hottest chilies right off the bush, like cherries, as some Texans do (I tried it once, in a gingerly way, and my mouth burned unpleasantly for a long time), but I am sure that I could learn, for every time I enjoy a hot chili dish I find myself hoping that the next one will be hotter.

The most famous of all chili dishes is, of course, chili con carne *(Recipe Index),* which is something of an obsession in Texas. Men assert loudly that they are hopelessly addicted to it, and yearn for it unhappily when in foreign parts. Several books and innumerable newspaper and magazine articles have been written about it. Chili-cooking contests attract thousands of asbestos-throated fans from Texas and neighboring states. And the International Chili Appreciation Society, founded in 1951 and based in Dallas, now has chapters all over the world—including one impudent group in Mexico City, which, according to one member, was "a 'chili desert' until the Appreciation Society did some missionary work."

One thing, in fact, that Texas chili lovers want to have understood right off is that the celebrated dish called chili con carne is *not* Mexican. This assertion is hard to prove—but equally hard to disprove. It is certain that modern Mexicans consider the dish to be Texan. It is also certain that the Indians of Mexico were making concoctions of chilies and meat long before Columbus and Cortés. Soon after the first Spaniards entered Tenochtitlán (Mexico City), Fra Bernardino de Sahagún described the thousand dishes that made up the fare at the court of the Aztec Emperor Moctezuma. Many of them consisted of chilies cooked with what must have been every kind of meat, fish or fowl available to the Aztecs. And in modern Mexico, women stand in the great markets beside simmering pots of chili peppers cooked with all sorts of ingredients. When these stews—which Americans should sample only with the utmost caution— contain a substantial amount of meat, they are essentially chili con carne.

Despite these facts, it remains likely that Texas-style chili con carne, which purists call "a bowl of red," was invented somewhere in Texas, possibly in San Antonio. It is not very liquid, as the Mexican market stews generally are, and its main ingredient is beef, which is too expensive in Mexico to be eaten in quantity by many of the people who frequent the markets. A fair compromise might be to say that chili con carne is a Texas dish inspired by Mexico. It is, in other words, an ideal example of "Tex-Mex," or Texas-Mexican cooking.

The second point that chili lovers want understood is that chili con carne is perverted, insulted and desecrated everywhere outside Texas and perhaps New Mexico. They will not admit that the sloppy mixtures of beans, a little hamburger and chili powder that are offered as chili con carne in New York or Chicago are anything like the real thing. In this con-

tention, at least, they are absolutely right. Though distinctly a food of the people, real chili con carne is a far nobler dish than its mealy imitations.

In one traditional form it is made essentially of half-inch cubes of beef, preferably rather tough, and of dried red chilies, about 12 pods to each three pounds of beef. The beef cubes are browned in a little fat. The chilies are boiled until soft in a minimum of water, and the seeds and skin are then separated from the pulp in any convenient way, such as being rubbed through a strainer. The meat and chili pulp are then cooked together with a little ground oregano and cumin and perhaps a clove or two of garlic. If water is needed, one adds some of the peppery liquid in which the chilies were boiled, and when the meat is properly tender, enough cornmeal or *masa* (the cornmeal used for tortillas) to give a little thickening. That is all.

Please note, the chili lovers insist, that beans have not been mentioned. Not that they are against beans; if they are traditional Texans they may have beans for breakfast, and they expect them frequently at other meals. But beans should not intrude on chili con carne. They have muscled their way into the dish only because they are cheaper than meat and because New Yorkers, Chicagoans and the buyers of most kinds of canned chili don't know when they are being imposed on.

On the patio of her Houston home, Mrs. Jayne Robinson *(seated, left)* presents her own version of chili con carne to a party of relatives and friends. Mrs. Robinson, an assistant professor of home economics at Texas Southern University, departs from tradition in using ground beef instead of cubed beef, and in adding fresh hot chili peppers, ketchup, Worcestershire sauce and—a heresy to some devotees—beans. With the chili she serves fresh onion rings, pickled *jalapeño* chilies and carrots, corn muffins, salad and fruit punch.

The true, old-time chili religion is not always followed nowadays, even in Texas. The beef for the chili is now generally ground, though the grinder may have extra-large holes to cut it in comparatively large pieces. Onions and tomatoes are sometimes added (Lyndon Johnson, for one, insists on this) and chili powder may be substituted for the dried chilies and the minor spices. There are many other variations. Some of them, designed for sissies, are comparatively mild or even non-hot. Others are fortified to the limit with red pepper, Tabasco sauce or *chiletepín*. They make strong men weep and weak men beg to be put out of their misery.

Nothing I have said should be taken to imply that Texans are gastronomic masochists. Most of them simply like hot chili, and they like to boast frankly about how hot they can take it. They also like other kinds of Mexican-influenced cooking, but the fact is that when their reputation as chili-eaters is not at stake, they often consume versions that are only slightly hot or not hot at all. One of the best of all chili purveyors, the Caliente (literally, "hot") Chili Company of Austin, offers packets of good, hot ingredients for a standard "Two-Alarm" chili and instructs its customers in the preparation of an even hotter "Three-Alarm." But the company also halves the peppers for a mild "One-Alarm" chili, and (presumably for the faint heart and sensitive palate) gives a recipe for a completely pepperless dish. It calls that last version a "False-Alarm" chili —but obviously some customers enjoy it.

Tex-Mex cooking, whether in chili con carne or in other dishes, can be better understood in the light of the original cuisine developed by the civilized Indians of Mexico. The backbone of that cuisine was corn, supplemented by beans for protein and by chili peppers, squash and tomatoes for taste and vitamins. The corn was eaten in many forms. Some of them, such as *atole,* or corn gruel, are convenient but uninteresting; others, such as the cornmeal pancakes called tortillas, are delightful in themselves and form a base for innumerable culinary ingenuities.

To make tortillas, the Indians heated whole corn grains in water containing a little dissolved lime to make the skins come off. Then they ground the softened kernels into a smooth dough called *masa,* which the women tossed and patted into thin cakes between their hands. (This graceful performance looks easy but is in fact so difficult that hardly anyone can do it who did not learn in childhood.) The cakes, about one eighth inch thick and up to eight inches in diameter, were cooked briefly without fat on a griddle.

Tortillas were the bread of Mexico, and they still are. They are excellent eating when hot or warm and, like bread, lend themselves beautifully to simple combinations with meat or vegetables. (The Mexican equivalent of a sandwich, called a taco, is simply a fresh tortilla rolled around almost any filling the eater pleases.) But I do not think that the indigenous Mexican tortilla-based cuisine would have spread far into the United States if it had not been for new foodstuffs introduced by the Spanish conquerors of Mexico. The most important of these foodstuffs were cattle and hogs. For all the surprising sophistication of their cooking, the Indians had little meat except turkey and wild game, and no handy sources of fat for frying. The Spaniards' pigs supplied not only meat but lard, and lard revolutionized Mexican cooking. When frying became possible, the humble tortilla became a base for many new and excellent dishes.

Even when tortillas are limp and stale, they fry to delicious, nutty crispness; nearly all Americans know and like these *tostaditas (Recipe Index)* as "corn chips." And fried tortillas, either slightly or crisply fried, are used in innumerable ways. They can be fried lightly, rolled around a filling and served covered with another sauce. These are enchiladas *(Recipe Index)*. When a tortilla is fried crisp and covered with any of several toppings, it is a *tostada.* When an uncooked tortilla is made into a turnover with a cheese or other filling, the edges are crimped, and the whole is deep-fried, it becomes a *quesadilla.* Other traditional corn preparations, such as tamales, are sometimes served along with beans and meat dishes. Literally hundreds of kinds of chilies can go into the sauces for these dishes, and Mexican gourmets can tell the difference when one is substituted for another.

This elaborate cuisine has regional variations, and it was the cooking of northeast Mexico that crossed the border to become a major element in Tex-Mex food. Northeastern Mexicans made more use of beef, because that part of Mexico is prime cattle country, and also of wheat. It was they who produced the wheat-flour tortilla, which looks like a pale tortilla but is thicker and stiffer. When I, a Cape Codder born and bred, first saw a wheat tortilla, I took it for some kind of ship biscuit.

I had known and liked Mexican food for a good many years before I tried much Tex-Mex. Now I must admit that I like the Tex-Mex cuisine better. If it lacks certain standard Mexican dishes (usually because the ingredients are hard to get) or prepares them poorly, it more than makes up for its deficiencies with enthusiasm, willingness to innovate and the lavish use of good materials. Tex-Mex is more generous with meat and cheese, which in Mexico are expensive items that cooks are apt to skimp on. Many proprietors and chefs of Mexican restaurants in Texas are native Texans, often for many generations, and they know that their customers expect a lot of animal protein in their food.

Matt Martinez, a Texan of Mexican ancestry who is proprietor of the excellent El Rancho Restaurant in Austin, is an enthusiastic innovator in Tex-Mex cooking. Periodically he visits Mexico to pick up ideas, then returns to Austin to adapt them to Texas tastes. One of his recent and most popular innovations he calls "Mexican pizza." It consists of the crust of a large, thin round of puffy fried wheat bread, piled with meat, chicken, shrimp or beans, covered with the sauce called *salsa ranchera* and an onion ring, and sprinkled with cheese that is melted under a broiler. Topped off with a dollop of sour cream, Matt's high-profile Mexican pizza makes most of the standardized Italian pizzas look steam-rollered.

For his version of *salsa ranchera,* which forms part of most Mexican dishes and is usually made of hot chilies, onions and tomatoes, Matt leaves out most of the hot chili (the customers can add it to their own taste from separate saucers) and includes celery, which is not used in Mexico. He makes his own tortillas from the whole corn kernels right in the kitchen, as in the best restaurants in Mexico, but when he fries them for any purpose he drains them under the heat of infrared lamps so they keep piping hot and are practically grease-free. An extra-rich dish that Matt calls a *quesadilla* does not resemble its Mexican namesake. Its underpinning is sliced cheese which is covered with chopped meat, *salsa ranchera,* bits of *jalapeño* chili and an onion ring. It is put in the oven until the cheese melts. The trick is to use mild Monterey Jack cheese, a kind that does not stick to the plate.

It is not only Texas restaurants that prepare and expand upon Tex-Mex food. Private homes do it too, and with excellent results. They do not have to start with the crude ingredients, such as corn kernels. Almost every Texas town of any size now has little tortilla factories that soak the corn, grind it into *masa* and make the *masa* into raw tortillas with a machine that delivers them on a conveyor belt. Some of the tortillas are sold cooked and hot, ready to be eaten before they cool off. Others are sold raw, to be cooked just before the family and guests sit down at the dinner table or to be made into enchiladas or some other tortilla-based dish.

Very popular as canapés are *nachos,* which I first encountered in Texas. You cut raw tortillas into pie-shaped segments and fry them in oil until they are crisp and golden brown. Drain them (they do not absorb much fat), put on each some grated cheese and a slice of *jalapeño* chili, and leave under the broiler until the cheese melts. They have the advantage of being self-regulating in their degree of hotness; though they are best eaten whole, people who cannot take chili can remove the *jalapeño* and get only the faintest trace of the chili's burn. You had better make a lot of *nachos;* they vanish almost instantaneously.

Another Texas invention, or rather a combination of Southern and Mexican cooking, is the hush-*jalapeño.* I myself have never liked hushpuppies, those cornmeal balls fried in deep fat that so many Southerners admire as a traditional part of their cuisine, but at the elegant D. J. Sibley ranch in West Texas I had a fine variation on that dish. Jane Sibley wrapped canned *jalapeños* in about one eighth inch of *masa* dough, to which a touch of milk had been added to make it less stiff. Fried just long enough to make the dough crisp on the outside, they made an enlivening breakfast dish for people with strong palates. I ate half a dozen of them.

A Mexican breakfast dish that Texans improve in many ways is *huevos rancheros* (ranch-style eggs). The traditional way to serve this is on an oval plate, with two fried eggs in the center placed on a tortilla and covered with *salsa ranchera.* Small piles of "refried" beans (cooked pinto or pink beans, mashed and warmed up in lard; *Recipe Index*) are placed at each end with bits of toasted tortilla stuck into them. At the Sibley ranch, Mahala Sibley, the daughter of the house, omitted the beans. She made an egg-and-milk mixture, cooked it just enough to hold together, put *salsa ranchera* in the center, folded the edges of the egg over it and topped it off with slices of *jalapeño.* It was a dish to start the day off right.

Anyone who travels in Texas can come up with examples galore of Texas variations on the theme of Mexican cooking, many of which are, in my opinion, distinct improvements on an exotic cuisine that was already good. Tex-Mex food now is spreading fast beyond the boundaries of Texas. It should be welcomed and applauded. Its success testifies to the benefits of mingling cultures.

A boatload of fiesta celebrants dines on such choice Mexican dishes as enchiladas and tamales while cruising a canal in downtown San Antonio. One of four boats operated by the Casa Rio, a waterfront restaurant, the floating dining room puts into port for a new cargo of fine food halfway through the three-course meal. The diners aboard this craft are members of the self-styled Shallow Water Navy, an organization whose sole function is to hold such shipboard feasts once a year, during the fiesta.

A Heady Mixture of Frolic and Food at a Fiesta in Old San Antonio

Every April the people of San Antonio combine civic pride and local energies in an uninhibited 10-day fiesta commemorating the Battle of San Jacinto (1836), at which Texas won its independence from Mexico. A procession of water-borne floats, a torchlight parade, dancing in the streets and solemn visits to such historic landmarks as the Alamo—all celebrate the city's varied traditions and joie de vivre. Another vital feature of the fiesta is the intake of specially prepared foods, Mexican and Tex-Mex for the most part, but with other influences as well: a German touch in sausages, sauerkraut and beer, a French one in such dishes as *quiche lorraine.* Adding a special fillip to the festivities is a happy local custom that involves *cascarones,* which are richly decorated eggshells stuffed with confetti. To confer good luck upon a special amigo, one has only to buy a *cascarón* and break it over his head.

43

The fiesta reaches its peak of revelry in La Villita, or Little Village, in San Antonio's oldest quarter. Here, for four nights, throngs of strollers, entertained by wandering street musicians called *mariachis (left)*, partake of a movable feast. The food reflects the city's mixed past; there are, for example, Southern ham and biscuits, German *wurst,* Irish corned beef and Chinese egg rolls. Most popular of all are Tex-Mex dishes, which run from *jalapeño* cornbread to *empanadillas* (deep-fried pastries filled with honey) to *buñuelos* (large, round pastries sprinkled with sugar and cinnamon). The ones most frequently consumed are variations on the tortilla. Friendly cooks fry thousands of them at stands like the one shown at right, and some glorify the humble tortilla with fillings or toppings in combinations of beans, beef, chicken, cheese, tomato and other ingredients.

Tacos can be eaten daringly, without spilling the filling

. . . or daintily, with a cautiously balanced plate.

There are also grilled beef *anticuchos*

. . . and *chalupas,* tortillas with beans, cheese and lettuce.

45

Date, Pecan and Orange Bread

Preheat the oven to 350°. With a pastry brush, spread 1 tablespoon of the softened butter over the bottom and sides of a 9-by-5-by-3-inch loaf pan. Add 2 tablespoons of the flour and tip the pan from side to side to distribute it evenly. Invert the pan and rap it sharply to remove excess flour.

Place the dates, pecans and orange peel in a bowl, add 2 tablespoons of flour, and toss together gently but thoroughly. Combine the remaining 2 cups of flour, the baking powder, soda and salt, and sift them together into a bowl. Set aside.

In a deep bowl, cream the remaining 4 tablespoons of butter and the sugar by beating and mashing them against the sides of the bowl with the back of a large spoon until the mixture is light and fluffy. Beat in the egg. Add about ½ cup of the flour mixture and, when it is incorporated, beat in ¼ cup of the orange juice. Repeat three times, alternating ½ cup of the flour with ¼ cup of orange juice and beating well after each addition. Stir in the reserved floured fruit and nuts.

Pour the batter into the prepared pan and bake in the middle of the oven for 50 to 60 minutes, or until a toothpick or cake tester inserted in the center comes out clean. Let the bread cool in the pan for 4 or 5 minutes, then turn it out on a wire rack to cool completely to room temperature before serving.

To make one 9-by-5-by-3-inch loaf

5 tablespoons butter, softened
4 tablespoons plus 2 cups unsifted flour
8 ounces pitted dates, cut into small bits with kitchen scissors (about 1 cup)
½ cup finely chopped pecans
4 teaspoons finely chopped fresh orange peel
1 teaspoon double-acting baking powder
1 teaspoon baking soda
1 teaspoon salt
1 cup sugar
1 egg
1 cup strained fresh orange juice

Pecan Tassies

Preheat the oven to 350°. Combine the flour and butter bits in a bowl and, with your fingertips, rub them together until the mixture resembles flakes of coarse meal. Add the cream cheese and continue to rub until the dough is smooth. Shape into a ball, wrap in wax paper and refrigerate the dough for at least 1 hour.

Pecan tassies are baked in a miniature muffin pan with 12 cups, each 1¾ inches across the top and ¾ inch deep. To make a pastry shell, cut off about 1 tablespoon of the dough and press it firmly into the bottom and against the sides of an ungreased muffin cup; repeat the process until you have filled two muffin pans. Smooth the inside surface of the pastry shells with a pestle or the bottom of a small glass.

To prepare the filling, beat the eggs lightly with a wire whisk or a rotary or electric beater. Beat in the brown sugar ½ cup at a time, then add the cooled melted butter and the vanilla extract and salt.

Place 1 teaspoon of chopped pecans in the bottom of a pastry shell, pour in about 1 tablespoon of filling, and set a pecan half on top. Bake the tarts in the middle of the oven for 15 to 20 minutes, or until the filling has puffed slightly and the top begins to crack. The filling will be somewhat firm to the touch.

Turn the pecan tassies out on wire racks to cool completely to room temperature before serving them.

To make about 2 dozen miniature tarts

CRUST
1 cup unsifted flour
8 tablespoons butter, chilled and cut into ¼-inch bits
A 3-ounce package cream cheese, cut into ¼-inch bits and softened

FILLING
2 eggs
1 cup dark brown sugar
2 tablespoons butter, melted and cooled
1 teaspoon vanilla extract
⅛ teaspoon salt

½ cup finely chopped pecans
24 shelled pecan halves (about 2 ounces)

At a ball given by the Order of the Alamo at San Antonio's Menger Hotel, one of the fiesta's more exclusive events, guests line up for a buffet.

To serve 4 to 6 as a first course or
    6 to 8 as an appetizer

1 pound uncooked medium-sized
    shrimp (about 20 to 24 to the
    pound)
1 cup vegetable oil
¼ cup strained fresh lemon juice
2 or 3 large garlic cloves, peeled
    and crushed with a kitchen mallet
    or the flat of a heavy cleaver
¼ cup finely chopped fresh parsley
Salt
Freshly ground black pepper

Texas Broiled Shrimp

Shell the shrimp, leaving the tail and the last segment of shell intact. Devein the shrimp by making a shallow incision down their backs with a small sharp knife and lifting out the black or white intestinal vein with the point of the knife. Wash the shrimp under cold running water and pat them completely dry with paper towels.

Combine the vegetable oil, lemon juice and garlic in a bowl and mix well. Drop in the shrimp and turn them about with a spoon to coat them evenly. Then cover the bowl tightly with aluminum foil or plastic wrap and marinate the shrimp in the refrigerator for about 12 hours, turning them over occasionally.

Immerse two dozen individual Oriental bamboo skewers in water and soak them for at least an hour to prevent the skewers from charring when the shrimp are broiled. Then light a layer of charcoal briquettes in a hibachi and let them burn until a white ash appears on the surface. Or preheat the broiler of the oven to its highest setting.

Remove the shrimp from the marinade and spear each one with a skewer. Broil the shrimp about 4 inches from the heat for 2 to 3 minutes on each side, or until they are delicately browned.

Arrange the skewered shrimp attractively on a heated platter and sprinkle them with the chopped parsley. Season the shrimp lightly with salt and a few grindings of pepper and serve at once.

A purist's version of chili con carne is free of tomatoes or chili powder, and accompanied by separate bowls of beans and rice.

Osgood Pie

Preheat the oven to 350°. With a wire whisk or a rotary or electric beater, beat the egg whites until they are stiff enough to stand in unwavering peaks on the whisk or beater when it is lifted from the bowl.

In a separate bowl but with the same beater unwashed, beat the egg yolks to a froth. Combine the sugar, flour, cinnamon, cloves and nutmeg in a sifter and sprinkle them over the yolks about ½ cup at a time, beating well after each addition. Beat in the vinegar, bourbon or sherry, and cooled melted butter and, when they are thoroughly incorporated, stir in the pecans and raisins.

With a rubber spatula, scoop the egg whites over the egg-yolk mixture and fold them together gently until no trace of white remains. Pour the filling mixture into the pie shell and smooth the top with the spatula. Bake in the middle of the oven for 25 to 30 minutes, or until the top is puffed and delicately browned and the filling remains firm when the pie is shaken gently.

Cool the Osgood pie to room temperature before serving.

To make one 9-inch pie

4 egg whites
4 egg yolks
1 cup sugar
1 tablespoon flour
1 teaspoon ground cinnamon
½ teaspoon ground cloves
½ teaspoon ground nutmeg
3 tablespoons distilled white vinegar
2 tablespoons bourbon or dry sherry
1 tablespoon butter, melted and cooled
1 cup finely chopped pecans
1 cup seedless raisins
A 9-inch short-crust pastry shell partially baked and cooled *(Recipe Booklet)*

Texas Chili con Carne

Under cold running water, pull the stems off the *ancho* and red chilies. Tear the chilies in half and brush out their seeds. With a small sharp knife, cut away any large ribs. Crumble the chilies coarsely, drop them into a bowl, and pour the boiling water over them. Let them soak for at least 30 minutes, then strain the soaking liquid through a sieve set over a bowl and reserve it. Set the chilies aside.

In a heavy 5- to 6-quart casserole, cook the beef suet over moderate heat, stirring frequently until it has rendered all its fat. With a slotted spoon, remove and discard the suet bits. Pour off all but about ¼ cup of the fat remaining in the pot.

Add the venison or beef cubes to the casserole and, stirring constantly, cook over moderate heat until the pieces of meat are firm but not brown. Add 2½ cups of the reserved chili-soaking liquid and bring it to a boil over high heat. Drop in the bay leaves and reduce the heat to low. Simmer partially covered for 1 hour, stirring the mixture from time to time.

Meanwhile, place the cumin seeds in a small ungreased skillet and, sliding the pan back and forth frequently, toast the seeds over low heat for 10 minutes. Drop the seeds into the jar of an electric blender and blend at high speed for 30 seconds. Turn off the machine, add the *ancho* and red chilies, the remaining chili-soaking liquid, the garlic, oregano, paprika, sugar and salt, and blend again at high speed until all of the ingredients are reduced to a smooth purée.

When the meat has cooked its allotted time, stir in the chili purée. Simmer partially covered for 30 minutes. Then, stirring constantly, pour in the cornmeal in a slow stream and cook over high heat until the chili comes to a boil and thickens lightly. Taste the chili for seasoning and add the ground hot red pepper if desired.

Serve the chili con carne directly from the casserole, or from a heated tureen or serving bowl. Mound the pinto beans and the rice in separate bowls and present them with the chili.

To serve 6 to 8

6 dried *ancho* chilies, plus 8 dried hot red chilies, each about 2 inches long *(caution: see note, page 20)*
3½ cups boiling water
½ pound beef suet, preferably kidney suet, cut into ½-inch bits
3 pounds lean boneless venison or beef chuck, trimmed of excess fat, sliced ½ inch thick and cut into ½-inch cubes
3 medium-sized bay leaves, finely crumbled
1 tablespoon cumin seeds
2 tablespoons coarsely chopped garlic
4 teaspoons dried oregano
3 tablespoons paprika
1 tablespoon sugar
1 tablespoon salt
3 tablespoons yellow cornmeal
1 teaspoon ground hot red pepper (cayenne; optional)
Freshly cooked pinto beans *(Recipe Booklet)*
9 cups freshly cooked rice made from 3 cups long-grain white rice

Dear to the Hearts of Texans

Most Texans love pecans. The state is second only to
Georgia as a producer of the meaty, full-flavored nuts,
and Texas cooks turn out such varied sweets as *(from
bottom left, clockwise)* tiny tarts called pecan tassies;
pecan cake; date, pecan and orange bread; and so-
called Osgood pie with a pecan-and-raisin filling. The
basket at center holds pecan-stuffed date cookies.

To serve 4

1 pound fresh okra, or substitute
   two 10-ounce packages frozen
   okra, thoroughly defrosted
4 lean slices bacon, cut crosswise
   into halves
1 medium-sized onion, peeled and
   coarsely chopped
1½ teaspoons salt
3 medium-sized firm ripe tomatoes,
   peeled and coarsely chopped (see
   chile con queso, page 20)
1 teaspoon finely chopped fresh hot
   red chili (caution: see note, page
   20)

Okra and Tomatoes

Wash the fresh okra under cold running water, and with a small sharp knife scrape the skin lightly to remove any surface fuzz. (Frozen okra needs only to be thoroughly defrosted and drained.) Pat the okra completely dry with paper towels, cut off the stems and slice the okra crosswise into ¼-inch-thick rounds.

In a heavy 10-inch skillet, fry the bacon over moderate heat, turning the pieces frequently with tongs until they are crisp and brown and have rendered all their fat. Transfer the bacon to paper towels to drain.

Add the okra, onion and salt to the fat remaining in the skillet and, stirring constantly, cook over moderate heat for 10 minutes. Watch carefully and regulate the heat so that the vegetables do not burn. Add the tomatoes and chili and cook over high heat for 2 minutes, still stirring constantly. Reduce the heat to low and, stirring the mixture occasionally, simmer uncovered for about 15 minutes, or until the okra and tomatoes are soft. Taste for seasoning.

To serve, transfer the entire contents of the skillet to a heated bowl and arrange the bacon on top.

To make one 10-inch cake ring

2½ cups seedless raisins
¾ to 1¼ cups bourbon
13 tablespoons butter, softened
2 tablespoons plus 3 cups unsifted
   flour
1½ teaspoons double-acting
   baking powder
1½ teaspoons ground nutmeg
1 teaspoon salt
1½ cups sugar
5 eggs
3 cups coarsely chopped pecans
   (about 12 ounces)

Pecan Cake

Mix the raisins and ¾ cup of bourbon together in a bowl and let them steep for at least 30 minutes, stirring from time to time.

Preheat the oven to 325°. With a pastry brush, spread 1 tablespoon of softened butter over the bottom and sides of a 10-inch tube cake pan. Add 2 tablespoons of the flour and tip the pan from side to side to distribute it evenly. Invert the pan and rap the bottom sharply to remove the excess flour. Set the pan aside.

Combine 2½ cups of the remaining flour with the baking powder, nutmeg and salt, and sift them together into a bowl.

In a deep mixing bowl, cream the remaining 12 tablespoons of softened butter and the sugar by beating and mashing them against the sides of the bowl with the back of a spoon until the mixture is light and fluffy. Beat in the eggs, one at a time, then add the flour-nutmeg mixture by the cupful, beating the batter well after each addition.

With a slotted spoon, transfer the raisins to a small bowl and pour the ¾ cup of bourbon into the batter. Mix well. Add the pecans and the remaining ½ cup of flour to the raisins and toss them together thoroughly. Then stir the raisin-and-nut mixture into the batter.

Pour the batter into the prepared pan, filling it about three quarters full and smoothing the top with a rubber spatula. Bake in the middle of the oven for about 1 hour and 10 minutes, or until a toothpick or cake tester inserted in the center comes out clean.

Let the cake cool in the pan for about 10 minutes, then turn it out on a wire rack to cool completely. Serve at once or, if you prefer, soak a double-thick 16-inch square of cheesecloth in ½ cup of additional bourbon and wrap the cloth around the cake. Cover it tightly with foil or plastic wrap and let it stand at room temperature for at least 48 hours before serving.

Okra cooked in the Texas style, crisp and never sticky, is combined with tomatoes, laced with onion and red chilies, and served with a bacon topping.

III

Frontier Foods of Desert and Mountain

Cattle and mountains, classic
features of a Western landscape,
meet in the spacious grandeur
of Fraser, Colorado, where herds
of Herefords graze below the pine-
and aspen-clad foothills of the
Rockies. Though most of Colorado's
terrain is rugged and mountainous,
food production is one of its basic
industries. Two thirds of the state's
output comes from livestock, mainly
in the form of beef and veal.

Colorado, Utah, Nevada, Arizona and New Mexico form the monumental heart of what was once called, in a great oversimplification, the Great American Desert. Much of the region is mountainous and well forested, and catches a lot of rain. Many of the flatlands are, indeed, desert or semidesert country, but they are now laced with highways and dotted with irrigated oases. Only about six million people live in all five states, most of them in and around Denver, Salt Lake City, Phoenix, Albuquerque and a few smaller cities. Between such urban intervals, a visitor drives through some of the world's most spectacular scenery, including the Grand Canyon in Arizona and the Garden of the Gods in Colorado. But he also travels, for mile after mile, through uninhabited mountain terrain or across enormous stretches of low-lying arid land where nothing moves but horned toads, sidewinder rattlesnakes and roadrunners.

Although the five states share a more or less common geography, their historical backgrounds are quite dissimilar, and this has dramatically influenced their present culture, including their cuisine. White men came into this difficult region at various times and by various arduous routes. In Colorado, Utah and Nevada the mainstream of settlers was from the East. The gold seekers, the cattlemen, the Mormons and other homesteaders who flocked into these states from the 1840s on brought with them Eastern ways of cooking, and as a result the cuisine there is largely Anglo in style and distinguished mainly by its bounty.

History followed a different course in New Mexico and Arizona. New Mexico, long a domain of the communal Pueblo Indians, was the first of

Found in a thousand-year-old pueblo ruin in Arizona, a trough-shaped stone *metate,* or hand mill *(above),* and its *mano,* or grinding stone, symbolize the Indians' greatest single gift to the world's cuisine—corn. Pueblo women still use such utensils to grind corn kernels into meal. In pre-Columbian days, their ancestors grew as many as 40 different varieties of corn, and the Indians continue to prefer such diversity. Each of the varieties shown above at right, when ground into meal, will lend its own distinctive flavor to Indian dishes. Surplus ears, husked, dried and sorted by colors, will be stacked like cordwood and stored for future use.

the five states to be settled by white men—Spaniards moving north from Mexico who began to establish outposts along the Rio Grande at the close of the 16th Century. Since the Indian-Spanish-Mexican tradition has such deep roots in New Mexico, it has inevitably and strongly influenced the cuisine of present-day New Mexicans. Neighboring Arizona shares this tradition, but to a lesser degree. Lacking New Mexico's natural oases, it was largely ignored by the Spanish for another century and remained sparsely settled, primarily by Pueblo Indians and nomadic tribes, until the advent of large-scale copper mining and cattle raising in the 1870s and 1880s. Thus much of Arizona's cooking too is Anglo, although in the extreme southern part of the state, near the Mexican border, it has a distinctively Mexican character.

Spanish explorers and a few settlers from Spanish-ruled New Mexico were the first non-Indians to enter Colorado. But the state's most celebrated pioneers were hardy frontiersmen of French or Anglo origin who came westward across the plains early in the 19th Century to trap beaver among the towering ranges of the Continental Divide. They lived on game—venison, buffalo, antelope, sometimes beaver—and on any other food, including dog meat and sunflower meal, which the friendlier Indians would trade for goods and whiskey.

I was lucky to get my first glimpse of the Colorado Rockies just as the trappers had usually seen them—from the plains to the east. For two days my train lumbered across the Mississippi Valley and the prairies of Kansas and eastern Colorado; with each passing mile the country became drier, emptier and more monotonous. Then someone shouted "Pikes Peak!" and we all rushed to the windows to admire a sharp white point thrusting itself above the distant horizon. Soon a whole chain of rugged snow peaks rose majestically into sight, their summits glistening in the sunlight, and we felt some of the awe and exhilaration that the old trappers must have experienced as they left the dreary plains and approached the beautiful mountains.

The epoch of the mountain man lasted only a generation: by the late

1830s beaver hats for men were going out of fashion in American and European cities, and beaver pelts were no longer in such demand. Cattlemen and a wild stampede of gold miners soon replaced the trappers. But the old mountain men are still a part of Colorado's legend, and every story and relic they left is cherished.

A center of this he-man cult is a colorful restaurant called The Fort, located at Morrison in the foothills of the Rockies about a half-hour drive from Denver. It is a careful reconstruction of the fort built on the Arkansas River in 1834 by the Bent brothers, the most important trading post of its day in the Rocky Mountain region. The Fort's proprietor, Sam Arnold, is a gold mine of information about the mountain men and the Indians they fought, lived with and often married; he has gone to great lengths to recapture the atmosphere of that lusty era. As in the original fort, long since destroyed, the 15-foot-high walls are of large adobe bricks, and the rounded bastions at two corners are loopholed for muskets. Even the tableware and furniture of The Fort's dining rooms retain some of the character of the frontier. The knives are of an old-fashioned pistol-grip pattern, and the forks have three tines instead of the more familiar four. The tables and chairs, hand-carved and put together with wooden pegs, are copied from Spanish Colonial designs of the 1840s.

The Fort is famous for its thick steaks grilled in the aromatic smoke of aspen coals, but it also offers some of the game meats that were the mainstay of the early West. One of these is buffalo, which today is raised commercially or comes from surplus herds on reservations. My introduction to buffalo was a buffalo-and-green-pepper stew that Sam Arnold personally prepared for me. It resembled a fine beef stew except that the meat, while tender as prime beef, was richer and somewhat sweeter in flavor. Buffalo tongue, which the mountain men considered an outstanding delicacy and which was once smoked and shipped to the finest restaurants back East and in Europe, makes an even tastier dish. I sampled a tongue that had been boiled with peppercorns, grated onion, bay leaves and a pinch of salt, and admired the discrimination shown by the old trappers and hunters. The tongue was indeed splendid, its meat firmer, leaner, darker and smoother in texture than beef tongue and with a distinctive, most agreeable "wild" flavor.

A gourmet and social club calling itself the Green River Scalping and Joy Society meets at The Fort from time to time to feast on exotic foods favored by the old mountain men. The society takes its name from the Green River skinning knife that was widely used in frontier days and was originally manufactured by a factory near the Green River in Massachusetts. In earlier times it often served purposes more sinister than skinning game and gave rise to the expression "Give it to 'em right up to Green"—meaning up to the trademark stamped on the blade near the hilt. At the Green River Scalping and Joy Society dinners, the menu includes such rarities as bighorn sheep steaks, wild pig, fresh rattlesnake, roast beaver and boiled moose nose.

Some of The Fort's adaptations of old-time Western recipes have a more universal appeal. One of these rejuvenated dishes is Bowl of the Wife of Kit Carson *(Recipe Index)*. The famous guide and Indian fighter was once employed as a hunter by the original Bent's Fort, and the bowl of his wife—possibly but not necessarily her invention—is a savory Mexican-style "dry soup" of rice, chicken, chilies, *garbanzos* and cheese, with avocado (a recent innovation) added mainly to lend color. Another frontier food served at The Fort as a side dish or dessert is trappers' fruit *(Recipe Index),* the main ingredients of which are dried apples, sugar or honey, and nuts. I tried it as a dessert, hot, laced with rum and topped with a generous swirl of whipped cream, and found it rapturous, but I doubt if a mountain man ever ate such a fancied-up version.

Just west of Denver the foothills of the Rockies rise abruptly, but east of the city there are hundreds of square miles of tawny plains, crawling with herds of cattle. So it is not surprising that until fairly recently Denver lived primarily on beef; in fact, it may have rivaled Chicago as the nation's greatest meat-eating town. When the average citizen went to a restaurant, his idea of a fine meal was simply a large, juicy cut of Colorado's excellent beef, fattened in nearby feed lots.

Those simplistic days have passed. Denver still eats a spectacular amount of meat, but its dining habits, like the city itself, have become highly sophisticated. The change is largely due to an influx of newcomers from more crowded parts of the country who were accustomed to a more cosmopolitan diet. Restaurants serving the dishes of many nationalities have opened and are prospering, and specialties like chicken *teriyaki* and beef Stroganov now appear on menus formerly dominated by steak and roast beef. In summer Denver families stage elaborate picnics amid the uncluttered mountain scenery nearby, each trying to outdo the other in the quality and variety of offerings. A friend in Denver once invited me to such a picnic in a fragrant pine grove beside a fast-flowing mountain stream. So many tempting foods were spread before me that I had a hard time deciding which to try first—the venison paté, the smoked rainbow trout or the pickled wild mushrooms. I finally decided on the smoked trout, accompanying it with a zesty, stream-chilled white wine that my host himself had made with choice grapes from California.

Denver was founded in 1858, a year before the "Pikes Peak or Bust" rush to the newly discovered Colorado gold fields. Still, the city treasures reminders of its relatively brief past. Although most of its flamboyant Victorian mansions, built by miners-turned-millionaires, have given way to blocks of apartment buildings, one outstanding relic of the wildly booming mining era is still going strong. It is the Brown Palace Hotel, built mainly of massive red granite and opened in 1892. It is still Denver's prestige hotel. In its lobby and other public rooms, the turn-of-the-century furnishings and décor have been lovingly preserved. Likewise the hotel's tradition of fine cuisine. The menu of its opening banquet began with littleneck clams followed by *consommé renaissance,* and included such elegant dishes as mountain trout *ravigote, terrapin en caisse à la Maryland* and golden plover. Among the wines served were Josefshöfer, a distinguished Moselle, and for those who preferred champagne, a Brut Imperial. I do not recall seeing terrapin in its shell or golden plover listed on any recent menus, but dining at the Brown Palace is still a notable experience in old-fashioned opulence and deft service.

Continued on page 64

At an outlying community of the Acoma pueblo, Mrs. Santana Antonio lifts newly fired pots from the smoldering remains of a cow-dung fire. Firing is the final step in the Indian method of pottery making, traditionally a woman's craft. Each vessel is first built up of coils of clay, rather than turned on a wheel. It is then smoothed inside and out, dried and skillfully decorated with mineral or vegetable paints in traditional freehand patterns. Completed vessels are used to store water and dry foodstuffs —or are sold to collectors.

Indian Customs and Foods Reflect an Ancient Mode of Life

Centuries before Spanish explorers and settlers first ventured north of the Mexican border, the Pueblo Indians of the Southwest had achieved what many authorities consider the highest level of civilization among all the Indians who lived in what is now the United States. The region is scattered with remains of their sturdy communal dwellings, their elaborate irrigation projects, their simple but efficient utensils and their sophisticated artistry. Even today, some of their multistoried strongholds, built on fertile valley floors or atop easily defended cliffs and mesas, still flourish in New Mexico and Arizona; one of them, the Acoma pueblo in north-central New Mexico, has been continuously inhabited for nearly seven hundred years. Although the present-day pueblo dwellers have adopted a number of modern customs and conveniences, they and certain other Southwestern Indians, such as the once-nomadic Navajos, cling tenaciously and proudly to many of their old-time ways, among them the preparation of both traditional Indian foods and dishes borrowed from or inspired by their Spanish conquerors.

Two mainstays of the Navajo diet—fry bread *(Recipe Index)*, deep-fried to a crisp golden brown, and savory mutton stew —are here photographed against the dramatic backdrop of Window Rock, a natural arch on Arizona's Navajo reservation. Both foods trace their origin to the Spaniards, who introduced wheat and sheep into the region. The traditional recipe for the stew calls only for mutton, potatoes, onions and water, but present-day Navajos sometimes enrich the dish with a carrot or two and slices of green pepper.

When Tirzah Honanie, a sturdy Hopi grandmother, makes *piki* bread, she uses a method that exemplifies her people's changeless way of life. Centuries ago her ancestors found safe homes atop high sun-baked mesas northeast of Arizona's Painted Desert. These refuges were ringed with irrigable land, and the pueblo-dwelling Hopi became skilled farmers. Corn was and still is their chief food, often in the form of *piki*.

Tirzah makes *piki* almost exactly as her forebears did. She roasts blue corn *(page 56)* for about an hour, crushes and grinds it with stone implements and makes a batter by mixing the meal with water. To make blue *piki (below),* the bread for everyday use, Tirzah adds sage ash to darken the batter; yellow *piki* and red *piki,* prepared chiefly for special occasions, are made with white cornmeal and the appropriate vegetable dyes.

Tirzah spreads a thin layer of batter by hand over a hot stone greased with sheep's brains. When the *piki* curls at the edges, she peels it off the grill *(top)* and spreads another batch. She deftly rolls two crêpe-thin sheets of hot *piki* into long, flaky rolls—and at this point invariably loses at least one roll to her hungry granddaughter *(opposite).* Normally, Tirzah makes 50 rolls of blue *piki* at a time, a job that takes about three hours and provides a week's supply of bread for the five members of her family. But demand rises in summer, when her menfolk are busy with new crops in the family plot 25 miles away. "It takes five rolls a day just to fill each of them up then," Tirzah explains, "and it's really the only thing that tastes good when you're working hard."

Other reminders of Denver's lively past survive in the original city center. A few blocks on Larimer Street were never converted into office buildings; instead, the business center moved away from them and left their fancy Victorian facades to vagrants. Ladies did not ordinarily venture there, but a few years ago one vigorous Denverite, Mrs. Dana Hudkins Crawford, became interested in the picturesque old buildings and found them sturdy enough for rehabilitation. She created an organization that bought the most interesting block, carefully restored it and turned it into a now-fashionable complex of elegant boutiques and restaurants. Even the memory of the luxurious brothels that flourished in Denver's most boisterous day is kept alive in Larimer Square. One antique shop there is called Mattie Silk's, after a bawdyhouse run by an especially successful madam; it sells faithful replicas of the brass tokens that entitled customers to trade at her popular establishment.

There is plenty of good eating to be found throughout Colorado. It ranges from the simple but plentiful fare served at dude ranches that pride themselves on their old-style Western cooking to the international cuisine favored at such resort towns as Colorado Springs and Aspen. Nestled at the foot of Pikes Peak, Colorado Springs has long been famous as a posh watering place and summer vacation spot, but Aspen, perched in the lofty heart of the Rockies and Colorado's major ski resort as well as a cultural center, has become an immensely popular attraction only within the past 25 years or so.

In the 1890s Aspen was a lusty silver-mining town, and there are still some ornate mansions of the silver barons that recall the big years before Aspen declined to little more than a ghost town. After World War II, as new entrepreneurs moved in to exploit the surrounding mountainsides that are deep in dry powdery snow from November to mid-April, Aspen came back bigger than ever. To accommodate the thousands who challenge its ski slopes each year (and other thousands who come to its summer music festival or to attend the Aspen Institute for Humanistic Studies), Alpine-style lodges, apartments and luxurious condominiums have sprung up, and the restaurants that cater to these visitors are mostly first-rate and varied enough to suit all tastes. In one of them huddled at the base of the ski slopes I enjoyed my most satisfying lamb chops in years —so tender, juicy and thick that they must have come from a burly but still adolescent lamb. Aspen apparently has not yet decided that lamb chops should be ladylike little things with delicate trimmed bones and a small kernel of meat. Another restaurant features sophisticated dishes from a different nation or area of the world each night of the week, and yet another, Swiss in style, is justly celebrated for its creamy cheese fondue prepared with dry white wine and Kirschwasser.

West of Colorado lies Utah, another state with an extraordinary past and an unusual present. Salt Lake City, its capital, was settled not by brawling gold seekers as Denver was, but by the orderly and industrious Mormons, members of the Church of Jesus Christ of Latter-day Saints. Today about three fourths of the population of Utah is still Mormon, so that everything that happens in the state is affected in some way by the rules and customs of their church. The food is no exception. A stranger spending a few days in Salt Lake City may be surprised that the city, though obviously prosperous, has so few good restaurants. If he has much contact with the Mormons, he soon learns why: it is because Mormons eat at home. They also eat extremely well, and what they eat is strongly influenced by their religion.

In 1847 Mormon pioneers, fleeing from religious persecution in the Middle West, came to Utah. Led by Brigham Young, they entered the wide, mountain-sheltered valley that contains the Great Salt Lake. The site where they decided to build their holy city was on the edge of sagebrush desert, but streams from the nearby mountains offered abundant water. One of their first acts was to divert the streams, to irrigate the dry earth and prepare it for planting.

The first years were hard. Isolated from civilization and with only the scantiest imported supplies, the original settlers and hundreds of other Mormons who soon joined them eked out their meals with such native foods as sego lily bulbs, thistle greens, hawks, owls and crows. When some of the settlers showed an inclination for prospecting, Brigham Young decreed otherwise. "Instead of hunting gold," he ordered, "let every man go to work at raising wheat, oats, barley, corn and vegetables and fruit in abundance that there may be plenty in the land." As the fields and orchards began to yield good crops, a rich oasis developed, and well-planned Mormon expeditions set out from around Salt Lake City to create similar centers in other parts of Utah and in Idaho, Nevada and Ar-

Workers at the Santa Cruz Chili and Spice Company in Amado, Arizona, remove the stems from newly harvested chilies. The deep-red pods, ripened in fields near the Mexican border, are the basic ingredient of chili paste, a hot, spicy seasoning that is used to enliven any number of Mexican or Mexican-inspired dishes.

Rosalia Contreras blends tomatoes, chilies and other ingredients for a Santa Cruz Chili and Spice Company product, taco sauce.

izona. To this day only a tiny part of Utah's total area is cultivated, but that part is beautifully lush and productive.

Although Utah is increasingly urban and industrial, the all-pervasive Mormon influence is responsible for its attachment to customs of its agricultural past. The church, which is rich, efficient and progressive, has not forgotten less-affluent times. It remembers, for instance, the famines that more than once threatened the early settlers, and urges Mormon families to store a year's supply of food. Many do, and it is not unusual for a family to keep more than the designated amount. One young housewife showed me her storeroom, a dry basement cut into a hillside off her kitchen. In it was a full ton of wheat packed in metal drums, 300 pounds of dried milk, 700 pounds of sugar and large quantities of beans, macaroni and commercial canned goods. Every summer she augments these provisions with shelf after shelf of peas, tomatoes, corn, celery and other fruits and vegetables that she cans herself, and once a year she bakes enough fruitcake to last 12 months. She also stores a broad assortment of home-dried fruits, a Mormon specialty that is especially easy to make in Utah's dry air and bright sunshine.

In addition to all this, she has a monster freezer stuffed with meat, including the meat of two deer shot by the head of the house. Some of the venison, his wife said, would be made into mincemeat for old-fashioned pies. Her husband also contributes to the family food stockpile by fishing, and she cans the plump trout he catches in mountain lakes and streams. The containers are steamed in a pressure cooker, and the trout bones become tenderized like those of canned salmon.

She rotates all these foodstuffs systematically so that none of them will get too old. Some of the wheat she boils whole as breakfast food. "It costs six cents a breakfast to feed my family of eight," she told me. Some of it is ground into whole-wheat flour, which she uses to make pancakes or waffles. Many Mormon brides receive as a wedding present a small, hand-operated flour mill somewhat like those used by their pioneer ancestors, although modern Mormon women usually have their wheat ground in a church-owned mill.

Another old-time custom encouraged by the church is bread baking. A great many Utah households still bake their own bread, and it is indeed superb, especially the whole-wheat variety made from an early Mormon recipe that includes a liberal amount of honey and molasses. Even the stores in Utah sell richly textured and flavorsome bread that is almost indistinguishable from the homemade kind.

The church forbids the use of tobacco, alcoholic drinks, coffee and tea, and it is easy to theorize that the Mormon emphasis on good food and lots of it is at least partly an effort to compensate for these deprivations. The prohibitions may also account for Utah's large per capita consumption of candy, almost twice as much as the national average. The figure would probably be considerably higher if it included homemade candy. Church policy encourages each Mormon family to have a "family evening" once a week, usually on Monday. A popular entertainment on such an occasion, for children and grownups alike, is to make candy. Some is as simple as popcorn balls, some as complex as "pioneer fruit

The Old-fashioned Way with a Wheat Tortilla

An Arizona staple is the wheat tortilla, here made by Luisa Rojas, a descendant of Spanish settlers in the state. In these pictures, Mrs. Rojas is dressed in the Spanish colonial style of the 1770s; her kitchen, in a museum at Tubac, near Nogales, is a restoration of a kitchen of the era. After mixing dough in a wooden tray *(above)*, she shapes it into balls *(above)*, pats them into thin disks *(left)* and cooks them on the earthenware griddle. Her efforts culminate on a table *(opposite)* of traditional Arizona dishes: a *chimichango*, a tortilla wrapped around a mixture of meat, potatoes, onion and chilies and deep-fried *(left foreground)*; a tortilla topped with cheese, lettuce, green chilies and red chili powder *(center)*; chili con carne ringed with pieces of tortilla used as scoops *(far right)*; and beef tamales *(right rear)*.

candy," consisting of raisins, figs, dates, stoned prunes and orange peel ground together and blended with orange juice and chopped walnuts. This mixture is molded into balls or bars, and to make these even more toothsome they are dipped in melted milk chocolate. Confections as tricky to make as soft-centered chocolates are also produced in Mormon kitchens; and one of my pleasantest memories of Utah is the parting gift from another young housewife: some of her homemade chocolate creams, as perfectly formed as if they had come from the shop of a professional candymaker—and better tasting.

Because many early converts to Mormonism came from abroad, cooking in Utah has been influenced by European cuisines as well as by the church. For example, spiced red cabbage, a dish that has been popular here for more than a century, is typically German, and Mormon sour-cream raisin pie, topped with a fluffy meringue, is also inspired by an old German recipe. Pepper cookies, another great favorite, trace their ancestry to Scandinavia. The ground black pepper in them is unobtrusive, and along with goodly amounts of ginger, cloves and cinnamon, it gives the cookies a delightful, lingering spiciness, rather like a souped-up gingersnap. Some Mormon dishes are even influenced by Spanish-speaking regions to the south. The traditional Mormon casserole of lima beans and pork sausage is enlivened by chili powder, and it is a bit startling to find that another time-honored dish of the faithful, hamburger bean goulash, is actually a naturalized version of chili con carne.

The Mormon expeditions that fanned out from Salt Lake City to establish fruitful garden spots elsewhere met one of the continent's most awesome landscapes when they crossed into what is now Nevada. The country was strewn with jagged mountains interspersed with valleys even more arid and barren than Utah's had been. In the midst of this wasteland loomed rocky masses eroded into twisted, eerie shapes, and hot springs bubbled up from deep underground. But in far-western Nevada, near the eastern slopes of the Sierras, the venturers found some well-watered valleys. In one of these, in 1850, a group of Mormons built the state's first white settlement, a crude temporary station for trading with gold hunters and emigrants on their way to California. During the next decade a few longer-lasting Mormon settlements appeared in Nevada, but signs of civilization were few and far between. They still are today. Almost all of Nevada remains uninhabited desert. Although it is the fourth largest of the continental states, it has only about 500,000 people, most of them located in the resort and gambling centers of Reno and Las Vegas, but it is growing fast as more and more newcomers move into the population vacuum.

With the discovery in 1859 of the fabulously rich Comstock Lode in the Sierra Nevada foothills, life in Nevada perked up dramatically. Once the Comstock mines began to yield fortunes in gold and silver, Nevada was no longer simply a formidable obstacle on the way to California; it became an irresistible magnet for hordes of people dreaming of sudden wealth. Virginia City, Gold Hill and other turbulent mining towns mushroomed in the Comstock region and other parts of western Nevada. By 1880, when the Comstock Lode was nearing exhaustion, some of the mining communities that had begun as mere collections of tent shanties boasted not only elaborate gambling halls and ornately furnished homes but elegant restaurants as well, patronized by newly rich miners and speculators determined to enjoy the finest food that money could buy.

Virginia City in particular knew an opulence that has become legendary. Its wealthier citizens rode in fine carriages, attended performances by famous singers and actors in the city's opera house and theaters, and ate lavishly at its luxurious hotels, clubs and restaurants, some of which imported internationally celebrated chefs. A reporter for the New York *Daily Tribune* visited Virginia City in 1872 and reported that its restaurants "are as fine as any in the world . . . There are drinking saloons more gorgeous in their appointments than any in San Francisco, Philadelphia or New York, and there are shops and stores that are dazzlingly splendid . . . the number of diamonds displayed in their windows quite overwhelms the senses."

When the bonanza era was over, many of Nevada's mining communities faded into ghost towns. Virginia City managed to survive, if only as a small, quiet tourist attraction. But eating as sophisticated as anything known in its rambunctious days still is to be found in Nevada's more modern cities. Reno, about 25 miles northwest of Virginia City and best known for its gambling casinos and divorce mills, is within easy reach of the state's great cattle and sheep ranches. Inevitably its cooking features a great deal of beef and lamb, and the meat offered by Reno's many excellent restaurants is highly praised even by visiting Coloradans, especially when it is served in such elegant, mouth-watering guises as *châteaubriand béarnaise* or rack of lamb.

The nation's gaudiest gambling den is Las Vegas, surrounded by barren desert down in Nevada's extreme south. Besides the roulette wheels, slot machines, nightclubs and extravagant hotels of the neon-lit street called The Strip, Las Vegas boasts a cuisine whose variety and quality make the city one of the most cosmopolitan dining places in the country.

Since gambling is a pursuit that acknowledges no set timetable, eating in Las Vegas is geared to a 24-hour-a-day schedule. With people getting up and going to bed at all hours, breakfast is a round-the-clock affair, and so are other meals. You can get almost anything you want to eat at any time of the day—from snails and lobster to corned beef and cabbage—and no demand is too exotic. The city's population is polyglot, made up largely of people born and raised elsewhere, who have brought their culinary pleasures along with them. Consequently, Las Vegas abounds with restaurants that serve foreign foods, among them French, Italian, Chinese, Japanese, Greek and Syrian specialties, as well as traditional dishes from northern Spain introduced by the Basques, who have been coming to Nevada as sheepherders for more than 50 years.

Unlike Nevada, Utah and Colorado, the desert states of New Mexico and Arizona owe a deep debt to the cuisine of their common neighbor to the south, Mexico. The cooking of New Mexico, in particular, preserves a high proportion of authentically Mexican and Spanish dishes, as well as culinary legacies from the far older Indian tradition. To some visitors to the Southwest, the differences that separate the two Latin kinds of cook-

Genoveva Martinez, a cook at Rancho de Chimayó, inspects an array of the restaurant's specialties *(left)*. The display includes: (1) a combination platter of refried beans, rice, *chile relleno,* enchiladas, a taco and *guacamole* with *tostaditas;* (2) red chili sauce; (3) chicken Chimayó with peas and rice; (4) *sopaipillas;* (5) *carne adobada* (pork steaks in hot sauce) with *posole* (hominy) and salad; (6) *chile relleno* (chopped chilies, cheese and meat fried in an egg batter) with rice and salad; (7) pinto beans; (8) blue-corn tortillas; (9) white-corn tortillas; (10) dried Chimayó chilies; (11) green chili sauce; (12) *tostaditas* (tortilla chips).

An Authentic yet Creative New Mexican Restaurant

Southwestern gourmets sometimes drive for hours to reach the picturesque 400-year-old village of Chimayó, about 30 miles north of Santa Fe. Here, in a lovely orchard-studded valley, is Arturo Jaramillo's Rancho de Chimayó, a rambling old farmhouse that has become a restaurant famous for the authenticity of its cooking. Jaramillo offers classic versions of such standard Mexican-American dishes as enchiladas and tacos. But he has also created such new dishes as chicken Chimayó, for which a chicken is parboiled, roasted, broiled with a savory coating of hot chili sauce and cheese, and served with Spanish rice. Another example of the Rancho's inventive use of traditional ingredients is the heady Chimayó cocktail with which Mr. and Mrs. Jaramillo toast each other in the picture below. To make one, put 1½ ounces of tequila, 1 ounce of apple cider, and ¼ ounce each of lemon juice and crème de cassis in a shaker with cracked ice or ice cubes, shake well and serve.

ing may frequently be so subtle as to defy recognition; to the initiated, however, they are unmistakable.

The first Spaniards to settle permanently in what is now New Mexico must have felt that they had entered an earthly paradise when they finally reached the fertile upper Rio Grande Valley in 1598. They had struggled northward from Mexico through rugged mountains and across ghastly deserts. At the end of the worst desert of all, the Jornada del Muerto (Dead Man's March) in southern New Mexico, they came to the river, running cool and fresh from the towering Rockies far to the north. Strung along or near the Rio Grande at long intervals were thriving communities of the peaceful Pueblo Indians, with their slope-sided, multistoried adobe buildings and the fields in which they cultivated corn, beans, squash, pumpkins and cotton.

It is still a moving experience to glimpse this green valley for the first time. Most highways approach it across scrub-covered plains or dry, rocky ridges. Then you top a rise and look down into an utterly different world, as rich and productive as its surroundings are barren, spreading for miles from the New Mexican capital of Santa Fe. There are fields of corn, lush pastures dotted with cows, prosperous farms and an occasional Indian pueblo, a sight from another age.

The early settlers in this favored land suffered from its extreme isolation. Except for intermittent supplies from Spanish Mexico, they were cut off from the world by desert and by hostile nomadic Indians. To add to their troubles, the power of Spain began to decline not long after they arrived in New Mexico, and aid from Mexico dwindled to a trickle. Left to their own resources, the settlers of the beautiful valley turned their farms and villages into fortresses to stand off marauding Indians. They made utensils out of local materials, wove their own cloth, grew their own food. They survived, and their descendants survive today as a sizable portion of New Mexico's population. They call themselves Spanish-Americans, and pursue a way of life that clings to many of their ancestral customs, including habits of eating.

Although their delicious and distinctive cuisine, like that of New Mexico in general, shows many Mexican influences—including a fondness for chilies—it is by no means wholly Mexican. It has much that is Spanish and not a little that is inherited from the Pueblo Indians, with whom the Spaniards lived amicably side by side for centuries. The Indians, whose only domesticated animal in pre-Spanish days was the dog, quickly added beef, lamb and goat to their diet, and the early colonists just as readily adopted Indian foods, especially the corn that, in one form or another, still figures prominently in many Spanish-American dishes. Perhaps the most visually startling of these is cornbread made from a strain of blue corn that is still cultivated around the pueblos; while blue cornbread does not taste very different from the ordinary kind made from white or yellow corn, its impact on the eye is considerable.

The purely Spanish elements in the Spanish-American cuisine tend to show up in the desserts. In the old days, when the settlers of the upper Rio Grande Valley could only rarely count on such imported ingredients as sugar and spices, rich desserts from Spanish recipes were reserved for

At Taos Ski Valley in the Sangre de Cristo Mountains, high above the sun-baked plains of northern New Mexico, skiers enjoy an *alfresco* lunch break as another skier swoops down a slope in the background. The people shown here are guests at the St. Bernard Hotel, situated at the foot of the ski slopes and known for its fine French foods; their meal, prepared in the hotel kitchen, includes hot vichyssoise and roast New Mexican pheasant accompanied by a Bordeaux claret.

special festive occasions. Some, like the anise-flavored cookies baked at Christmas, still are.

Among the desserts that maintain their Spanish integrity, one of the most delicious is *empanaditas de frutas,* turnovers filled with mincemeat, baked or fried to a golden brown and sprinkled with a powdering of sugar. The ones I ate in New Mexico, stuffed with an aromatic mixture of finely chopped boiled tongue, sugar, molasses, raisins, apples and spices, were practically indistinguishable from some I had recently tasted in Spain. The only noticeable difference, but an intriguing one, was the addition of piñon nuts.

Another especially rich and flavorful dish derived from Spain is a kind of bread pudding called *capirotada.* The recipe given me by Mrs. Joseph M. Montoya, wife of the United States Senator from New Mexico, is fancier than most. It calls for slices of toasted white bread fried in butter and arranged in layers in a casserole with piñon nuts, raisins and slivers of longhorn cheese, a very mild Cheddar. The whole is sprinkled with cinnamon, after which a syrup of wine, water and caramelized sugar is poured over it. The casserole is then put in the oven until the bread has absorbed all the syrup and has browned nicely on top. The dessert is even more compelling when brandy or whiskey is added just before serving. Then it is called *capirotada borracha* (drunken bread pudding).

75

The piñon nuts, incidentally, are an Indian contribution to Southwestern cuisine. The seeds of a smallish Southwestern pine tree, with a sweet, somewhat oily taste, they were once a staple of the Indian diet throughout this region, but the demand for them became so great that they are now a rather costly item. The Indians simply gathered the nuts as soon as they ripened on the tree, but I learned a different and less honorable way to acquire them. Once on a visit to a laboratory in New Mexico, I was driven out into wild country by a scientist whose hobby was archeology. He was searching for traces of ancient Indian burials by raking the loose dirt of anthills and looking for tiny turquoise beads that are sometimes brought up by the ants from graves below. On this trip we found no beads, but we were among piñon trees, and the scientist showed me how to forage for the nuts in the storage bins of pack rats. We found two, each with about a quart of piñon nuts in it. I felt a bit guilty about this larceny, but the scientist assured me that pack rats store many more nuts than they really need for the winter.

For anyone who wants to savor traditional New Mexican cooking at its best, I strongly recommend dining at the Rancho de Chimayó, about 25 miles north of Santa Fe, where the atmosphere is as authentic as the Spanish and Mexican dishes that are served. The restaurant is owned and operated by a handsome young man named Arturo Jaramillo, who is descended from a family of New Mexico's original Spanish settlers and looks as Spanish as a Velázquez portrait. Arturo married an Anglo and lived for a while in Connecticut, but soon came back to New Mexico to manage the ancestral ranch, set amid apple orchards and fields of chili plants in the charming little valley of Chimayó, which is kept green by two small tributaries of the Rio Grande.

The upper Rio Grande Valley, whose 7,000-foot altitude gives it a refreshingly cool climate, is a popular summer resort, and it did not take Arturo Jaramillo long to discover that discerning vacationers were hungry for New Mexican food prepared from appetizing, time-honored recipes. So he turned part of his rambling old adobe ranch house into a restaurant and started offering local dishes cooked as he remembered them from his grandmother's kitchen, using local ingredients wherever possible. Success was immediate.

The flourishing Rancho de Chimayó occupies three large rooms whose whitewashed walls, heavy hand-hewn beams and hand-carved furniture recall the charm of a typical Spanish Colonial home. The last time I ate there, while the main course was being prepared my appetite was whetted by a plate of *sopaipillas,* the world's most ethereal kind of hot bread. These triangular or pillow-shaped puffs, three or four inches across and with a thin, delicate crust, not quite crisp, are customarily brought to the table before anything else in New Mexican restaurants that feature traditional Spanish or Mexican food. Golden brown and so airy that they almost waft away, *sopaipillas* are eaten with honey or a delectable syrup of brown sugar, wine, raisins and cinnamon.

The main course, *carne adobada*—pork steaks marinated in chili and baked with a chili sauce—was a memorable experience. Not only was it as hot as any Tex-Mex or Mexican dish I have ever eaten, but it had a special flavor imparted by Chimayó-grown chilies, which chili fanciers claim are among the best produced anywhere. Unlike some Southwestern restaurateurs, Arturo does not compromise on the question of chili. When he serves a dish that was traditionally hot, it is still hot, and he will not pamper the tender-tongued by serving an insipid version.

As the finale to my Rancho de Chimayó meal, I chose a traditional New Mexican dessert called *panocha,* a baked pudding made with flour ground from sprouted wheat and given a spicy taste by a dash of cinnamon. New Mexico is too cold for growing sugar cane, and in the old days, honey, the only other sweetener available, was always scarce. To satisfy their families' craving for sweetness, New Mexican housewives moistened wheat kernels, and when they began to sprout, dried and ground them. Such meal is naturally sweet because enzymes produced by the sprouting germs have turned some of the kernels' starch to sugar. Nowadays sugar may be added to *panocha,* but even without sugar it is still pleasantly and likably sweet.

Although firmly entrenched in New Mexico, all this authentic Spanish and Mexican cooking is less widespread in neighboring Arizona. One reason is the state's relatively recent settlement, begun by Anglo cattlemen and copper miners. Another is the fact that today most Arizonans old enough to vote seem to have been born somewhere else. But interest in the old cuisines—and in Arizona's Spanish-Mexican heritage in general— is very much on the rise throughout the state and especially in the kind of Mexican cooking called Sonoran, from the Mexican state across Arizona's southern border.

Sonora grows more wheat than corn, and one of the identifying marks of Sonoran-style cooking is the *tortilla de harina,* or wheat-flour tortilla. Another feature is the comparative mildness of many of the chili dishes; many Sonoran recipes call for no chilies at all. One form of the distinctively Sonoran wheat tortilla that I am especially partial to is about the size of a large pizza, but so thin that it is almost translucent *(Southwestern pizza, Recipe Index).* It is first baked on a griddle, then sometimes spread with butter and sprinkled with grated cheese; sometimes sliced chilies are added. A short time in the oven melts the cheese and turns the tortilla into a crisp, billowing thing like an enormous potato chip. Such a tortilla often serves as an hors d'oeuvre to a Sonoran-style meal on either side of the border. It is placed in the center of the table on a special footed stand with room around it for bottles of various seasonings. From then on it is every man for himself, as the diners break off bits around the edges until the tortilla is replaced by a fresh, hot one.

Another Sonoran specialty that is delicious in its own right has also won popularity among Arizonans as a cure for the aftereffects of a night of partying. This is *menudo (Recipe Index),* a soup made of tripe and hominy or, in a more elaborate version, of tripe, green chilies, onion and mint leaves. After a party in Yuma that went on into the small hours, I stopped off with local friends at a restaurant featuring Sonoran cooking and was introduced to a big, steaming bowl of *menudo.* It was indeed revivifying, and I could well appreciate why it is a great favorite on New Year's Day. If it works that well in Yuma, why not everywhere?

A Monument to Mormon Faith and Ingenuity

The 14-room mansion of the Mormon leader Brigham Young, its cupola crowned by a carved beehive symbolizing the Mormon virtue of unremitting industry, stands in the center of Salt Lake City. Completed in 1854, the house has walls of adobe, the ubiquitous building material of the early West, but the severe elegance of its square-columned façade reflects the New England heritage of the Vermont-born pioneer and patriarch. Here Young lived with several of his 27 wives and 56 children (the rest of the family was lodged in adjoining buildings), gave both spiritual and secular direction to the Mormon church, governed the vast area then known as Utah Territory and received distinguished visitors such as Ulysses S. Grant and Horace Greeley. A unique feature of the Beehive House, its "family store" *(above, right)*, is a carefully preserved witness to Mormon ingenuity and practicality. With a host of dependents to feed and clothe, Young found it expedient to set up a fully equipped commissary in a corner of his home for the exclusive use of his family. No money was exchanged at the "store," but wives and children could requisition supplies from the "mother" in charge of the little establishment.

Lovingly restored to its original state, Beehive House is both a memorial to a man and an absorbing museum of 19th Century Americana. The shelves of its "family store" *(above)* are stocked with calico and dry goods, the jars on the counter are filled with candies and spices, and the big barrels hold onions, potatoes and other produce. In the kitchen *(below)*, where Young's immediate household usually ate, a soup pot stands on the stove, just as it customarily did over a century ago.

Minted Trout

To serve 4

48 fresh leafy mint stalks, each 5 or 6 inches long, thoroughly washed and patted dry with paper towels
1 cup plus 1 tablespoon vegetable oil
4 teaspoons salt
Four 10- to 12-ounce trout, thoroughly defrosted if frozen
8 slices lean bacon

Position the broiler pan and rack 4 inches below the source of heat, then preheat the broiler to its highest setting.

Drop 32 of the mint stalks into a deep bowl and bruise the leaves and stems with the back of a large spoon to release their flavor. Dribble 1 cup of the oil over the mint, add 2 teaspoons of the salt, and turn the stalks about with a spoon to coat them evenly.

Wash the trout briefly under cold running water and pat them dry inside and out with paper towels. Rub the cavities of the fish with the remaining 2 teaspoons of salt, dividing it evenly among them. Then stuff the cavities with the bruised mint stalks.

To wrap each fish, lay 2 bacon slices parallel to one another on a flat surface, spacing them about ½ inch apart. Place 2 of the remaining mint stalks at right angles to the bacon slices in the center of the row and lay a trout over the mint. Place 2 more mint stalks on top of the fish, lift the ends of the bacon slices and wrap them snugly around the mint and fish. Secure the bacon in place with wooden toothpicks. Repeat, arranging 2 of the mint stalks on both sides of each fish and holding the stalks in place with 2 slices of the bacon.

With a pastry brush, spread the remaining tablespoon of oil evenly over the broiler pan rack. Arrange the trout side by side on the rack and, turning them once with a metal spatula, broil for 4 to 5 minutes on each side, or until they feel firm when prodded gently with a finger.

Using a sharp knife or kitchen scissors, cut the bacon slices along the cavity of each fish and remove and discard the mint stuffing but leave the bacon and the whole mint stalks in place. Arrange the minted trout attractively on a large heated platter and serve them at once, garnished if you like by decoratively cut lemons.

Mormon Johnnycake

To make one 9-by-9-inch cake

1 tablespoon butter, softened, plus 2 tablespoons butter, melted and cooled
2 eggs
2 cups buttermilk
2 tablespoons honey
½ cup unsifted flour
1 teaspoon baking soda
1 teaspoon salt
2 cups yellow cornmeal

Preheat the oven to 425°. With a pastry brush, spread the tablespoon of softened butter evenly over the bottom and sides of a 9-by-9-by-2-inch baking dish. Set the dish aside.

In a deep mixing bowl, beat the eggs to a froth with a wire whisk. Beat in the buttermilk and honey, then add the flour, baking soda and salt. When the batter is smooth, beat in the cornmeal about ½ cup at a time. Stir in the 2 tablespoons of cooled melted butter and pour the batter into the buttered dish, spreading it evenly and smoothing the top with a rubber spatula.

Bake the johnnycake in the middle of the oven for about 20 minutes, or until the cake begins to pull away from the sides of the dish and the top is golden brown and crusty. Serve the Mormon johnnycake at once, directly from the baking dish.

Broiled Rocky Mountain trout, stuffed and wrapped with mint, is a Western delicacy featured at The Fort restaurant *(shown at right)* near Denver. The source of the original recipe was an Indian woman of Taos, New Mexico.

To make one 9-by-5-by-3-inch loaf

1 cup lukewarm water (110° to 115°)
1 package active dry yeast
1 teaspoon granulated sugar
1 cup rye flour
2½ to 3 cups unsifted all-purpose flour
¼ cup dark brown sugar
1 teaspoon salt
¼ cup honey
½ cup vegetable shortening, cut into ½-inch bits and softened
2 tablespoons butter, softened
1 egg, beaten lightly with 1 tablespoon milk

To serve 6 to 8

1 cup (½ pound) dried chick-peas (garbanzos)
2 quarts water
Two 1½- to 2-pound turkey legs, thoroughly defrosted if frozen
2 medium-sized onions, peeled and coarsely chopped
1 medium-sized bay leaf, crumbled
1 tablespoon salt
8 whole black peppercorns
3 tablespoons uncooked long-grain white rice (not the converted variety)
1½ teaspoons crumbled dried oregano
3 tablespoons finely chopped seeded canned green chilies (not the jalapeño variety; caution: see note, page 20)
½ pound Monterey Jack cheese, cut into ¼-inch dice, or substitute ½ pound diced Münster cheese
2 tablespoons finely chopped fresh parsley
1 large firm ripe avocado, halved, seeded, peeled and cut lengthwise into thin slices (see poor man's butter, Recipe Booklet)

Mormon Rye Bread

Pour ¼ cup of the lukewarm water into a small bowl and sprinkle the yeast and granulated sugar over it. Let the yeast and sugar rest for 2 or 3 minutes, then mix well. Set in a warm, draft-free place (such as an un-lighted oven) for about 10 minutes, or until the yeast bubbles up and the mixture almost doubles in volume.

Place the rye flour, 2 cups of all-purpose flour, the brown sugar and salt in a deep mixing bowl and make a well in the center. Add the yeast mixture, the remaining ¾ cup of lukewarm water, the honey and vege-table-shortening bits. With a large spoon, gradually incorporate the dry ingredients into the liquid ones and continue to stir until the mixture is smooth and can be gathered into a medium-soft ball. If the dough be-comes too stiff to stir easily, mix it with your hands.

Transfer the ball to a lightly floured surface and knead, pushing the dough down with the heels of your hands, pressing it forward and fold-ing it back on itself. Incorporate up to 1 cup more all-purpose flour by the tablespoonful as you knead, adding only enough to make a smooth dough that is no longer sticky. Then continue kneading for about 10 min-utes, until the dough is smooth and elastic.

With a pastry brush, spread 1 tablespoon of the softened butter evenly inside a large bowl. Place the dough in the bowl and turn the ball about to butter the entire surface. Drape the bowl with a kitchen towel and set it aside in the warm, draft-free place for approximately 1½ hours, or until the dough doubles in volume.

Brush the remaining tablespoon of softened butter over the bottom and sides of a 9-by-5-by-3-inch loaf pan. Punch the dough down with a blow of your fist and, on a lightly floured surface, shape the dough into a loaf about 8 inches long and 4 inches wide. Place the loaf in the buttered pan and set it in the warm, draft-free place for about 45 minutes, or until it has doubled in volume.

Preheat the oven to 375°. (If you have used the oven to let the loaf rise, gently transfer it to another warm place to rest while the oven heats.) Brush the loaf with the egg-and-milk mixture and bake in the middle of the oven for 30 to 35 minutes, or until the top is golden brown. To test for doneness, turn the loaf out and rap the bottom sharply with your knuckles. The loaf should sound hollow; if not, return it to the pan and bake for 5 to 10 minutes longer. Place the Mormon rye bread on a wire rack and cool completely to room temperature before serving.

Bowl of the Wife of Kit Carson
TURKEY, CHICK-PEA AND GREEN CHILI SOUP

When Sam Arnold built The Fort restaurant near Denver as a repro-duction of a historic adobe fort, he sought out early foods as well. A granddaughter of Kit Carson, the famed frontiersman, gave Mr. Arnold the original family recipe for this savory turkey soup; he has embellished it with a garnish of avocado slices.

Starting a day ahead, wash the chick-peas in a sieve under cold running water, place them in a large bowl or pan, and pour in enough cold water to cover them by 2 inches. Soak at room temperature for at least 12 hours.

Drain the peas in a sieve or colander and discard the soaking water. Then place the peas in a heavy 4- to 5-quart casserole, add the 2 quarts of water, and bring to a boil over high heat. Reduce the heat to low and simmer partially covered for about 1 hour, or until the chick-peas are tender. With a slotted spoon, transfer them to a bowl and set aside.

Add the turkey legs to the chick-pea cooking liquid. The liquid should cover the turkey completely; if necessary, add water. Bring to a boil over high heat, meanwhile skimming off the foam and scum that rise to the surface. Add the onions, bay leaf, salt and peppercorns, reduce the heat to low, and simmer partially covered for about 45 minutes, or until the turkey legs show no resistance when pierced deeply with the point of a small sharp knife.

Transfer the turkey legs to a plate. Then strain the stock through a fine sieve set over a bowl, and return it to the pot. Remove the skin from the turkey legs with a small knife or your fingers. Cut or pull the meat away from the bones and discard the skin and bones. Cut the meat into 1-inch cubes and set them aside.

Over high heat, bring the stock in the casserole to a boil. Add the rice and oregano, stir well and reduce the heat to low. Cover tightly and simmer for 20 minutes, or until the rice is tender. Stir in the chick-peas, cubed turkey and chilies, and simmer for 4 or 5 minutes longer to heat all the ingredients through.

Taste for seasoning and ladle the soup into a heated tureen or serving bowl. Scatter the diced cheese and the parsley over the soup, arrange the avocado slices on top, and serve at once.

The so-called "bowl of the wife of Kit Carson" is a robust turkey and chick-pea soup, overlaid with cheese and avocado slices.

Basque Sheepherders' Potatoes

To serve 6 to 8

3 tablespoons bacon fat
9 medium-sized boiling potatoes
  (about 3 pounds), peeled and cut
  crosswise into ⅛-inch-thick
  slices
Salt
Freshly ground black pepper
4 eggs
2 tablespoons finely cut fresh chives
1 tablespoon finely chopped fresh
  parsley
¼ teaspoon crumbled dried thyme

Preheat the oven to 375°. Put 2 tablespoons of the bacon fat into a 10-inch enameled or cast-iron skillet and tip the pan from side to side to spread the fat evenly. Arrange about one third of the potato slices in a flat layer in the skillet and season them lightly with salt and pepper. Repeat two more times, then dribble or dot the remaining tablespoon of bacon fat over the top. Cover tightly and bake in the middle of the oven for about 1 hour, or until the potatoes are tender.

Beat the eggs lightly with a wire whisk or a fork, add the chives, parsley and thyme, and mix well. Then pour the egg mixture over the potatoes, cover again and continue baking for 5 minutes, or until the eggs are just firm to the touch. Do not overcook.

To unmold and serve the sheepherders' potatoes, loosen the edges by running a knife around the sides of the skillet and as far beneath the potatoes as possible without breaking them apart. Place an inverted plate on top of the skillet and, grasping plate and skillet together firmly, turn them over. The potatoes should slide out easily. Serve at once.

Trappers' Fruit

To make about 5 cups

3 cups (about 12 ounces) coarsely
  chopped dried apples
1 cup canned puréed pumpkin
½ cup dark brown sugar
¼ cup roasted sunflower seeds
¼ cup seedless raisins
¼ teaspoon coriander seeds
1 teaspoon salt
1 quart water

Combine the dried apples, pumpkin, brown sugar, sunflower seeds, raisins, coriander, salt and water in a heavy 3- to 4-quart casserole and mix well. Bring to a boil over high heat, reduce the heat to low, cover tightly and simmer for about 1½ hours, or until the apples are tender. Check the pan occasionally and, if the fruit seems dry, add more water ¼ cup at a time. Transfer the fruit to a bowl and cool to room temperature before serving. Trappers' fruit, so called because it was easy for Colorado fur trappers of the mid-19th Century to prepare, is served as an accompaniment to roasted and broiled meats.

Cowboy Soda Biscuits

To make about 15 biscuits

2¼ cups unsifted flour
1 teaspoon baking soda
1 teaspoon salt
3 tablespoons lard, cut into ½-inch
  bits, plus ½ pound lard for deep
  frying
1 cup buttermilk or sour milk

Combine the flour, baking soda and salt in a deep bowl. Add the 3 tablespoons of lard bits and, with your fingertips, rub the flour and fat together until they resemble flakes of coarse meal. Pour in the buttermilk or sour milk and beat vigorously with a spoon to make a smooth dough.

Over moderate heat, melt the remaining ½ pound of lard in a Dutch oven or heavy casserole about 8 inches in diameter and 4 or 5 inches deep. Heat the fat until it is very hot but not smoking.

To shape each biscuit, cut off about 2 tablespoons of the dough and, flouring your hands lightly as you proceed, pat the dough into a ball about 1½ inches in diameter. Drop two or three biscuits at a time into the hot fat, turning them about with a slotted spoon to coat them on all sides with the fat. When all the biscuits have been added to the pot, cover it tightly and fry the biscuits over moderate heat for 4 minutes. Turn the biscuits over with a slotted spoon, cover again and fry for 4 minutes longer, or until they are evenly browned and puffed. Transfer the biscuits to paper towels to drain briefly, and serve them hot.

At The Fort restaurant *(page 81)* grilled steaks stuffed with green chili strips come to the table with trappers' fruit *(above)* and vegetables.

Flat round cakes of dough deep-fried in a pot of bubbling lard quickly turn into crispy puffs of Navajo fry bread *(above, right)*.

To make three 8-inch round breads

2 cups unsifted flour
½ cup dry milk solids
2 teaspoons double-acting baking
    powder
½ teaspoon salt
2 tablespoons lard, cut into ½-inch
    bits, plus 1 pound lard for deep
    frying
½ cup ice water

Navajo Fry Bread

Combine the flour, dry milk solids, baking powder and salt, and sift them into a deep bowl. Add the 2 tablespoons of lard bits and, with your fingertips, rub the flour and fat together until the mixture resembles flakes of coarse meal. Pour in the water and toss the ingredients together until the dough can be gathered into a ball. Drape the bowl with a kitchen towel and let the dough rest at room temperature for about 2 hours.

After the resting period, cut the dough into three equal pieces. Then, on a lightly floured surface, roll each piece into a rough circle about 8 inches in diameter and ¼ inch thick. With a small sharp knife, cut two 4- to 5-inch-long parallel slits completely through the dough down the center of each round, spacing the slits about 1 inch apart.

In a heavy 10-inch skillet, melt the remaining pound of lard over moderate heat until it is very hot but not smoking. The melted fat should be about 1 inch deep; add more lard if necessary. Fry the breads one at a time for about 2 minutes on each side, turning them once with tongs or a slotted spatula. The bread will puff slightly and become crisp and brown. Drain the Navajo fry bread on paper towels and serve warm.

To serve 6 to 8

2 tablespoons butter
1 cup finely chopped onions
½ cup finely chopped celery
2 cups (1 pound) dried green split
    peas, washed in a sieve under
    cold running water
3 quarts water
3 medium-sized boiling potatoes
    (about 1 pound), peeled and
    coarsely grated
½ teaspoon crumbled dried
    marjoram
3½ teaspoons salt
¼ teaspoon freshly ground black
    pepper
1 pound lean ground pork
1 teaspoon ground sage
¼ teaspoon ground white pepper

Mormon Split-Pea Soup

In a heavy 5- to 6-quart casserole, melt the butter over moderate heat. When the foam begins to subside, add the onions and celery and, stirring frequently, cook for about 5 minutes, until the vegetables are soft but not brown. Stir in the peas and water, then bring to a boil over high heat, meanwhile skimming off the foam and scum that rise to the surface. Add the potatoes, marjoram, 2 teaspoons of the salt and the black pepper, reduce the heat to low, and simmer partially covered for 1 hour.

Meanwhile, combine the ground pork, sage, the remaining 1½ teaspoons of salt and the white pepper in a bowl. Knead vigorously with both hands, then beat with a wooden spoon until the mixture is smooth. Moistening your hands in cold water occasionally, pinch off about 1 tablespoon of the pork mixture at a time and shape each piece into a ball about 1 inch in diameter.

When the soup has cooked its allotted time, drop in the pork balls and return the soup to a simmer. Cover the pot partially and continue to simmer for 30 minutes. To test the pork for doneness, lift one of the balls out of the water with a slotted spoon and pierce it deeply with the point of a small sharp knife. If the liquid that trickles out is clear yellow, the pork is done even though the meat itself appears somewhat pink; however, if the liquid is pink, simmer the soup for 5 to 10 minutes longer.

Taste for seasoning and serve the soup at once from a heated tureen or individual soup plates.

Sopaipillas
DEEP-FRIED BREADS

Combine the flour, baking powder and salt, and sift them into a deep bowl. Add the shortening bits, then, with your fingers, rub the flour and fat together until the mixture resembles flakes of coarse meal. Pour in the lukewarm water all at once and toss the dough together until it can be gathered into a compact ball.

On a lightly floured surface, knead the dough by pushing it down with the heels of your hands, pressing it forward and folding it back on itself. Knead for about 5 minutes, until the dough is smooth, shiny and elastic, then gather it into a ball, drape a kitchen towel over the top, and let the dough rest for about 15 minutes.

Meanwhile, pour vegetable oil into a deep fryer or large heavy saucepan to a depth of about 3 inches and heat the oil until it reaches a temperature of 400° on a deep-frying thermometer.

To make the wedge-shaped *sopaipillas* shown below, divide the dough in half and roll out each portion into a circle about 8 inches in diameter and ⅛ inch thick. With a pastry wheel or sharp knife, cut each circle into four equal wedges. To make square *sopaipillas*, roll out the dough into a rectangle about 12 inches long, 9 inches wide and ⅛ inch thick and cut the rectangle into 3-inch squares.

Two or three at a time, deep-fry the *sopaipillas* for about 3 minutes, turning them frequently with a slotted spoon. As they fry, the *sopaipillas* will puff up and brown. When they are crisp and golden on both sides, transfer them to paper towels to drain while you deep-fry the rest.

Serve the *sopaipillas* warm or at room temperature, accompanied with butter and honey.

To make 8 wedge-shaped or 12 three-inch square *sopaipillas*

1½ cups unsifted flour
2 teaspoons double-acting baking powder
¾ teaspoon salt
2 tablespoons vegetable shortening, cut into ½-inch bits
½ cup lukewarm water (110° to 115°)
Vegetable oil for deep frying

Sopaipilla dough is cut into either wedges *(below, left)* or squares that are deep-fried until they swell up like "sofa pillows."

IV

The Cornucopia
of California

California grapefruit, the "aristocrat of the breakfast table," also shines at dinner in a fruit-flavored cake swathed in a cream-cheese icing *(Recipe Index).* The icing bears a tracery of fine strips of grapefruit peel, and the top of the cake is ornamented with grapefruit segments and icing roses.

Most people go to California by air, but that is too easy a way to approach this splendid land, for the plane puts mountains and deserts behind it in a matter of minutes. A slower yet far more dramatic way is to arrive by road, preferably from the Arizona side. For a long while the country gets drier, dustier and emptier. The ground, especially in summer, is almost bare; even cacti have a hard time making a living here. The rocky ridges look as lifeless as mountains on the moon. Yuma, Arizona, which is situated on the Colorado River, is a small oasis, but right across the bridge the desert begins again in its most awesome form. Just west of the river great dunes of loose brown sand march cross-country, sometimes threatening the highway. Where the sand is not moving, nothing grows but bushes a few inches high, widely spaced, gray-green and seemingly only half alive.

Then, almost without warning, the road crosses an irrigation canal and enters the wonderfully fertile Imperial Valley, which, thanks to water from the Colorado River, grows a wealth of crops all the year round. Suddenly the countryside around you is bright green, and from then on California opens like a flower.

No one ever described this transformation better than John Steinbeck, one of the state's most famous native sons. In *The Grapes of Wrath* Steinbeck takes his Okie family, the Joads, across "the broken rock glaring under the sun . . . the terrible ramparts of Arizona" to the rim of a valley much like the Imperial. They drive westward in a morning glow, the sun coming up behind them, and then:

PACOAST BRAND

Pacific Ocean

CALIFORNIA

PRODUCE OF U.S.A.

DISTRIBUTED BY **PACIFIC COAST FRUIT DISTRIBUTORS INC.** LOS ANGELES, CALIF.

A shipping-crate label recalls the heyday of a colorful American art form. In the 1880s California packers and distributors began to identify their products with labels glued to wooden crates; by the 1930s, when this label appeared, artists vied with one another in producing picturesque or humorous designs. But the school of American label artists died out about 1950, when wooden crates were replaced by preprinted cardboard cartons.

Suddenly they saw the great valley below them. . . . The vineyards, the orchards, the great flat valley, green and beautiful, the trees set in rows, and the farm houses. . . . The grain fields golden in the morning, and the willow lines, the eucalyptus trees . . . the peach trees and the walnut groves, and the dark green patches of oranges. And red roofs among the trees, and barns—rich barns. . . .

Ruthie and Winfield scrambled down from the car, and then they stood, silent and awestruck, embarrassed before the great valley. The distance was thinned with haze, and the land grew softer and softer in the distance. A windmill flashed in the sun, and its turning blades were like a little heliograph, far away. Ruthie and Winfield looked at it, and Ruthie whispered, "It's California."

The first Imperial Valley town across the border from Arizona is Holtville, whose great sprawling fields of feathery-leaved carrots in endless, geometrically straight rows eminently justify its claim to be the "Carrot Capital of the World." Farther along, there are fields of tomatoes, melons, onions, lettuce—almost every vegetable that grows, and almost all of them destined for Eastern markets. Only a few farm workers are visible, for much of the sowing, cultivating and harvesting is done by enormous machines that look like strange metal dinosaurs.

California grows plenty of such workaday produce as barley and cotton, but much more conspicuous are crops with a strong appeal to the palate. Among them are almonds, artichokes, olives, walnuts, pears, lemons, grapes, plums, dates, peaches, raisins, apricots and figs—every one originally an import from the Old World, and every one a food with a long and glamorous history. Mild rainy winters and hot dry summers enable large parts of the state to grow the crops characteristic of the Mediterranean region—crops that have been familiar to Western civilization from time immemorial and have become choice ingredients in all Western cuisines. The juice of almost any fruit, for instance, can be fermented into a "wine" of sorts, but only the Old World wine grape, *Vitis vinifera,* produces the traditional wine that has been beloved by several millennia of drinkers. *Vitis vinifera* flourishes in California, and so do all the other gourmet crops of the Mediterranean world.

Many of the places that specialize in these pleasant edibles are like creative culinary laboratories in which Old World foods are given New World improvements, for almost all of these places have discovered new ways to cook or prepare their local product. Some of these ways are delicious, most are interesting; what is more, the places themselves are fascinating in their own right.

The town of Indio, a garden of green and stately palms in the Coachella Valley, grows nearly all the dates produced in the United States. It lies more than 20 feet below sea level, in the same great depression that includes the Imperial Valley. Its annual rainfall is hardly enough to lay the dust, but a canal brings water from the Colorado, and the sun shines hot nearly all the time. These are exactly the conditions—"feet in the water, heads in the sun"—that date palms proverbially love. At Indio they bloom as luxuriantly as in any Arabian oasis. The town returns the compliment every February, when the dates have been harvested, with a festival that lasts 10 days. The prettiest girl in the county is crowned Queen Scheherazade, and on each of the 10 days a scene from the Arabian Nights is enthusiastically enacted. In their native home the dates of Araby never had such a festive fuss made over them.

Dates demand tender, loving care, as I know from experience. As a boy in Mesa, Arizona, I was observed climbing one of a half-dozen date palms at the ranch school where my father taught. I was doing so out of either exuberance or curiosity, I cannot remember which, but the owner of the property remarked that since I obviously liked to climb his palms I might as well pollinate them while I was at it, so that the dates would ripen properly. I was therefore provided with sprigs taken from male date flowers, which release an enormous amount of pollen, and told to climb the trees and shake the powdery pollen onto the female flowers. I did the job and was thoroughly scratched by the thorns of the date palm —but never got to know how effective I was as an amateur honeybee. My family left the ranch before the dates ripened.

All 18 fruits and vegetables shown on the overleaf and identified below may be found in a single California market. Some are exotics, some are everyday fare; taken together, they testify to the state's fertility and the amazing diversity of its produce.

1 Bean sprouts
2 Strawberries
3 Purple runner beans
4 Rhubarb
5 Loose-leaf lettuce
6 Radishes
7 Zucchini
8 Concord grapes
9 Valencia oranges
10 Okra
11 Prickly pears, or Indian figs
12 Chayote, or vegetable pear (originally Central American, sometimes prepared as a dessert)
13 Lemon cucumbers (true cucumbers, despite their color and shape, usually pickled or preserved)
14 Prickly-pear leaves (cooked and used in salads or as a vegetable)
15 Eggplant
16 McIntosh apples
17 Red cabbage
18 Acorn squash

The result of the date grower's effort is a glorious natural confection. All of California's fresh dates are, to my mind, so far superior to their imported rivals, mostly from the Middle East, that there is no comparison. But the California dates that appear in most out-of-state markets do not represent the best the Coachella Valley can do. The date that makes up the bulk of the crop is the Deglet Noor, yet other varieties are much better. The Medjhool is so big it is hard to believe it is a date; a mature fruit is almost as long as a hen's egg, though not as thick. The Khadrawi, somewhat smaller, has its own distinctive, smooth flavor. The Bahri is my personal favorite; it is honey-blond when freshly ripened, almost spherical and so soft that it bursts when dropped a foot or so. And its exquisite sweetness is so unforgettable that no weak-willed weight watcher should ever be exposed to its temptation.

Most dates are eaten like candy, but they can be consumed in other appealing ways. One of them is in the form of a "date shake." I once stopped at Be-Bee's Date Shop in Indio to buy some enormous Medjhools, simply to prove to friends back East that such things can exist. While Be-Bee was wrapping my package, a determined lady struggled toward the counter, slowed by her husband pulling at her sleeve.

"I've got to have one," she cried.

"You'll spoil your supper."

"No, I've got to have one. I've been thinking about it all day."

"You better remember that diet."

The lady prevailed. Be-Bee prepared a stupendous date milk shake that the lady consumed with joy while her husband watched with scowls.

To make your own date shake, put about three quarters of a cup of pitted dates in a blender with half a cup of milk and blend until they are nearly smooth. Then add a pint of vanilla ice cream and another half cup of milk, and blend some more. (The proportions can be varied according to taste, but you really can't go wrong.)

Dates are superb, of course, in any number of pastries and confections, but they can also be used in some unexpected and equally superb combinations wherever a sweet, mild flavor is in order. The date dish I most enjoy consists of sweet potatoes boiled, cut in halves and baked in a casserole with a syrup of sugar, orange juice, butter and chopped dates. The dates add a solid touch to the dish, and their flavor blends in perfect harmony with that of the sweet potatoes.

The date industry is comparatively new to California, brought there after 1902, but most of the state's large-scale Mediterranean crops were introduced much earlier by Spanish missionaries, mostly Franciscan friars sent in a dual attempt to convert and civilize the Indians and to secure California against Russian and Anglo-Saxon encroachment. The missions were, in effect, large agricultural estates, managed by the friars and worked by Indian converts. It took years to get organized, but after a short hungry period the people in the more prosperous missions were eating fairly well. Some of the kitchens in these missions have been preserved or restored. They have large, well-built stoves and ovens capable of turning out sumptuous meals.

In one respect the padres had a great advantage from the start. Prac-

94

tically every familiar Spanish crop they introduced was a success here in the New World. They were also, fortunately, old hands at plant introduction. For centuries the missionaries had made a practice of collecting promising plants, both wild and cultivated, in every far land they ventured to and shipping them to places where they might prove useful. At the California missions this sort of agricultural enterprise had its greatest success; its legacy includes both the Mission grape and the Mission fig. Olives, which are so basic to Spanish cookery, did as well along the Pacific as at home in Europe.

Like many another visitor I was introduced to California olives by having a large ripe one picked from a tree and handed to me. It was black and shiny, and looked delicious—but when I bit into it my mouth puckered unpleasantly. In their natural state olives are full of a bitter material called oleuropein, which must be eliminated before they are palatable. This is generally done by long soaking in alternate solutions of weak lye and brine. Some Californians who own a few olive trees do this at home, but they are taking a chance, for olives that are not cured properly can spoil and become poisonous.

Outside of the West, few Americans cook with olives; they are usually content to serve them as appetizers or as accents in a salad. (Even for these purposes, incidentally, canned ripe olives can be much improved by marinating them in wine vinegar, garlic and such herbs as basil, oregano or dill—and perhaps a bit of hot red chili.) Californians do not limit themselves to such minor uses for olives. They not only use them as a principal feature in salads, but mix them in egg or cheese dishes, cook them with meat gravies, and bake them in "olive bread," which sounds odd but is excellent: a baking-powder biscuit dough made with a cup and a half of chopped olives to two cups of dry ingredients. For an extra fillip of flavor, the baking pan is greased with olive oil.

Dates and olives are but two examples of California's bounty at its best. The state is dotted with towns that specialize in single crops and grow them with zest and precision. There's an artichoke town, several lettuce towns, many grape, peach and prune towns. Some of these places consist of little more than a cluster of packing sheds on the margins of broad fields; others are cozy and pleasant places, the homes of prosperous, skilled farmers. Many put on annual festivals to honor—and promote—their special product. In California the crop is king, and it molds the lives of the people who cultivate it.

A familiar sight is miles and miles of fruit trees. During much of the year the long, straight rows are monotonous-looking. They are generally planted on level ground so they can be irrigated evenly, and the trees in each great orchard are all alike, except perhaps in areas where the fumes of the highway have sickened the nearest ones. They lack the charm of smaller Eastern orchards, which are apt to be draped gracefully around knolls and hillsides. But in springtime California's fruit lands become glorious spectacles. Enormous rectangles of land turn pink or white as the buds of plums, pears, peaches and apricots open their fragile petals. The display lasts only a short time, but the trees stage a second show when their fruits begin to color. Then the branches bend with their heavy crop,

The three kinds of California figs shown above—the Black Mission *(top)*, the Calimyrna *(middle)* and the Kadota *(bottom)*—dominate the U.S. crop. All three are raised chiefly in the San Joaquin Valley.

95

and armies of men and machines descend upon them. At harvesttime the fruit lands inspire a wonderful feeling of overflowing plenty.

In Southern California the orchards are apt to be citrus: oranges, lemons, grapefruit, tangerines and such less-familiar relatives as kumquats. Citrus groves are evergreen and also ever decorative, especially when their intensely fragrant blossoms are open or their intensely colored fruit hangs bright among the glossy green leaves. The trees themselves like to live dangerously; they bear best in places that are sometimes threatened with frost. The citrus growers have to be alert and cautious men. An outlander may ask why so many "windmills" stand high above the groves. Most of them are not windmills at all but powerful mechanical blowers, which stir up the air on clear, cold nights and keep low-lying frost from damaging the vulnerable trees.

To many Americans, citrus fruits mean orange juice for breakfast and a twist of lemon peel for the martini, but Californians have put them to many uses in cookery, from candies to breads and meat dishes. Traveling in citrus country, I have encountered and enjoyed some fairly unusual citrus dishes. Tangerine cheesecake is excellent. So is baked acorn squash with the hollows filled, part-way through the baking, with peeled orange sections as well as the usual sugar and butter. In Los Angeles I had a magnificent grapefruit cake *(Recipe Index)* with bits of grapefruit embedded in the white frosting. The tart flavor of the fruit mingled with the sweetness of cake and frosting to produce a blissful blend.

I have dwelt on California's agriculture because it is one of the major elements in the special regional cuisine that is beginning to take shape in the state. There are other elements, of course, but the availability of really fresh produce all the year round has a powerful influence. It shows up most noticeably in the statewide passion for salads. These salads are not mere side dishes or minor courses but serious parts of almost every meal. Usually they contain several of the many kinds of greens that California markets stock in impressive variety. In one market, not an especially large one, I counted iceberg lettuce, Boston lettuce, bibb lettuce, red lettuce, escarole, romaine, endive, chicory and watercress. I saw Chinese bean sprouts, a frequent addition to local salads, and sprouted alfalfa seeds, fine white threads that make a lacy decoration when scattered over a salad. All of these vegetables were beautifully fresh, tender and crisp. Because of the climate that equably permits them to be grown in some nearby place throughout the year, they never need suffer a wilting week on the way to market.

Some California aficionados of the salad argue that it is never better than when combining three or four kinds of greens tossed with a simple dressing of oil, vinegar, salt, pepper and a hint of garlic. The point, they say, is to emphasize the utter freshness and tenderness of the greens. Other salad enthusiasts are less purist. To them the greens are only a preamble; then they add crisp bacon bits, pimiento and red cabbage, diced avocado and chopped green onions. They also insist on special dressing ingredients, such as pear vinegar. One of the most memorable tossed salads I ever ate contained practically all these things, but also a spiced vinegar suffused with 14 flavorings, including horseradish and anchovies.

The kaki, or Oriental persimmon, is one of many exotic aliens that flourish in California's climate. Every year the state reaps a bumper crop of the fruit, which reaches maturity after the leaves fall from the tree *(above)*. Most of the crop is shipped out of the state, but there is still some opportunity for local enterprise, too: the MacGeraghty children *(opposite)*, Brian, Killian, Erin and Tara—with Daisy Mae, their dog, as shop assistant—peddle persimmons picked from a tree in the yard of their Palo Alto home.

The Kiwi, or Chinese gooseberry, a recent import from New Zealand, is grown on a small scale in California. An average Kiwi vine, which flowers in late April or early May, bears up to 300 pounds of rather ugly, brown-skinned fruit *(top)* at the November harvest. But the ugliness is only skin deep: the fruit beneath the skin *(bottom)* is colorful and eminently edible.

On many a California table, salads have been expanded to full-sized meals. A comparatively conservative one is the famous Green Goddess salad served by San Francisco's great old Palace Hotel. Invented in 1915 in honor of the actor George Arliss, who was then starring in the play *The Green Goddess,* the salad is still popular. Traditionally, the dressing of mayonnaise and tarragon vinegar is combined with fresh herbs, a green onion and anchovy fillets. It is then tossed with crisp leaves of romaine in a bowl well rubbed with garlic. The salad is often topped with chicken, crab or shrimp to make it a substantial meal.

Caesar salad is another celebrated California creation—though according to one legend it actually originated in Tijuana, the wide-open Mexican border town a few miles south of San Diego. The story goes that during the Prohibition era a crowd of Hollywood movie people took refuge in the town for a Fourth of July weekend of serious drinking and dining. The drinks seem to have held out well enough, but one evening Caesar Cardini's restaurant almost ran out of food. The local stores were either cleaned out or closed, and Caesar desperately took inventory of his store-room. All he found was crates of romaine lettuce (in those days a little-known delicacy), a huge slab of Romano cheese, some bread, some bottles of olive oil and half a crate of eggs.

With hungry guests clamoring, Caesar frantically improvised several salads with the ingredients at hand. Not one of these efforts satisfied him. Then he remembered something his mother in Italy had told him: an egg coddled for *exactly* 60 seconds somehow makes a dressing stick to salad greens. He coddled an egg to the precise second and dropped it into a garlic-rubbed salad bowl. Then he added romaine torn into small pieces, grated cheese, vinegar, lemon juice, seasonings and croutons made of bread cubes fried in olive oil. The guests, says the story, were so delighted that they did not ask for anything else to eat, and the fame of Caesar's salad spread across the continent.

Whatever the truth of this tale, Caesar salad is uncommonly good. As with most enduringly popular recipes, all sorts of changes have been rung on the basic theme. Nowadays chopped anchovies are often added to the dressing, and sometimes blue and Parmesan cheese. Some latter-day heretics scoff at the idea of coddling the eggs; beaten raw eggs, they say, do just as well. But in my opinion the fundamental secret of the salad's success is the croutons, which are added at the last minute so they do not soak up dressing and lose their crispness. They contribute something to Caesar salad that all other salads lack.

For a more ambitious dish—indeed, for a substantial meal—there is Cobb's salad. Named after the proprietor of Hollywood's Brown Derby restaurant, it is described on the restaurant's flamboyant menu as: "Finely Chopped Lettuce, Romaine, Celery, Chicory, Chives, Watercress, Avocado, Peeled Tomato, Crisp Bacon, Breast of Chicken, Hard-Cooked Egg and Bleu Cheese all tastefully mixed with Our Special Old-Fashioned French Dressing." As served at the Brown Derby, the ingredients are chopped separately and laid out in stripes of many colors in a huge wooden salad bowl. The waiter displays the ingredients to the guest, then mixes them with the dressing. I have had this salad several times, and I have always regretted failing to intercept it in the unmixed state, to do the mixing myself. Its taste was splendid, but everything was chopped so fine and mixed so thoroughly that each forkful was like all the others. Rather monotonous; next time I shall remember.

Besides their salad mystique, Californians have a fanatical love of very young, very tender vegetables. I particularly remember a dinner I had with food authority Sylvia Vaughn Thompson at her house in Malibu, a beachside community near Los Angeles. Never had I tasted such vegetables since I tended my own kitchen garden 20 years earlier. Indeed they were better than mine, for Sylvia had more kinds than I ever produced at one time and she cooked them better. In a great Mexican bowl were wonderful peas, slender green beans, zucchini about three inches long, baby carrots, turnips, beets and tiny nubbins of broccoli and cauliflower. Sylvia had blanched all the vegetables separately and briefly, and they were crisply tender. She placed them in a large frying pan with butter and chased them around very fast until they were uniformly hot and the butter had browned just a little. Of all the splendid dishes that I ate that night, those virgin vegetables remain uppermost in my memory. I shall not be able to buy their like in New York.

If I were writing this book a decade or so hence I am sure I would be singing the praises of a California cuisine as distinctive as those of New England or the Deep South. This is not possible now; too many millions of people have moved too recently into California, each family bringing its own cooking traditions and eating more or less what they or their parents ate in Iowa, New York, Italy or wherever. But this random patchwork of imported cuisines is beginning to blend into a pattern peculiar to California. Some of the blending is due to local conditions not particularly admirable in themselves. Los Angeles, for instance, is a city that lives on wheels, with people moving incessantly from parking place to parking place. Many of these people snack rather than dine, and an incredible number and variety of informal restaurants, each with its spacious parking lot, stand ready to serve them. Generally these drive-ins are characterized by garish architecture and glaring neon signs. Some boast fanciful names and slogans, such as The Broken Drum ("You can't beat it!") and Piece of Pizza ("Had a piece lately?"). Many are undistinguished, especially those that belong to large chains and have prepared food trucked in from distant factories.

But some of the roadside places are remarkably good. I have had excellent lunches at Hamburger Hamlets, a small chain that claims to provide the best hamburgers, in many varieties, that money can buy. And it was in California that I learned what is now my favorite way of cooking this staple dish. You buy fairly lean chopped chuck and divide it with as little handling as possible into half-pound patties about one inch thick. Sprinkle each with a heaping teaspoon of coarsely chopped onion. Take a large knife and chop, chop, chop rapidly, until most of the onion has been worked into the meat. Sprinkle each patty with one teaspoon of red wine, for moisture—and chop, chop, chop some more. The patties will now be somewhat loose, and must be pushed gently together with the knife to make them an inch thick again and permit them to be handled.

The chunky, russet pomegranate *(top)*, borne on trees that reach a height of 15 to 20 feet, was Middle Eastern in origin, and probably brought to the New World by Spanish colonists. In California, which produces almost all of the U.S. commercial crop, the somewhat tart fruits, filled with crimson seeds *(bottom)*, ripen in September and are harvested by men on ladders.

Put a tablespoon of olive oil in a frying pan, preferably cast iron, and heat it so hot that the oil smokes. Add the patties one at a time with a spatula and let them fry until only one half their thickness still looks rare. When you turn them over, the high spots on the underside should be crisply brown. Let them cook 30 seconds or so on the other side, and they will be done: moist, medium rare, oniony and wonderful. If you do not like the taste of olive oil as much as I do, use some neutral cooking fat— but not butter, which will burn too much.

Other Los Angeles drive-in restaurants are as good in their own ways as the Hamburger Hamlets. Some of them, too, provide good examples of another California trend that I have watched over the years: a growing tendency to mix cuisines. In one Los Angeles suburb, a small drive-in restaurant offers fish and chips (British), tacos (Mexican), pizza (Italian), "broasted" chicken (American) and *sukiyaki* (Japanese). Apparently they all come from the same stoves and ovens.

Of all California cities, San Diego is one of the most eclectic in cuisine. It is less than 20 miles from the border, so Mexican influence is strong. There are many good Mexican restaurants, and non-Mexicans often "cook Mexican" in their homes. When San Diego kids have picnics or other get-togethers, they are apt to choose tacos instead of hot dogs and to prepare them themselves.

A seafaring and Navy town, San Diego also has a considerable Oriental population: Chinese, Japanese, Koreans, Filipinos and quite a few Southeast Asians and Indonesians. Besides many small shops to supply their national foods, there is a large and attractive supermarket that appeals to them all. Run by a Chinese-American family, it is called the Woo Chee Chong, which roughly means "Peace, Harmony, Fruitfulness." Inside are row upon row of shelves packed with foods from all over the Orient: dozens of kinds of Japanese crackers, noodles and canned seafoods; Chinese dried mushrooms, sauces and many kinds of tea, including a block tea that is believed to have a weight-reducing effect. Koreans find the spices needed to make *kimchee,* their fiery-hot pickled cabbage, and even a press for squashing it down as it ferments. Filipinos find their own favored flavorings and a great variety of preserved fish, some no more than an inch long.

Most of the customers of the Woo Chee Chong are Oriental, but Caucasians are coming in ever-increasing numbers, especially on days after a local television station has described an Oriental dish. When I was last at the store, Caucasian schoolchildren were running around the aisles delightedly and selecting such exotic treasures as *krupuk* (dried shrimp wafers) and *bagoong* (fermented fish paste) to take home with them. On my next visit to San Diego I fully expect to hear that the teenagers are putting *kimchee* in their tacos.

Another trend that may help shape the California cuisine is the notable number of men who take a passionate interest in the fine points of cooking. I recall with special pleasure a dinner in Pasadena cooked by food expert Philip Brown. The main course was leg of lamb, a California favorite, with the bone end cut short. Philip told me he had punctured the lamb all over with a fork and baked it in a covered pan with a quart of white

California apricots dry in the sun outside a Santa Clara packing company. Blenheim and Royal apricots, the two major varieties used for drying, are picked ripe from early June through mid-July, cut in half and pitted, then placed centers up in shallow wooden trays for about four to six hours of sulfur-smoking, which preserves their color. The final sun-drying takes two to six days, depending on the temperature. In a recent year about a fifth of California's apricots were marketed in dried form—and the total crop made up 97 per cent of all the apricots grown in the U.S.

California Dates: The Sweet That Grows on Trees

California's Coachella Valley is the only place in the Western Hemisphere in which dates are raised on a commercial basis. More than a hundred varieties of dates grow here, often planted, as shown at left, in mixed groves of date palms and citrus trees. Because pollen from the nonbearing male date palm does not attract insect carriers, it must be transferred by hand to the blossoms of the smaller female trees. The date clusters that develop two or three months later are covered with paper to protect them against ruinous rains and pests. Finally, six to nine months after pollination, the ripened date clusters are harvested from raised platforms. All of these processes are both painstaking and expensive, but they pay handsome dividends: the palms of the Coachella Valley produce an annual date crop worth from $8 to $10 million.

The five major varieties of dates grown in the Coachella Valley are displayed in the tray at right. They are, from left: Halawy (native to Persia and Iraq), Black Abbada (Egypt), Zahidi (Iran), Medjhool (Morocco) and Deglet Noor (Algeria and Tunisia). Dates of all varieties reach the market in any of several forms—whole, pitted, or chopped. Contrary to popular belief, however, the dates are not dried; they are carefully packed in their natural, fully ripe state. To keep them fresh and moist, they should be refrigerated after purchase and between servings. Since dates quickly absorb the aromas of other foods, they should be stored in covered containers.

A male date palm *(left foreground)* pollinates 49 females, whose dates are protected by paper wrapping *(center)* until picked *(right)*.

wine and a dozen cloves of garlic. While the wine simmers, the garlic softens and loses the most pungent part of its flavor. For the last half hour of baking Philip removes the cover and bastes the lamb with the garlicky wine. The final step is to discard the garlic and most of the fat released by the meat, then boil the liquid down and make gravy of it.

I have never had more deliciously flavored lamb. Garlic has an affinity for lamb, but when garlic cloves are embedded in the meat there are always hot spots of excessive flavor. Philip's lamb, on the other hand, was evenly and gently garlicked. Along with the lamb he served rice mixed with chopped onion, paprika and pine nuts sautéed in olive oil. (It had to be California oil, he told me; European oils are "undependable.") Just before serving the rice he added chopped pimiento and parsley. For a vegetable he cooked peas and thin-sliced mushrooms together until all the moisture was absorbed. The mushrooms were not those little pale things that one too often gets in the East; they were robust, fully flavored California mushrooms that had been spared by the pickers until their caps grew large and open.

I had asked Philip to prepare a characteristically Californian dessert. He selected some very large oranges and peeled them spirally with a sharp knife. The parings were long and thin and less than a quarter of an inch wide. Philip simmered them in a little vanilla-flavored sugar syrup until they were soft enough to be eaten. He then removed the remaining white pith from the oranges, cut the fruit in halves and partially separated the sections so they could be eaten individually. Finally, he poured the syrup over the sections and arranged the parings about the dish in colorful swirls. The result was a simple but highly appealing dessert, with a subtle flavor that was partly fresh orange, partly orange liqueur.

Though Southern California may be catching up, the state's apex of taste and grace is still San Francisco. This marvelous city has almost everything: a climate that is never really hot or cold, a spectacular setting, a rich and beautiful hinterland and citizens who enjoy themselves hugely and seldom appear to work too hard. The people of few American cities

Certain varieties of California olives, among them the popular Manzanillo *(below),* are still cured by an old European method in wooden tanks like the one shown below at right. (Most modern processors prefer stainless-steel tanks, but follow the same method.) Over a period of four days, the olives in the tank are treated with two baths of lye solution (to neutralize their bitterness) and three of plain water (to wash off the lye); then they are pumped into 50-gallon oak barrels and exposed for seven months to the heat of the sun, which speeds fermentation. Finally, the cured olives are washed, sorted and packed for market.

—indeed, of few cities outside France—talk so much about food and cooking as do San Franciscans *(Chapter 5)*. No detail about food is too small to escape their interest. I know one man who insists that only in the damp salt air on the seaward side of San Francisco can salami ripen properly. Another is watching with confidence a project to inoculate the roots of California's live oak trees with the fungus that produces truffles. They will be better than the French ones, he predicts.

San Francisco is also one of the few American cities that get really excited about bread. Woe to a restaurant that serves an inferior loaf. San Franciscans demand homemade-type bread even though it is slower to produce and therefore costs more. Their prime and famous favorite is sourdough bread, leavened not with commercial yeast but with a sourdough starter in which yeast cells have been happily multiplying. Many families keep their own sourdough starter bubbling in a crock and claim a history for their strain of yeast going back dozens of years.

San Franciscans insist that their local sourdough bread cannot be equaled anywhere in the world. Some say simply that it is due to "something about the air." Others give a more elaborate explanation: that its magical leaven is actually "wine yeast" from the nearby vineyards and wineries. I cannot altogether credit these explanations, or the widespread belief that a crock of San Francisco sourdough taken away from its native city loses its power to produce top-quality bread—but I must grant that San Francisco sourdough, whether baked in large rounds or in long, French-style loaves, is better than any bread of its type I have ever tasted. The attractively sour flavor varies in intensity (some kinds are advertised as extra-sour) but all the varieties are excellent. When a San Franciscan leaves his city—usually not for long—he gets a last chance to buy his native bread at the airport.

A pleasant and recent feature of San Francisco life is the gourmet cooking school that also functions as a social club. One of them is run by Thomas Cara, the owner of an elegant store that sells fancy cooking utensils. Connected with the school as a semisecret elite is the only chartered American chapter of the *Confrérie de la Marmite*—translated, the Brotherhood of the Cooking Pot—a Swiss society in which male gourmets (no women have breached its ramparts as yet) prepare meals for each other. As a signal honor I was invited to a Confrérie dinner.

I particularly remember the soup, called "garbage soup" by its author, a local writer named Jinx Kragen. Its basic ingredient was leftover salad, two cups' worth. Confrérie member Jeff Morgan sautéed a sliced peeled potato and some chopped shallots in plenty of butter, added about six cups of chicken broth and simmered the mixture until the potato was very tender. He then added the salad greens along with their dressing and simmered the soup for 10 minutes more. At this point, he warned me, it will invariably look awful—but you simply whirl it in a blender for a while to turn it into delicious green soup. There is no fixed recipe; the soup changes a little each time it is prepared because the "garbage" is different. (When I brought word of this concoction back across the continent, my wife fell in love with garbage soup—but she is trying to think up another name for it.)

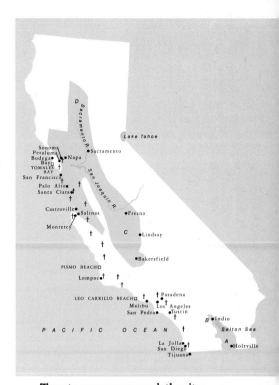

Twenty-one crosses mark the sites of Franciscan missions established on or near the California coast between 1769 and 1823. These missions introduced many crops that are now staples of the American diet, but they did not remain centers of intensive farming. Today agriculture in the state is concentrated in four fertile areas, shown in green: (A) the Imperial Valley, (B) the Coachella Valley, (C) the San Joaquin Valley, and (D) the Sacramento Valley.

The main course at the Confrérie dinner was veal *scaloppini* cooked by Cara himself. He was guarded about the full range of herbs and seasonings he had used, but I watched him pound veal cutlets thin between sheets of wax paper and brown them; he tossed in a lot of brandy and touched it with a match so it flared almost to the ceiling. After the flaming, which gave a glaze to the pan and a special flavor to the veal, Cara simmered the cutlets with chicken stock, wine, sliced mushrooms, garlic and slender asparagus spears, blending all the flavors of the ingredients for half an hour into delightful harmony. Whatever his secret may have been, it worked; all *scaloppini* should be as good as Thomas Cara's.

Each course of the Confrérie dinner was accompanied by a wine, and the veal course had two—one Californian and the other French, for purposes of comparison—and both were first-rate. With dessert came a remarkable sweet wine, Moscato Amabile, produced in small quantities by the Martini winery. I was told that the wine is fermented a second time, exactly like champagne, to give it a bit of sparkle. It tastes rather like *Asti spumante* and it is delightful with a sweet dessert. Somewhat smugly, my hosts told me that Moscato Amabile rarely travels beyond California because it must be held under deep refrigeration to keep the fermentation from starting up again.

Another elegant cooking school in San Francisco is run by a charming young lady named Joyce Goldstein. One afternoon at the school I watched her make a dessert to end all desserts, a *gâteau Rolla* constructed of four layers of almond meringue filled with chocolate, beaten egg whites and butter; next day I went to dinner at her home to enjoy this delicacy along with others. We had artichoke bottoms (the enormous California kind) cooked with oil and saffron and filled with crabmeat in herb mayonnaise. We had a salad of raw sliced mushrooms, romaine, watercress and endive. We had roast pheasant with wild rice, and sauerkraut mixed with pineapple, raisins, carrots and juniper berries. We had that marvelous dessert. With each course went wine—enough in all to make up at least a bottle per person. I expected the conversation to lag after dinner but it continued to scintillate. For this was San Francisco, where great meals are stimulants, not soporifics.

Opposite: Lovingly made and sinfully rich, serried ranks of cakes and pastries adorn the shelves of San Francisco's Fantasia bakery. To turn out these regal concoctions Fantasia's founder, Ernest Weil, employs pastry chefs from Austria, Denmark, Germany, Switzerland and his native France. His clientele includes restaurants, hotels, clubs and an army of mail-order customers, but the best proof of his success is the patronage of gourmets who prefer desserts more elegant than they can prepare themselves.

To make about 2½ cups

⅔ cup white distilled vinegar
2 teaspoons finely grated onion
1 cup sugar
2 teaspoons dry mustard
2 teaspoons salt
2 cups vegetable oil
3 tablespoons poppy seeds

To make about 2 cups

A 10-ounce package frozen sliced
   sweetened strawberries,
   thoroughly defrosted, and their
   syrup
1½ cups sour cream
A pinch of salt
Confectioners' sugar (optional)

To make about 3 cups

½ cup dried apricots
3 tablespoons confectioners' sugar
1 cup heavy cream, chilled

To make about 1 cup

1 cup (8 ounces) plain unflavored
   yoghurt
2 tablespoons honey
1 tablespoon finely cut fresh mint
   leaves
1 to 2 teaspoons strained fresh
   lemon juice

Poppy-Seed Dressing

Combine the vinegar, onion, sugar, mustard and salt in a bowl and stir vigorously with a wire whisk until the sugar, mustard and salt dissolve. Whisking constantly, pour in the oil in a slow, thin stream and continue to beat until the dressing is smooth and thick. Stir in the poppy seeds and taste for seasoning.

Serve the poppy-seed dressing at once with any fruit salad or cover tightly with plastic wrap and store in a cool place or the refrigerator until ready to serve. Tightly covered and refrigerated, the dressing can safely be kept for 6 to 10 days.

Strawberry-and-Sour-Cream Dressing

Place the strawberries and their syrup in a bowl and crush the berries slightly with the back of a large spoon. Add the sour cream and salt, and stir until the ingredients are thoroughly blended. Taste for sweetness and add up to 1 tablespoon of confectioners' sugar if desired. Cover with foil or plastic wrap and refrigerate the dressing for at least 1 hour before serving. Strawberry-and-sour-cream dressing may accompany any fruit salad.

Apricot-Cream Dressing

Place the apricots in a bowl and pour in enough boiling water to cover them completely. Let them soak for 10 to 15 minutes, or until they are soft, then drain them in a sieve set over a bowl. Combine the apricots and ¼ cup of the soaking liquid in the jar of an electric blender and blend at medium speed for 15 seconds. Turn the machine off, scrape down the sides of the jar with a rubber spatula and blend again until the apricots are a smooth purée. Scrape the purée into a bowl and stir in the sugar.

In a chilled bowl, whip the cream with a wire whisk or a rotary or electric beater until stiff enough to stand in unwavering peaks on the beater when it is lifted from the bowl. With a rubber spatula, scoop the apricot purée over the cream and fold them together gently but thoroughly.

Taste the apricot-cream dressing for sweetness and serve it with any fruit salad. Tightly covered with plastic wrap, the dressing can safely be stored in the refrigerator for up to 3 hours before serving.

Yoghurt-and-Honey Dressing

Combine the yoghurt, honey and mint in a bowl and beat with a wire whisk until the mixture is smooth. Whisk in 1 teaspoon of the lemon juice, then taste the dressing and add up to 1 teaspoon more lemon juice if desired. Cover tightly with foil or plastic wrap and refrigerate until ready to serve.

Yoghurt-and-honey dressing may be served with any fruit salad.

A fruit salad changes character according to its dressing. The dressings shown are: (1) tangy strawberry-and-sour-cream, (2) minty yoghurt-and-honey, (3) tart apricot-cream, and (4) sweet-and-sour poppy seed.

To serve 6 to 8

Two 12- to 14-ounce artichokes
6 cups chicken stock, fresh or
   canned
¼ cup strained fresh lemon juice
1 cup cold water combined with
   1 tablespoon strained fresh lemon
   juice
2 tablespoons butter
2 tablespoons finely chopped
   shallots
2 tablespoons flour
1 cup light cream

To serve 6 to 8

1 tablespoon vegetable oil
1 small Temple or navel orange
½ cup cold water
1 envelope unflavored gelatin
¼ cup sugar
1½ cups ginger ale
2 tablespoons strained fresh lemon
   juice
2 medium-sized firm ripe peaches,
   peeled, halved, pitted and cut
   lengthwise into ⅓-inch-thick
   slices
½ cup fresh ripe strawberries,
   washed, hulled and cut
   lengthwise into ⅓-inch-thick
   slices
½ cup table grapes, washed,
   halved and seeded if necessary
1 tablespoon very finely chopped
   crystallized ginger

Artichoke Soup

With a small sharp knife, trim about ⅛ inch off the stem end of each artichoke and peel the tough outer skin from the remaining stem. Cut the artichokes lengthwise in half, drop them into a 4- to 5-quart enameled or stainless-steel saucepan, and pour in the chicken stock and the ¼ cup of lemon juice. Bring to a boil over high heat, reduce the heat to low, cover the pan partially and simmer the artichokes for 20 to 30 minutes, or until their bases show no resistance when pierced with the point of a small sharp knife.

With tongs or a slotted spoon, transfer the artichokes to a cutting board. Cut or pull off the green artichoke leaves, return them to the saucepan, and simmer partially covered for 10 minutes longer.

Meanwhile, cut or pull the thistlelike yellow leaves and hairy inner chokes away from the artichoke bottoms (drawings, Recipe Booklet) and discard them. Trim the artichoke bottoms, drop them into a bowl and pour the water-and-lemon-juice mixture over them. Set the bottoms aside; they can safely wait at room temperature for 2 or 3 hours.

Scoop the green leaves out of the stock with a slotted spoon. With a teaspoon, scrape the soft flesh from each artichoke leaf. Return the pulp to the stock and discard the scraped leaves. Simmer the stock, partially covered, for 30 minutes more, then purée the mixture through a food mill set over a bowl or rub it through a fine sieve with the back of a spoon.

In a heavy 3- to 4-quart saucepan, melt the butter over moderate heat. When the foam begins to subside, add the shallots and stir for about 5 minutes, or until they are soft and translucent but not brown. Mix in the flour and stir over low heat for 2 or 3 minutes to remove the taste of raw flour. Stirring the mixture constantly, pour in the artichoke purée in a slow, thin stream and cook over high heat until the soup comes to a boil, thickens slightly and is smooth. Stir in the cream, simmer for 2 or 3 minutes, then taste for seasoning. Pour the soup into a bowl and cool it to room temperature. Cover with foil or plastic wrap and refrigerate for 1 or 2 hours, or until the soup is thoroughly chilled.

Just before serving, rinse the artichoke bottoms briefly under cold running water, pat them completely dry with paper towels and cut them into ¼-inch dice. Pour the soup into a chilled tureen or individual soup plates, scatter the pieces of artichoke bottom on top and serve at once.

Ginger-Ale Salad

With a pastry brush, spread the vegetable oil evenly inside a 1-quart decorative mold. Invert the mold on paper towels to drain off the excess oil.

Remove the peel and all of the white membrane of the orange with a small sharp knife, using short sawing motions. Section the orange by cutting along both sides of each membrane division to the core. As each section is freed, carefully lift it out and set it aside on paper towels to drain.

Pour the water into a heatproof measuring cup and sprinkle the gelatin over it. When the gelatin has softened for 2 or 3 minutes, set the cup in a small skillet of simmering water and stir over low heat until the gelatin dissolves completely. Add the sugar and stir until it dissolves.

Pour the gelatin mixture into a deep bowl and stir in the ginger ale

A welcome addition to a summer menu, chilled artichoke soup garnished with bits of artichoke bottom offers a creamy mixture of subtle flavors.

Molded mounds of lime gelatin, cucumber "leaves," watercress and strawberries set off a shimmering ring of ginger-ale salad.

and lemon juice. Then set the bowl into a larger bowl half filled with crushed ice or ice cubes and cold water. With a metal spoon, stir the mixture until it thickens enough to flow sluggishly off the spoon. Stir in the orange sections, peaches, strawberries, grapes and the crystallized ginger.

Pour the mixture into the oiled mold, cover with foil or plastic wrap, and refrigerate for at least 4 hours, or until it is firm to the touch.

To unmold the salad, run a thin knife around the sides of the mold and dip the bottom briefly into hot water. Place an inverted serving plate on top of the mold and, grasping plate and mold together firmly, turn them over. Rap the plate on a table and the ginger-ale salad should slide out easily. Refrigerate until ready to serve. Ginger-ale salad may be served with poppy-seed or strawberry-and-sour-cream dressing *(Recipe Index)*.

Lime-Gelatin Salad

To serve 6 to 8

1 medium-sized firm ripe cucumber
1 teaspoon salt
1 tablespoon vegetable oil
2 packages lime-flavored gelatin
1 quart boiling water
2 eight-ounce packages cream cheese, cut into ½-inch bits and softened
2 tablespoons strained fresh lime juice
2 teaspoons Worcestershire sauce
¼ teaspoon Tabasco sauce
1 cup finely chopped celery
¼ cup finely chopped onions
¼ cup finely cut fresh dill

With a small sharp knife, peel the cucumber and slice it lengthwise in half. Scoop out the seeds by running the tip of a teaspoon down the center of each half. Then cut the cucumber into ¼-inch dice. Place the dice in a fine sieve set over a bowl, add the salt and toss the cucumber about with a spoon to coat the dice evenly. Set aside to drain for at least 30 minutes, then pat the cucumber dice dry with paper towels.

Meanwhile, with a pastry brush, spread the vegetable oil evenly inside a 1-quart ring mold or eight individual 4-ounce molds. Invert the mold or molds on paper towels to allow the excess oil to drain off.

Place the powdered gelatin in a heatproof bowl, pour in the boiling water and mix well. Put the cream cheese in a large bowl, and with an electric mixer, beat it until it is light and fluffy. Beating the mixture constantly, pour in the gelatin in a slow thin stream and, when it is thoroughly incorporated, add the lime juice, Worcestershire sauce and Tabasco.

Set the bowl in a larger bowl half filled with crushed ice or ice cubes and cold water. Stir with a metal spoon until the gelatin mixture thickens enough to flow sluggishly off the spoon. Stir in the cucumber dice, the celery, onions and dill.

Pour the gelatin mixture into the oiled mold or molds, cover with plastic wrap and refrigerate for 4 hours, or until it is firm to the touch.

To unmold the salad, run a thin knife around the sides of the mold and dip the bottom briefly into hot water. Place an inverted serving plate on top of the mold and, grasping plate and mold together firmly, turn them over. Rap the plate on a table and the gelatin salad should slide out easily. Refrigerate until ready to serve.

Spit-roasted Wild Ducks with Olives

To serve 4

Light a 1- to 2-inch-thick layer of briquettes in a charcoal grill equipped with a rotating spit. Let the coals burn until white ash appears on the surface. (This may take as long as an hour.)

Meanwhile, wash the ducks briefly under cold running water and pat them dry with paper towels. Season the ducks inside and out with the salt, then secure the neck skin to the back of each bird with a small skewer and truss the ducks securely. String the ducks lengthwise end to end on the spit and anchor them in place with the sliding prongs.

Fit the spit into place above the coals and roast the birds for 1½ to 2 hours. To test for doneness, pierce a thigh with the point of a small sharp knife. The juice that trickles out should be pale yellow; if it is still tinged with pink, roast the ducks for another 5 to 10 minutes.

Meanwhile, prepare the sauce. In a heavy 10- to 12-inch skillet, melt the butter in the oil over moderate heat. When the foam begins to subside, add the chopped necks, gizzards and hearts. Fry the duck giblets for 4 or 5 minutes, stirring them frequently and regulating the heat so that the pieces brown richly and evenly without burning. Add the onions and, when they color lightly, mix in the flour. Then, stirring constantly, pour in the stock in a slow, thin stream and cook over high heat until the sauce comes to a boil and thickens slightly. Add the chopped olives, reduce the heat to low, and simmer the sauce partially covered for 30 minutes.

Strain the sauce through a fine sieve set over a small saucepan, pressing down hard on the giblets and olives with the back of a spoon to extract all their juices before discarding the pulp and neck bones. Skim as much fat as possible from the surface of the sauce and taste for seasoning.

To serve, remove the spit from the grill, unscrew the prongs and slide the ducks onto a heated platter. Remove the trussing strings, and garnish the birds with the whole olives. Reheat the sauce over low heat if necessary and serve it from a gravy boat or sauce bowl.

Two 1½- to 2-pound oven-ready wild ducks, with necks, gizzards and hearts coarsely chopped and reserved
1 teaspoon salt
3 tablespoons butter
1 tablespoon olive oil
½ cup finely chopped onions
2 tablespoons flour
1½ cups chicken stock, fresh or canned
¼ cup finely chopped pitted green olives
12 whole pitted green olives

New Role for a Time-honored Food

In California, where olive trees have flourished for some 200 years, cooks use the fruit as both an ingredient and a garnish. For an otherwise simple dish of spit-roasted wild ducks *(Recipe Index)*, chopped olives lend unexpected pungency to the sauce, while whole green olives adorn the platter.

MENU.

Huîtres.
Chablis.
Consommé Royale.
Sherry Isabella.
Saumon glacé au four à la Chambord.
Sauterne.
Boudin blanc à la Richelieu.
Château la Tour.
Filet de Boeuf à la Providence.
Champagne.
Paté de fois Gras.
Château Yquem.
Timbale de Volaille Américaine au Sénateur.
Clos Vougeot.
Côtelettes d'Agneau sauté au pointes d'Asperges.
Sorbet.
Bécassines au Cresson.
Château Margeaux.
Salade à la Française.
DESSERT.

V by JACK SHELTON and JACK JUHASZ. San Francisco, one of the great "restaurant cities" of America, boasts a monthly newsletter called *Jack Shelton's Private Guide to Restaurants in San Francisco.* Accordingly, TIME-LIFE BOOKS asked Shelton and his editor, Jack Juhasz, to write this chapter.

Dining Out in San Francisco

San Francisco's bonanza days are recalled in this reconstruction of a place setting for an 1876 dinner at the Palace Hotel, held in honor of Nevada Senator William Sharon. A menu for each guest was engraved —at a cost of $40—on silver from the Comstock Lode that had helped make Sharon a multimillionaire. Since the back of the menu bore the guest's name, it doubled as a place card and a personal souvenir.

San Franciscans are notoriously tolerant, and can forgive almost any transgression—corruption, bribery, loose morals, even earthquakes. But bad restaurant food, never! More than in any other city in America except New Orleans, dining out in San Francisco is a serious matter. It is also a matter of intense pleasure. What gives San Francisco restaurants their unique flavor and flair cannot be precisely or wholly defined. Part of it is the spectacular backdrop the city provides, with its roller-coaster hills and breathtaking water views. Part of it is a history of hospitality to strangers; San Franciscans have long been sufficiently self-assured to welcome all sorts of foreign ways and cuisines. Part of it, too, is the city's proximity to an immense bounty of fresh food from both sea and land, and the loving care with which that food is cooked and served. Care, perhaps, is the key: San Francisco restaurateurs and their staffs go to great lengths to deliver fine food and meticulous service because their customers care deeply about these things.

Restaurants are to San Franciscans what the theater is to New Yorkers: something to be enjoyed, of course, but also something to be evaluated and criticized. Eavesdropping on what looks like a parley on high finance, one is likely to hear a lively debate on who is cooking the best cioppino *(Recipe Index)* in town these days. It is a safe bet, because it is inevitable, that any social gathering of San Franciscans will include at least one discussion of the latest in dining places, for discovering a new restaurant before its fame begins to spread is one of the city's more prevalent forms of oneupmanship. Moreover, the grapevine is incredibly efficient: San Francisco is one of those rare cities where a restaurant can open without benefit of advertising, public relations or other forms of promotion and turn away crowds in its first week. But the same grapevine that makes a restaurant can break one, too; more often than not, a restaurant that falls from grace is abandoned immediately and completely. When a favorite chef leaves a favorite establishment, his followers simply follow him to his new one, leaving behind a chagrined restaurant owner presiding over a roomful of empty tables.

This diligent pursuit of the delights of dining out did not develop overnight. San Francisco has a tradition of respect for fine food that goes back to the 1840s, when the city suddenly grew from the isolated frontier village of Yerba Buena (the Spanish for "good herb"—in this case, a mint-scented plant that flourished in the region) to a metropolis bustling with hordes of migrants in quest of gold. By stagecoach and steamer, the gold hunters poured into San Francisco, seeking their dream of El Dorado. Hungry as they were for gold, the newcomers were hungry for good food, too; and somebody had to feed them.

Hotels and restaurants sprang up in the 1850s, some of them pleasantly homey in food and service. To accommodate both boarders and transients, many hotels and guest houses provided "family-style" dinners at which, for a few cents a head, the patrons shared a substantial meal at a communal table. (The tradition of family-style meals has persisted; even today, particularly in the bohemian North Beach area, one can dine at communal tables in Italian, French or Basque restaurants, many of them still located in small hotels.)

There were epicures back in the 1850s, too, and mostly they preferred the surprisingly numerous French restaurants of the young city. By the 1870s, however, other groups had made their mark on local menus: Russians, Germans, Swiss, Italians, English, Mexicans, Spaniards—and Chinese, many of whom had come from the Orient to labor on the transcontinental railroad.

With the opening in 1875 of the Palace, called "the world's grandest hotel," a special elegance arrived in San Francisco. Royalty, presidents, millionaires and stage and opera luminaries beat a path to the Palace to feast on its soon-to-be-legendary cuisine. Jules Harder, a chef at ultra-fashionable Delmonico's, in New York City, was lured west to supervise the Palace's kitchen. It was Harder who, in 1876, conceived and brought off a celebrated dinner in honor of William Sharon, owner of the Palace and United States Senator from Nevada. Not the least of the splendors of the occasion was the menu at each guest's place, engraved on a plaque of silver mined from the Comstock Lode, one source of the Senator's millions *(page 116)*.

The original mining barons of the opulent 1870s and 1880s may have been rough at the edges, gourmands rather than gourmets in their eating habits, but their children were often well schooled and well traveled, and this younger generation developed a sophisticated awareness of fine food. By the Gay '90s San Francisco, enriched by new fortunes and a growing culture, was also bejeweled by a galaxy of excellent restaurants that her citizens were well able to appreciate.

118

The thriving port city was looking forward to a new century in which it would play to the hilt its role of Gateway to the West when, on April 18, 1906, its dreams came tumbling down in the most destructive earthquake in North American history. But like the game grande dame she was, San Francisco picked herself up, brushed herself off and started all over again. Along with the rest of the city, many fine restaurants were rebuilt. The Tadich Grill, now the oldest dining establishment in town and one famous for its seafood, set up new quarters, and still preserves the atmosphere of the old days. Schroeder's, founded in 1893, reopened and resumed serving its hearty German fare; over the years it has relaxed, somewhat grudgingly, its old men-only policy, but there is still a part of the place tacitly reserved for males, where oldtimers share a common table. Jack's Restaurant, which first opened its doors in 1864, quickly recovered after the earthquake and is still serving some of the city's best food in its handsome rooms on Sacramento Street *(page 124)*.

The Palace Hotel was rebuilt, too. Its sumptuousness is now embodied in the majestic Garden Court, which many diners-out regard as the most beautiful public eating room in all of the United States. In 1954, when the Sheraton Corporation bought the Palace, the headquarters of the hotel chain hastily reassured shocked San Franciscans that no basic changes would be made in the time-honored Palace ways of doing things. Another hotel tradition has been less successfully defended. For many years stately San Francisco matrons gathered, all chapeaued and gloved, for lunch every Monday in the Mural Room of the St. Francis Hotel, often at the same tables that generations of their families had had reserved for them. According to some local historians, the tradition grew out of the custom among pacesetting San Francisco hostesses of taking their weekend guests to Monday luncheon "on the way to depositing them at the depot," thereby indicating more or less subtly that the guests should not expect to stay on *past* Monday. Whatever the origin, the Monday luncheons became a hallowed ritual—and then just went out of style around 1960.

And so an era ended. Today there are few places left in San Francisco that are "in" with the city's upper crust. One is the Captain's Cabin at Trader Vic's, an oasis for owner Vic Bergeron's steady customers in the middle of an essentially tourist-oriented restaurant. While elsewhere at Trader Vic's guests dine impersonally on Chinese and South Pacific dishes amidst gaudy Polynesian decor, in the Captain's Cabin a conscious attempt has been made to create a more intimate atmosphere. But more than exclusiveness accounts for the Cabin's cool éclat: the versatility of the food and the perfect service. For many resident Bay Area notables, dining in the Captain's Cabin is the closest thing to dining in their own mansions. "Good afternoon, Mr. Zellerbach. Egg foo yung, of course. Without onions, as usual," murmurs Hans Brandt, Trader Vic's famous captain, and a pampered regular's meal is quickly ordered.

The standards required of restaurant personnel in San Francisco were paradoxically demonstrated when Hans was fired for discussing with local society reporters the behavior of a well-known patron who dined at the Cabin, thereby violating Vic Bergeron's policy of giving his select customers complete privacy. Yet some of the same customers entreated Vic to bring Hans back, and after a year he did. When Hans reappeared at work, a roomful of patrons rose and applauded.

The city's elite eaters do not by any means confine their patronage to such posh places as Trader Vic's, Jack's and La Bourgogne *(page 121)*. It is not uncommon to see prominent San Franciscans perched atop rickety stools, alongside cab drivers and hardhats, at the marble-topped counter of a small fish house called Swan's Oyster Depot, all of them devouring some of the freshest Dungeness crab in the city. Where there is good food to be found, San Franciscans at every level of income and social status will seek it out, and for at least three good reasons: the astonishing variety of good ethnic restaurants, the mobility of the residents and the compactness of the city itself. From the downtown shopping area and business district, connoisseurs of fine food can easily walk to Chinatown. North Beach, the city's Little Italy, blends into Chinatown—and also into the Philippine community and into Fisherman's Wharf, that magnificent medley of waterfront restaurants and stalls to which many businessmen go every Friday for lunch.

Added to all these handy places are others well beyond the city limits that San Franciscans, for all intents and purposes, regard as "local." In hot pursuit of culinary excellence they will gladly drive for an hour or more—or even fly—out of town. For example, on Interstate Highway 80, about 60 miles northeast of San Francisco Bay, there is the Nut Tree Restaurant, which maintains its own small airstrip for private planes that fly in from the Bay Area and elsewhere. Perhaps the finest of all practitioners of Californian and other Western cooking, the Nut Tree puts special emphasis on dishes that feature such local produce as artichokes, walnuts, raisins, olives and all the other fruits and vegetables that grow in the state year round.

The six restaurants shown on the following pages were chosen by the authors of this chapter as representative of the variety, both in cost and in culinary style, available in San Francisco. Such restaurants are among the major reasons it has won the accolade, at home and abroad, of "America's favorite city."

In a Pantheon of Fine Restaurants, a Shrine of Grande Cuisine

The décor at La Bourgogne is luxurious, yet unobtrusive—a fitting backdrop for French service that is lavish without ostentation. Admirers of French cuisine, like these diners preparing to sample a 1967 Meursault, consider a visit to the restaurant the next best thing to a trip to Paris. But La Bourgogne also makes masterly use of native American foodstuffs, such as the Maine lobster in a faultless *homard à l'américaine,* or the West Coast's superb lamb for the *selle d'agneau.*

If, as many gourmets believe, the classic French cuisine represents the peak of man's achievement in the culinary arts, then La Bourgogne may well deserve the title of San Francisco's finest restaurant. Patron Jean Lapuyade and chef Marcel Perrin offer a menu that reads like a litany of *grande cuisine,* with specialties like *selle d'agneau des gastronomes* (boned and baked saddle of lamb, stuffed with mushrooms and *foie gras,* encased in a pastry crust, and served with a *sauce périgourdine*) and *carré d'agneau à la façon chevreuil Nesselrode* (roast rack of lamb marinated in wine and herbs, carved at the table and served with a chestnut purée). La Bourgogne flies in sole from Normandy and oysters from Belon, and owner Lapuyade has assembled a superb cellar of wines. Moreover, he maintains standards of service that, even in a city of great restaurants, place La Bourgogne in a class all its own.

Long, expendable bamboo chopsticks enable Mandarin diners to grill Mongolian lamb at this special barbecue table.

Classic Chinese Cooking Superbly Done

A specialty of the Mandarin's kitchen is four-happiness dumplings *(below)*. The exotic delicacy is made from a single continuous piece of dough, intricately folded into four open compartments containing chopped egg yolk, minced mushroom, shredded seafood and vegetables. Hidden beneath them is a fifth "secret" pocket of chicken or pork.

When, in 1960, Cecilia Chiang founded the Mandarin restaurant, fellow San Francisco restaurateurs gave it no more than six months. Not only was Mrs. Chiang trying to introduce a variety of Szechwan and northern Chinese dishes to a public that was accustomed to Cantonese cuisine, but she had chosen to open her restaurant in a location far from the Chinatown tourist path. To make matters worse, she opened without benefit of a liquor license and —because of her insistence on using the best of ingredients—with prices higher than those in many well-established Chinese restaurants. The Mandarin's tenure did indeed appear shaky.

Within weeks of the opening, however, the gastronomic grapevine quivered with reports of fantastic culinary achievements based on dishes never before seen in the West—dishes like a Mongolian fire pot or a "beggar's chicken" (chicken baked in clay). A hard core of sophisticated followers formed and grew, and competitors vied for alumni of the Mandarin kitchen. Dishes introduced by Mrs. Chiang began to appear on menus in other restaurants —but she originated new ones of her own. Then, in 1968, came an invitation to relocate in San Francisco's picturesque Ghirardelli Square. That is where the Mandarin thrives today—no longer an obscure hole-in-the-wall but a showplace, with what may be the most exciting Chinese menu in America.

Jack's preserves the atmosphere of an earlier age, with a high ceiling, potted plants and walls studded with brass coat hooks.

Character and Tradition in a Simple Setting

An occasional fresh coat of paint and some new lighting fixtures are the only discernible changes in Jack's décor in recent years, yet despite its uncompromisingly plain atmosphere, it has irresistibly drawn certain types of San Franciscans since 1864. People who dote on being pampered by elaborate service have never cared for Jack's. Others, however, have appreciated its honest, basically French approach to cooking, and on Sunday night (traditionally, cook's night off) some of the city's most prominent families gather here to enjoy rex sole *(right)*. Regulars also favor the rack of lamb with potatoes *boulangère,* deep-fried zucchini or eggplant, and salads liberally dotted with fresh seafood and generously doused, upon request, with Jack's own tarragon-flavored vinegar.

Rex sole *meunière* is perhaps the most popular dish at Jack's.

Jook and Noodles at Sam Wo

The Sam Wo restaurant is too small, too crowded, too plain and, most of all, "too Chinese" to attract many tourists—and San Franciscans like it that way. Patrons devour steaming bowls of rice-gruel *jook,* raw fish salad and Chinese crullers, and put up with constant kibbitzing from Sam Wo's famous waiter and part-owner, Edsel Ford Fung. The noodle dishes include some of the best tomato-beef chow mein in town.

Thirty years ago a San Francisco guidebook referred to the city's Chinatown as "alien in appearance to all the rest of San Francisco—hemmed within boundaries kept by tacit agreement with municipal authorities for almost a century." Local citizens and tourists alike were fascinated by this "alien" territory, but it was not until after World War II that dining in Chinatown became popular. Much of the credit for this is due to the restaurateur Johnny Kan, who hired authentic "side street" chefs from the heart of the district and presented their artistry in an attractive setting on Grant Avenue, Chinatown's main thoroughfare. The Cantonese banquet dishes featured at Kan's helped to educate a clientele whose only previous exposure to Chinese cookery may have been an occasional dish of chop suey (actually a Chinese-American invention). Today Grant Avenue is lined with luxuriously appointed—and often luxuriously priced—Chinese restaurants of varying merit, interspersed with hot-dog stands and patronized mainly by outsiders. Off on the side streets, though, there are a number of genuine ethnic establishments that cater primarily to the Chinese community but welcome Occidental visitors. Sam Wo, a *"jook* house," is typical. A stop there after midnight to sip some hot *jook* (a rice gruel hopefully regarded by some connoisseurs as a hangover curative) is a trip back in time to the exotic Chinatown of the past.

A Commanding Hostess Sets a Communal Table at La Pantera

At La Pantera, almost every night, sable-swathed dowagers rub elbows with dockhands, and well-groomed executives sit at communal tables alongside bearded hippies. What brings all of them together is their love of good food and their weakness for traditional San Franciscan-Italian-style family dinners. Ravioli *(below)*, filled with a spicy mixture of meat and spinach, and served with a rich meat sauce, is the perennial Saturday-night favorite.

Because San Franciscans have always been noted for their gregariousness it is not surprising that they favor certain family-style restaurants where they can sit at communal tables and gorge on substantial Italian dinners, sprinkled with conversation as well as with cheese. At the same time San Franciscans have always loved "characters." They have found a perfect blend of these attractions in the North Beach area at La Pantera, a superb family-style restaurant run by a remarkable character named Rena Nicolai. Her family has owned La Pantera (literally, "the panther," and appropriately in the feminine gender) for 75 years. Today Rena reigns over it much as a strict disciplinarian might reign over a boardinghouse —which is exactly what La Pantera was at the turn of the century. Endowed with a perpetual scowl, Rena will unhesitatingly eject anyone who does not conform to her personal code of punctilious behavior. But the *pastina in brodo,* minestrone and other soups, meat-stuffed zucchini, and the rich main courses (most notably a truly sensational ravioli) are well worth the risk of disfavor. And the modest check usually brings a smile to the face of the diner—if not to Rena's.

When in Morocco, one eats as the Moroccans eat—with the fingers. The same holds true at San Francisco's Marrakech, where guests are provided with Western dining implements only if they insist upon them. This rule is no mere restaurateur's gimmick, but an attempt to re-create completely the experience of Moroccan dining. The sights, sounds, odors and textures of a Moroccan dining room are recaptured as a setting for such dishes as *bastelah (opposite),* a flaky, layered pie stuffed with chicken, nuts and spices, and topped with a sugar-and-cinnamon heart.

The Marrakech: A Western Re-Creation of Morocco

Whatever ethnic cuisines deserve export from their native lands may usually be enjoyed somewhere among San Francisco's dining places. Considering the relatively small size of the city (its population is about 750,000), the fact testifies to San Francisco's venturesome, inquisitive palate, which is willing and even eager to try any style of cooking at least once. One of the newest members of the city's international culinary family is the cuisine of Morocco. The Marrakech restaurant began as an affair of the heart: Mr. and Mrs. Pierre Dupart, the owners of L'Orangerie, one of the city's best French restaurants, fell in love with Moroccan food on a trip to North Africa. They determined to share their enthusiasm with the people of San Francisco by re-creating their experience of Moroccan dining in every aspect. At the basement level of L'Orangerie, the Duparts built a suite of Moroccan-style dining rooms in meticulous and authentic detail, from tiled walls to low couches draped with Moroccan rugs. In the background Berber music is heard; even the Moroccan mealtime ritual of hand-washing is faithfully followed. But most important of all are the Moroccan dinners provided by chef Mehdi Ziani, which in these surroundings become a sensory pleasure in every particular.

130

VI

Ocean and Gulf: A Wealth of Seafood

A fishing boat, the *Santa Maria,* sails the waters of San Pedro harbor in a parade celebrating the famous annual Fishermen's Fiesta. Held in October at the time of the full moon, the festival traditionally marks the end of the tuna and the beginning of the anchovy season. It is observed on shore with a swordfish barbecue, a cioppino-cooking contest and the conspicuous consumption of a variety of foods.

The two seacoasts of the Great West, the Pacific Ocean and the Gulf of Mexico, could hardly be more different, and the good things to eat that they yield are very different too. In California, mountains crowd tumultuously upon the Pacific as if poised to plunge in; much of the coastline consists of cliffs or steep inclines with the surf foaming white at their bases. Far to the east, in Texas, level plains slope gradually out to the Gulf of Mexico. On these plains, rivers slow down and broaden into wide estuaries. The land becomes moist, then wet, then partly inundated marsh. Beyond lie shallow lagoons, separated from the Gulf by a line of narrow sandy islands. In season this Texas shore, like Louisiana's next door, is the playground of hurricanes.

So neither the Pacific nor the Gulf Coast is entirely benign, but each offers a marvelous bounty of seafood. California has what oceanographers call a "cold-water coast," which makes for fine fishing. A cold current sweeps down from Alaska, and cold northern water is rich with sea life. In addition, the current veers away from the land, pulling up bottom water with deep-lying nutrients that add to the richness of the surface water. The result is a sea that teems with life, from microscopic creatures to great whales. Sea lions bask on the rocks. Schools of anchovies cruise along, preyed upon by all sorts of natural enemies: sea birds, tuna, porpoise and fishermen. Vast beds of kelp—giant seaweed as much as 150 feet long—grow on the rocky bottoms and supply food for shellfish, including the beautiful and delicious abalone, a large mollusk with a mother-of-pearl-lined shell. Varicolored fish swim among the massive stems of

133

From a seine skiff off the California coast, tuna fishermen gather the fish trapped in a seine suspended between their skiff and the parent ship *(left)*. Their basic gathering implement, hidden in the water, is a brail—a huge power-driven nylon-net scoop that can raise a ton of tuna at a time to the deck of the parent ship. The fish will be frozen whole in the ship's hold, and later thawed and cut up for canning. After the entire catch has been secured in the hold, both seine and skiff are hoisted onto the deck of the parent ship to await the next sighting of a school of tuna.

the kelp. In the colder water live Dungeness crabs 10 inches across, their big legs and claws stuffed with delicate white meat.

There is even one species of fish that literally throws itself into the hands of fish lovers. This is the silvery five- to eight-inch grunion, which state law, in fact, requires to be taken *only* by the bare hands. Grunion gather off Southern California beaches during the especially high tides that accompany the full moon in spring and summer, the females swollen with ripe eggs and each with at least one male in attendance. A female waits until just after the crest of the high tide and then allows a wave to float her up onto the beach. As the water flows away, she frantically wiggles her tail to dig a hole in the semiliquid sand, and lays her eggs. The males press close beside her and discharge their fertilizing milt; then all go back to the sea on the next wave—unless, that is, human hands intervene. For it is during the spawning operation that grunion are permitted to be picked up. Only children under 16 and adults with state licenses are allowed to do so. Years ago I went grunion hunting on a beach near San Diego with a friend from an aerospace laboratory and a group of children. The moon was full and the beach was jammed with people, most of them wearing the correct hunting costume of sweatshirt, jeans and sneakers. For a while we saw not one grunion; then the tide began to fall, leaving a strip of wet beach above the waves, and suddenly thousands of the small fish were wriggling on the sand. The mob

More than 80 per cent of the California tuna catch is made up of only two of the five main varieties of tuna: the skipjack *(top)*, which generally weighs from 6 to 12 pounds, and the 30- to 200-pound yellowfin *(bottom)*. When packed and canned, both skipjack and yellowfin are rated as "light-meat" tuna, though the skipjack is markedly darker than the yellowfin. Tuna meat labeled "white," which comes from the blander albacore variety of the fish, amounts to less than 1 per cent of the catch.

scrambled into action, catching each other's bare ankles almost as often as the flopping grunion, but nevertheless enjoying the hunt. I caught no fish myself (I had no license) but my friend and the youngsters picked up a bucketful to take to his house for a late supper.

I felt a bit guilty about eating those pretty grunion, so rudely interrupted at a delicate moment in their lives, but when I smelled them cooking, my misgivings faded. My friend scaled and cleaned them; his wife dipped them in beaten egg, rolled them in bread crumbs and deep-fried them. They were crisp outside, tender and moist inside, with a light, pleasant flavor somewhat like that of a fresh-caught smelt.

Delightful as it is to hunt and to eat, the flyweight grunion has only amateur standing among California seafood. The heavyweight champion in tonnage caught both commercially and by sportsmen—and in terms of consumption canned and fresh—is the tuna. Like the Pacific salmon, it comes not in just one variety but several. Alphabetically they are the albacore, the bluefin, the skipjack and the yellowfin, and here are some basic facts about them:

Albacore (13 to 20 pounds) is the only variety that can be marketed under the term White Meat Tuna and, thanks to its flaky, moist flesh, is the one most prized for cooking fresh. In the temperate waters of the Pacific it is abundant in supply.

Bluefin (20 to 30 pounds) is marketed as Tano, or Dark Meat Tuna.

The flesh is high in oil content, which makes it a favorite for eating raw in Japanese-style dishes. The larger bluefin is the fighter of the family, and is thereby the favorite of sport fishermen, many of whom smoke it.

Skipjack (10 to 15 pounds), marketed as Light Meat Tuna, is soft and tender in texture. It roams all over the Pacific and is the quarry of the far-ranging California tuna boats that Ecuador "captures" from time to time within its 200-mile limit.

Yellowfin (20 to 30 pounds), also sold as Light Meat Tuna and often mixed with skipjack in canning, is less migratory and likes to stay in tropical waters. (In midsummer many laze about off Baja and Southern California, heading farther south in the fall.) Although they grow to impressive size (up to 450 pounds), smaller yellowfin are preferred for canning because the larger the specimen, the darker and tougher the flesh.

Once ashore, most tuna end up in cans, but they are a fine fish to eat fresh, even raw. In this form they are increasingly popular in Japanese restaurants all over the United States. The fish is cut into thin slices, called *sashimi,* served with a dipping sauce, or together with a vinegared rice dish, called *sushi.* Eaten this way, tuna has the texture of tender beef and a taste somewhere between cold rare beef and raw shellfish.

Fresh tuna for use in home cooking is not easy to come by, unless you have caught it or know a fish dealer who can fill a special order. One lucky friend of mine happened to find it easy to obtain. The 85-foot yacht on which he was a guest left Santa Barbara one summer morning, headed south. Before many miles the party snagged their first albacore, about 15 pounds. They cleaned it and put it on ice until late afternoon, when the host went to the galley and cut half of the fish into two-inch steaks. He placed them in a good-sized casserole along with tomato sauce, green peppers, Parmesan cheese, mushroom soup, sliced olives, onions, herbs, spices and white wine. All this baked for an hour and a half at low heat. At sunset the tender, flaky fish and its sauce was served over rice with French bread, white wine and, inevitably for Californians, a fresh green salad. That held everybody overnight. For snacks the next day they had only to dip into a great earthenware crock in which the remaining pieces of the raw tuna had soaked in a marinade of water, vinegar, salt, herbs and spices. For any thirst this aroused, there was plenty of beer.

It was on this same trip that my lucky friend was reminded of some other riches of the Pacific. In those waters turtles sometimes surface to take the sun. He and his shipmates corralled a big one and hoisted it aboard for later use as steaks and in soup and chowder, meanwhile keeping it refreshed and happy by occasional dousings with buckets of sea water. That evening the yacht anchored somewhere off Baja. The party went ashore and bought a dozen spiny lobsters from local fishermen, the only people allowed to catch these crustaceans in Mexican waters. Back aboard, the yachtsmen boiled the lobster tails briefly in seasoned salted water, slipped them under the broiler, and then gorged on them, dipping the chunks in lemon butter. The ensuing argument over which meal was better—albacore or spiny lobster—never did get settled.

Another West Coast fish, almost as unappreciated as fresh tuna, is the abundant anchovy. It is not the well-known European anchovy that comes in tubes of paste or spiced and coiled in cans, but an American cousin that averages four or five inches long. The Italian-American fishermen of California love these anchovies cleaned, strung in rows on bamboo skewers and grilled with a basting of lemon juice, tomatoes and such enliveners as parsley, garlic, basil and oregano. I like them best simply breaded and fried. In a San Pedro restaurant I had some very small ones that were dipped in batter and fried in butter so that they clustered together. Served as appetizers, they were crisp, crusty and delicious.

One of the most admired fish in Southern California, by those fortunate enough to get a taste of it, is the rare totuava, a large, grouperlike species found in the Gulf of California. Tasting like the striped bass of both Atlantic and Pacific waters, the totuava is a plump fish with flaky, moist meat. I like the steaks baked or steamed, but one California recipe I truly appreciated in a home at Playa del Rey calls for poaching the fish in water with sliced onion, white wine, pepper, allspice, bay leaf, salt and lemon juice. At the table the fish was anointed with a sinfully rich coating of butter mixed half-and-half with olive oil.

California shellfish are relatively scarce, because the shoreline has few of the mudflats and sheltered bays beloved by clams, scallops and oysters. Most of its shelled creatures must be tough enough to survive in open, storm-beaten waters. One that does survive is the Pismo clam, native to the neighborhood of Pismo Beach, north of Santa Barbara; it grows seven inches across and has a thick, strong shell. Once Pismo clams were plentiful; then, for a time, commercial exploitation almost exterminated them. Now they are strictly protected. Only amateurs may dig them and only for their own use; and the limit is 10 per day.

One favored implement for digging Pismo clams is a long garden fork. The digger wades in knee-deep water at low tide and pokes the sand until he feels something hard underneath. If it is a clam, it must be at least five inches long to be kept; anything smaller must be returned to the hole from which it came. Despite this technical problem there is something curiously satisfying about digging for Pismo clams. Unlike fishing, which requires hours of meditation and the emotional stability of a philosopher, or hunting, which calls for physical stamina and the courage to return empty-handed, clam-digging is one of the few remaining family sports that is nearly always successful. Now that they are protected by the state, the clams exist in plenty, and serious clam hunters know where they are. When a hunter spots a stretch of beach where clams are thick, he keeps it secret until he has organized a clamming party of friends and relatives, and since each digger is entitled to 10 large clams, the total haul is usually enough for a substantial clam dinner.

Pismo clams are packed almost solid with pinkish meat. The two large muscles that hold the shells together are excellent eating, raw or steamed, but the "foot" that the clam uses to get around with, though flavorful, is so tough that it is best ground up. The most common way to cook it is in a chowder. Californians are quite well aware of New England-style chowder, with potatoes and milk, and Manhattan-style, with tomatoes, but they usually prefer their own imaginative ways of dealing with Pismo clams in a chowder. They may, for example, sharpen an ordinary milk-

The Fun of Catching and Feasting on Grunion

For a combination of free-wheeling sport and alfresco feasting, nothing compares with a late-night picnic on a Southern California beach when the grunion are running. The silvery fish, five to eight inches long at maturity, swim ashore just after high tide to lay their eggs in the wet sand, and anyone who knows their timetable can scoop up all he can eat. Invariably, the grunion run brings out teenagers with flashlights and huge appetites. Their catch is quickly cleaned, then even more quickly grilled or fried (*right*). Well-prepared parties bring forks for their side dishes, but when it comes to the grunion themselves everyone remembers that fingers were made before forks.

This menu for a typical beach picnic consists of deep-fried grunion, potato salad and a composite salad containing green beans, kidney beans and chick-peas. The fish are simply fried in oil until golden brown.

Meeting the grunion run near Leo Carrillo Beach, north of Los Angeles, teenagers catch a dinner barehanded, as the law requires.

Seated at the fire, Rick LaGrasse and his sister, Sue, set out to beat the average grunion consumption—about six per person per sitting.

California clam diggers forage on Pismo Beach, famous for the large, hard-shell clam of the same name that abounds in the area. The digging itself is relatively easy, especially with a rented potato-digging fork, for Pismo clams seldom burrow deeper than six inches into the sand. But strict state regulations, aimed at protecting the species, make the sport tricky: diggers must have licenses, must take no more than 10 clams a day, and must rebury any clam less than four and one half inches across.

and-potato chowder with hefty slugs of Worcestershire and Tabasco; to make the chowder richer still, they will add minced or puréed garlic and throw in a handful of chopped, garden-fresh scallions and green peppers. The result is an exciting dish that any Easterner would envy.

Better known than Pismo clams—indeed, the most famous of all California shellfish—is the abalone. Californians love it, and use it as a multipurpose food; the California poet George Sterling begins his lengthy "Abalone Song" with these lines:

> Oh! some folks boast of quail on toast,
> Because they think it's tony;
> But I'm content to owe my rent,
> And live on abalone.

The abalone can do without poetic embellishment. It is delicious eating, has a shell lined with iridescent mother-of-pearl and is hunted in a romantic manner. Abalone are giant mollusks; those of the red variety —the largest of half a dozen kinds—may weigh as much as 10 pounds and measure almost a foot across. They cling to rocks with a sucker whose muscle, the part usually eaten, occupies a large area of the shell. In the early days, rocky shores from Oregon to Mexico were almost paved with abalone, but their dried meat brought a high price in China, and fishermen almost exhausted them. Now, like Pismo clams, they are protected and fairly plentiful, though none may be shipped out of the state. Most abalone are gathered by divers who work from small boats with pumps that supply them with air through hoses. An abalone holds its shell away from the rock in order to feed on seaweed and algae, and at that point it is easy to pry loose with a flat iron bar. But men have drowned when an outsized abalone caught their fingers under its shell and held them in a death grip with its powerful sucker.

Californians have developed a great many ways to cook abalone. The simplest way yields abalone steak, for which the big muscle is trimmed of the dark frilly membrane that surrounds it and is sliced into disks up to half an inch thick. These are placed on a firm surface and pounded with a wooden mallet. (Some authorities say two or three hard blows are enough to make the steaks tender; others pound them to half their original thickness.) Then they are fried very quickly at high heat, basted with butter and served with quartered lemons. Restaurants often bread their abalone steaks, but not much is gained except to make them look thicker, and the delicate flavor of the meat is masked by the butter-saturated breading.

When abalone is cooked any length of time it gets remarkably tough. The Chinese, who are masters of quick cooking, successfully incorporate bits of abalone in soup, but novices had better not take the chance. More often, when abalone is used in chowder or soup it is ground. Another good idea is to serve abalone soup in beautiful abalone shells, which are more capacious than soup bowls. I first had abalone soup in a Monterey restaurant, and still remember my enchantment with the pearl-lined service and my delight in the deep-sea flavor of the abalone bits.

For me, the seafood capital of California is San Francisco. One reason may be that it was originally populated by people from seafaring regions. Another is its large Italian-American colony, which includes many commercial fishermen. Whatever the reason, San Francisco has plenty of excellent fish markets. Its people eat a lot of seafood; the restaurants serve it and many specialize in it. Fisherman's Wharf is among the city's most popular attractions. Today, it is an odd combination of tourist magnet and businesslike commercial pier where fishermen tie up their boats, stock them with supplies and buy their gear. It was not always thus. Only a few decades ago the Wharf belonged exclusively to the fishermen and their friends, and the older San Franciscans remember those days with nostalgia. Doris Muscatine, one of the city's most knowledgeable writers, laments that it is too late to bring back "the men sitting in the sun mending the nets with large wooden shuttles; the lateen sails haven't been around for decades; the tasseled Sicilian fisherman's caps are worn by the waiters these days; the crab pots no longer bubble from the heat of the open fires beneath them—they use gas for their fuel; and party fishing boats don't rent out for three dollars a day, cioppino included."

Such wistful reminiscences may paint too dark a picture. The Wharf's curbside crab pots still steam in the sun, even though they are set aboil by gas, and passersby can still enjoy a crab tossed in to order. ("The best crab," say Californians, "is right out of the boiler pot, so hot you can't hold it.") If it is the waiters who now wear those Sicilian caps, they also serve some of the best seafood in the world. In the jumble of restaurants on the Wharf one may dine happily on a wide range of delicious fish cooked plain or in the Mediterranean fashion with tomato and garlic sauce. There are 52 varieties of rockfish alone in the nearby Pacific, and a great variety of flatfish, many of which come to the table under the name

In the Grange Hall in Bodega Bay, kitchen workers *(above)* immerse precooked Dungeness crab (a specimen is shown below) in a tomato- and herb-flavored sauce. Twenty minutes later the crab cioppino was on the table *(right)*.

A Crab Lover's Delight

All Californians know that any day is a good day to dine on Dungeness crab, which flourish in Western offshore waters all the way from Alaska to Mexico. Some days, though, are even better than others. In the San Francisco area, the high point of a crab lover's year comes on the first Sunday in February, when a mammoth cioppino feast is given at Bodega Bay, about 60 miles north of the city, for the benefit of the local Grange. The 1970 feast, depicted here, was the biggest yet, with some 5,000 eager guests. Volunteers cooked, washed and cracked 12,000 pounds of crab for crab cioppino and marinated crab, both served with garlic bread, salad and coffee. The crab-happy patrons, welcome to all they could eat at $3.75 a head, consumed an average of two 1½-pound crabs apiece: by noontime with incoming traffic backed up for miles on Highway 1, the Grange had to send out for an additional 4,000 pounds of crab.

of sole. Rex sole is popular, but my favorite is the sand dab, which is even tenderer and sweeter. Sand dabs are small, about eight inches long, and are delicious when sautéed whole in butter and sprinkled with chopped chives or parsley. At some San Francisco restaurants the waiter brings a plate of them to the table, deftly opens each fish and whisks away all the bones in a charming bit of culinary theatrics.

Even more important than fish to San Francisco gourmets is crab, specifically the Dungeness crab, found along the coast from Monterey to Alaska. They are savage-looking creatures with dangerous nippers. The males grow to be 10 inches across the shell; the females are smaller and, by law, the traps in which Dungeness crabs are caught must be provided with holes big enough to let the females escape. Crab can be bought all year round, but outside its season, December through May, it is marketed in frozen form and is inferior. Many San Franciscans scorn it and wait for the new catch. Then Fisherman's Wharf blossoms with stacks of pink boiled crabs, and everybody digs in and has a crab feast.

The classic way to eat Dungeness crab is "cracked." That is, the massive claws and legs, which contain most of the meat, are chopped off for serving along with a small part of the body, where a little more meat is found. The claws and legs ordinarily are cracked enough so the eater can pry the meat loose with a couple of forks. Every time I have done this, though, I have had trouble; I suspect the men who do the cracking leave most of the work undone so that I can have the joy of accomplishment as well as the pleasure of eating.

In any case the reward is worth the effort. Out of the armored claws and legs come thick, fingerlike chunks of meat, tender, sweet and juicy. The best way to enjoy the meat is without any sauce except melted butter. While adding a couple of teaspoons of sherry and a few drops of Tabasco to the butter gives variety and does no harm, I respect and share the purist point of view. As the food authority Shirley Sarvis sums it up, relaying a comment by one indignant San Franciscan: "Accompaniment to cracked crab? If I want to eat crab, I want crab. If I want mayonnaise, I'll get a bologna sandwich and have mayonnaise."

It is not always easy to hold the line. In many restaurants, Dungeness crab can be had in the form of fingers already extracted from the shells, and the guest must be wary. I ordered it once in a famous eating place and got a large sherbet glass overflowing with excellent fresh crab. But every finger was doused so completely with highly flavored tomato sauce that I could not tell from the taste whether I was eating crab or spaghetti. My own fault: all I had to say was, "No sauce, please."

When you tire of plain crab—if you ever do—there are dozens of other ways to serve it. Some Californians marinate cracked crab in olive oil, wine vinegar, minced garlic and parsley. Others use elaborate Chinese recipes with ginger root and many vegetables. Crab can be cooked with rice, eggplant or spaghetti, or included in any kind of green salad. By a pleasant culinary paradox, the delicate flavor of the crabmeat comes through in almost any dish in which it appears.

California's most famous crab concoction is cioppino (a coined word that can be said to mean "chopped a little"). According to one legend it originated in Sicily, but its real birthplace is California, where it developed as a version of the highly flavored seafood stew common to most Latin countries. San Francisco's Italian-Americans make it in many variations, almost as many as there are Italian-American cooks. Cioppino has always been in a state of evolution. A turn-of-the-century version included some of the Italian porridge called *polenta*. A modern version may contain fish, shrimp and other shellfish as well as crab, and always has tomato, garlic and olive oil. Any cioppino calls for generosity in seafood and restraint in everything else. Some restaurants make it with only a small amount of seafood submerged in a thick tomato sauce heavy with garlic, herbs and spices that overwhelm its delicate flavor. Homemade cioppino that goes heavy on the seafood and light on the tomato and spices is much better. When lovingly prepared it is a superb dish.

The 375-mile-long Texas Gulf Coast, like the Pacific Coast, is an immensely rich larder. I have seen king mackerel two to four feet long jumping out of the waters near the harbor at Port Aransas, Texas, and the lagoons behind the offshore islands and the open Gulf itself abound in fish that are legally protected from exploitation by commercial fishermen. One of the best kinds is redfish, which tastes rather like the bluefish of the Atlantic. The famous red snapper, a fish as delicate and delicious as trout, is also caught and eaten in Texas, but never reaches other markets.

While fish lovers are legion in California, they are still comparatively scarce in Texas. Until recently, with the construction of man-made, well-stocked lakes, most people in the vast inland reaches of the state simply had no easy access to fish, and the tradition of not eating much of it apparently held true for many Texans who lived on the coast as well. Texans do, however, appreciate their local oysters, which grow on reefs in the briny lagoons. Some of the reefs are natural, built of oyster shells that have accumulated for centuries. Others were created by oystermen who laid down thin layers of oyster shells and waited for young oysters to attach themselves to them. The oysters are of the same species that live along the Atlantic Coast, and like Eastern oysters they are excellent, either raw or cooked—but they must be fresh. The best-cooked Gulf oysters I have had were served in a restaurant in Corpus Christi conveniently located near an oyster fishery. They were grilled en brochette, and the Mexican-American chef showed me how he did it. He rolled shucked oysters in flour, folded them double and speared them in sixes on thin wooden skewers. From a small bucket, he poured a mixture of melted butter, garlic and paprika on the restaurant grill and laid the skewered oysters on top. After they had cooked a few seconds, he brushed more of the mixture on them and turned them over. The buttery oysters shrank hardly at all, and their flavor was enhanced by the liquid in which they were cooked.

The most important Texas seafood is shrimp, which swarm in the Gulf as nowhere else on earth, and are taken by boats equipped with huge trawls. The little ports along the coast are full of perky, high-bowed shrimp boats manned by hard-bitten crews from all over: native Texans, Portuguese-Americans from Cape Cod, Mexican-Americans, Louisiana Acadians. I have never heard such highly decorated language. The speech of one captain to whom I talked was so full of four-letter

Overleaf: A California creation, sole and crab mousse garnished and sauced with shrimp *(Recipe Index)* is elegant enough to justify a table setting of mother-of-pearl dishes and forks. Any one of the Pacific Ocean soles—petrale, rex, "Dover" and "English"—can be used in this dish. Although they are members of the flounder family, they have a delicate flavor and texture much like that of true Channel sole.

words that he took twice as long as necessary to say anything meaningful. But he showed me his boat and gear, took me for a ride around the Port Isabel harbor, and passed on some of the lore of his profession.

Shrimpers are full of secrets about how they find their shrimp. One captain told me "I smell 'em." Another, of a more scientific temper, had evolved a complicated detection system involving winds, currents and water temperatures. A third admitted that he simply tagged along where other boats seemed to be having good luck. Whatever the method, all boats carry small trawls to test the shrimping. If the little trawl brings up a few shrimp, the big trawls are likely to gather a good catch. Along with shrimp come all sorts of bottom creatures including flounder, grouper and snapper. But most of the catch is thrown away, because the shrimp boats do not have adequate facilities for keeping it fresh.

Some of the Texas shrimp boats make their cruises in the waters around their home ports; others go completely across the Gulf of Mexico, to fish as far away as the rich banks off Yucatán. They must keep out of Mexico's territorial waters, but small Mexican craft come out to sell them supplies. "We call them rum boats," that raffish captain told me. "They have everything. Rum, girls, marijuana, everything. Shrimping is the life."

As soon as shrimp are caught, the heads are broken off and they are put on ice. Big shrimp—about four inches long—bring better prices per pound than small ones do, and the experts at the processing plants can tell at a glance what the price of a batch should be. If the captains do not agree, they can take their catches to another plant. Such controversies generate some wonderfully piratical language and add a special zest to the joys of shrimping.

Almost everybody likes shrimp, and all along the shrimp coast cooks have developed favorite ways to prepare them. In Texas, not unexpectedly, they are often cooked with chilies. A dish I like combines shrimp with *jalapeño* chilies, garlic, onions, limes, potatoes and beer. It warms the stomach and makes you remember forever the place where you ate it. Another fine but milder dish is a casserole of cooked shrimp in a fairly thick sauce of buttered, toasted bread crumbs mixed with cream and sherry and flavored with chopped shallots, parsley and other herbs. It is sprinkled with more bread crumbs and baked for about 15 minutes. Then it can wait over a gentle warming flame until your guests call for it.

Some shrimp dishes, such as deep-fried breaded shrimp, are better known and more widely eaten than these specialties. The best I ever ate were in a small restaurant near Brownsville, Texas, a bougainvillea-bedecked semitropical city that calls itself the Shrimp Capital of the World. Texans disdain the dismal art so highly developed in Northern restaurants of combining little shrimp with so much butter and crumbs that they look like big shrimp. Those Brownsville shrimp were naturally big and fresh, with only a fine dusting of bread crumbs to turn them golden brown. I ate my portion voraciously, and when I complimented the waiter, who was also the chef, and told him about the horrible breaded shrimp I had endured far to the north, he insisted on cooking me a second plateful at no extra charge. I have long been waiting for something like this to happen again, outside Texas.

A Texas shrimp boat, its running lights aglow, sets out before dawn for the rich fishing grounds off Galveston in pursuit of white shrimp, which are caught during the day. Brown shrimp, which account for 70 per cent of the Texas haul, are taken at night. To catch either variety, Texas shrimp boats normally tow two huge nylon nets suspended from long outrigger booms.

A Texas-sized Sea Search for Millions of Shrimp Dinners

In the pursuit of shrimp, North America's most lucrative maritime harvest, Texas usually makes the biggest annual catch; in one recent year the state marketed over 70 million pounds of the toothsome crustaceans with a value of more than $40 million. The Texas-based shrimp fleet owes much of its success to a beneficent quirk of nature: the prolific shrimp (a single female lays up to a million eggs at a time) spawn in the Gulf of Mexico, and the new generation is carried by currents into the warm waters of the 375-mile-long, indented Texas coast. There they find the food and protection that they need to thrive and grow rapidly (a young shrimp may grow at the rate of an inch every 25 days) before returning to the Gulf. For the two- or three-man crew aboard each trawler, shrimping represents long, hard hours of work throughout the year—and most of this work must be done in the open Gulf, from 25 to 50 miles offshore. A typical crewman spends an average of 20 days a month at sea, and in a large trawler he may be out for as long as 10 days at a time.

When a shrimp boat enters a fishing ground, a small "try-net" is cast overboard; then, if the sample catch looks promising, the crew lowers two conical trawls, each some 50 feet across at the mouth. The tough nylon trawls, trailing brightly colored "whiskers," or chafing gear *(opposite),* are towed along the bottom and given about three hours to fill. As soon as a trawl is emptied on deck, the catch is culled *(left)* to eliminate such unwanted "trash" as jellyfish, starfish and sea catfish. On a trip lasting more than a day, the heads of the shrimp are removed on board and the tails are iced in the hold for better keeping on the journey back to port. At an up-to-date port, pipes connected to a powerful suction pump *(above)* draw shrimp out of the hold; a conveyor belt carries them to a plant for washing, sizing and packing.

To serve 6

1½ cups freshly made mayonnaise
  (Recipe Booklet), or substitute
  1½ cups unsweetened bottled
  mayonnaise
¼ cup bottled chili sauce
3 tablespoons finely chopped
  scallions, including 2 inches of
  the green tops
3 tablespoons finely chopped sweet
  green bell peppers
1 tablespoon strained fresh lemon juice
1½ teaspoons Worcestershire sauce
4 drops Tabasco
½ teaspoon salt
1½ pounds (about 3 cups) freshly
  cooked or defrosted frozen
  crabmeat, preferably Dungeness,
  drained and thoroughly picked
  over to remove all bits of shell and
  cartilage, then cut into 1-inch pieces
3 large firm ripe avocados
2 heads bibb or Boston lettuce,
  separated into leaves, trimmed,
  washed and thoroughly chilled
2 medium-sized firm ripe tomatoes,
  washed, stemmed and each cut
  lengthwise into 6 wedges
3 hard-cooked eggs, cut lengthwise
  into quarters

To serve 2 or 4

12 tablespoons unsalted butter
  (1½ quarter-pound sticks), cut
  into ½-inch bits
½ cup flour
1 cup soft crumbs made from day-
  old homemade-type white bread,
  pulverized in a blender
2 eggs, lightly beaten
4 four-ounce abalone steaks,
  thoroughly defrosted if frozen
1 teaspoon salt
¼ teaspoon ground white pepper
1 lemon, quartered

Crab Louis

Combine the mayonnaise, chili sauce, scallions, peppers, lemon juice, Worcestershire sauce, Tabasco and salt in a deep mixing bowl and stir with a wire whisk until the ingredients are well blended. Taste for seasoning, then add the crabmeat and toss it about gently with a spoon until the pieces are evenly coated.

Cut the avocados in half. With the tip of a small knife, loosen each seed and lift it out. Remove any brown tissuelike fibers clinging to the flesh. Strip off the skin with your fingers starting at the narrow stem end. (The dark-skinned variety does not peel easily; use a knife to pull the skin away, if necessary.)

To assemble the crab Louis, place the avocado halves on six individual serving plates and spoon the crab mixture into the cavities. Arrange the lettuce leaves in rings around the avocado, and garnish the leaves with the tomatoes and hard-cooked eggs. Serve at once.

Abalone Steaks

Clarify the butter in the following manner: Place the butter bits in a small heavy skillet and, stirring constantly, melt them over low heat. Do not let the butter brown.

Remove the skillet from the heat, then skim off the surface foam and discard it. Let the butter rest for a minute or so. Tipping the pan slightly, spoon the clear butter into a bowl and set it aside. Discard the milky solids at the bottom of the skillet.

Spread the flour on one piece of wax paper and the bread crumbs on another. Break the eggs into a shallow bowl and, with a wire whisk or a table fork, beat them only long enough to combine them.

Using the smooth side of a kitchen mallet or the flat side of a heavy cleaver, pound the abalone steaks to a uniform thickness of about ⅓ inch. Pat the steaks completely dry with paper towels and season them on both sides with salt and pepper.

Dip one steak at a time into the flour to coat it evenly, immerse it in the lightly beaten eggs, and turn it over and back in the bread crumbs. As they are coated, arrange the abalone steaks in one layer on wax paper. (At this stage, the steaks may be draped with wax paper and refrigerated for up to 1 hour if you like.)

Just before serving, heat 4 tablespoons of the clarified butter in a heavy 10- to 12-inch skillet over high heat. When the butter is very hot, add two of the steaks. Turning them with tongs, fry the steaks for 2 or 3 minutes on each side, or until the crust is golden brown. Transfer the fried abalone to a heated platter, add the remaining clarified butter to the skillet, and fry the other two steaks in the same fashion.

Garnish the platter with the lemon quarters and serve the abalone steaks at once.

No one can now identify the "Louis" of crab Louis, but—whoever he was— he inspired a masterful crab salad, piled high in an avocado shell *(right)*.

Texas Gulf shrimp and chilies flamed with sherry make a spectacular fish course that can be assembled in a matter of minutes.

To serve 4 to 6

1½ pounds medium-sized
  uncooked shrimp (about 20 to 24
  to the pound), thoroughly
  defrosted if frozen
1 cup flour
1½ teaspoons salt
½ cup peanut oil
3 canned green *jalapeño* chilies,
  drained, seeded and cut into
  matchlike strips 1 inch long and
  ⅛ inch wide *(caution: see note,
  page 20)*
½ cup pale dry sherry
6 cups freshly cooked rice made
  from 2 cups long-grain white rice
1 tablespoon finely chopped fresh
  parsley

Shrimp and Chilies with Sherry Sauce

Shell the shrimp. Devein them by making a shallow incision down their backs with a small sharp knife and lifting out the black or white intestinal vein with the point of the knife. Wash the shrimp in a sieve or colander set under cold running water, spread them on paper towels to drain, and pat them completely dry with fresh paper towels.

Combine the flour and salt in a paper bag, add the shrimp, and shake vigorously to coat them evenly. Remove the shrimp from the bag and shake each one to remove the excess flour. Lay the shrimp side by side on a sheet of wax paper.

In a heavy 10- to 12-inch skillet, heat the peanut oil over moderate heat until a light haze forms above it. Add the shrimp and, stirring constantly, cook for 4 to 5 minutes, until they are firm and delicately browned. Do not overcook the shrimp. Stir in the chilies, tip the skillet slightly and draw off the fat from the pan with a bulb baster.

Then warm the sherry in a small saucepan set over low heat. Carefully ignite the sherry with a long wooden match and pour it flaming over the shrimp and chilies. Gently slide the skillet back and forth over low heat until the flames die.

With a slotted spoon, arrange the shrimp and chilies attractively on a heated platter. Pour the sherry sauce over them. Mound the boiled rice in a bowl, sprinkle the top with the parsley and serve it at once as an accompaniment to the shrimp and chilies.

Cioppino

Though the name cioppino sounds Italian, and the savory blend of to-matoes, garlic, wine and herbs that give this fish stew its zest is remi-niscent of Mediterranean seafare, the word was actually coined in California—presumably by Italian fishermen who settled in the state. The stew itself bears a family resemblance to both the cacciucco alla li-vornese of Italy and the bouillabaisse of France. Like its European cous-ins, cioppino is made with whatever fish or seafood is available. Shrimp and even lobsters may be added; the mussels may be left out. Any firm white-fleshed fish, such as halibut or sea bass, may take the place of the cod. Live blue crabs may be substituted for the Dungeness variety, but blue crabs are small and should be cooked whole rather than cut up as are the larger Pacific crabs.

To prepare the fish stock, combine the fish trimmings and water in a 4- to 5-quart enameled or stainless-steel pot and bring to a boil over high heat, skimming off the foam and scum that rise to the surface. Add the coarse-ly chopped onion and the bay leaf, peppercorns and 1 teaspoon of salt, re-duce the heat to low, and simmer partially covered for 20 minutes.

Strain the contents of the pot through a fine sieve into a bowl, pressing down hard on the fish trimmings with the back of a spoon to extract all their juices. Measure and reserve 4 cups of the fish stock.

Wash the pot, add the oil and heat it over moderate heat until a light haze forms above it. Add the cup of coarsely chopped onions and the gar-lic, and, stirring frequently, cook for about 5 minutes, until the onions are soft and translucent but not brown. Stir in the reserved stock, the to-mato purée, wine and parsley, and bring to a boil over high heat. Reduce the heat and simmer partially covered for 15 minutes.

Meanwhile, prepare the crabs. Holding a crab tightly in one hand, lift off the top shell and discard it. Pull out the spongy gray lungs, or "dead man's fingers," from each side and scrape out the intestines in the center. Place the crab on its back and, with the point of a small sharp knife, pry off the pointed flap or apron. Cut away the head just behind the eyes. With a cleaver or heavy knife, cut the crab into quarters. Shell, clean and quarter the second crab in the same manner and set both aside on a plate.

Under cold running water, scrub the mussels and clams thoroughly with a stiff brush or soapless steel-mesh scouring pad, and remove the black ropelike tufts from the mussels. Season the cod on both sides with ½ teaspoon of salt. Set the mussels and clams and the cod aside on wax paper or plates.

To assemble the cioppino, arrange the pieces of crab in the bottom of a 6- to 8-quart enameled casserole. Lay the mussels and clams on top and pour in the tomato mixture. Bring to a boil over high heat, reduce the heat to low, cover tightly and cook for 10 minutes. Add the pieces of cod, cover the casserole again and continue to cook for 8 to 10 minutes longer. The cioppino is done when the mussel and clam shells have opened and the cod flakes easily when prodded gently with a fork. Discard any mus-sels or clams that remain closed.

Serve at once, directly from the casserole, or spoon the cod and shell-fish into a large heated tureen and pour the broth over them.

To serve 8

FISH STOCK

2 pounds fish trimmings: the heads, tails and bones of any firm white-fleshed fish
6 cups water
1 large onion, peeled and coarsely chopped
1 medium-sized bay leaf, crumbled
6 whole black peppercorns
1 teaspoon salt

FISH STEW

¼ cup olive or vegetable oil
1 cup coarsely chopped onions
1 tablespoon finely chopped garlic
3 medium-sized firm ripe tomatoes, washed, coarsely chopped and puréed in a food mill, or substitute 1 cup canned puréed tomatoes
1 cup dry white wine
2 tablespoons finely chopped fresh parsley
Two 1½-pound precooked Dungeness crabs, thoroughly defrosted if frozen
3 dozen large mussels in their shells
2 dozen small hard-shell clams in their shells
2 pounds fresh cod steaks, cut into 8 equal portions
½ teaspoon salt

Overleaf: Cioppino, a highly seasoned seafood stew, is at its best when made with a mixture of both finned- and shellfish. The version shown here includes crabs, mussels, clams and cod steaks. White wine adds flavor to the broth, but cioppino is normally served with a red wine. San Francisco sourdough bread *(Recipe Index)* is the classic accompaniment—good in itself and convenient for sopping up the last delicious drops of broth.

VII

A Stout Tradition of Outdoor Eating

A hillside terrace overlooking the Pacific provides a picture-book setting for an outdoor meal at the La Jolla home of the David S. Caseys. Here guests partake of an assortment of raw and cooked vegetables dipped in either a curry sauce or a garlic-based *aïoli* sauce.

Everybody likes to eat outdoors if the weather is right; the trouble is that in most of the United States it is wrong a lot of the time. But in much of the Great West and particularly in Southern California, the weather nearly always cooperates with devotees of the open air. Sometimes they do their cooking outside on a charcoal grill. Sometimes they cook the food indoors and carry it out to a patio. Either way adds joy to the intrinsic joy of eating.

The Spanish and ranch-style houses so common in the warmer parts of the West invite outdoor living and dining. Since they need not be compact for the sake of efficient heating, many of these houses ramble all over the place, with rooms wrapped around a patch of garden or a swimming pool. One house I know in Tucson, Arizona, has a 15-foot square of garden open to the sky and ablaze with tropical flowers, enclosed like a jewel in a case by plate-glass doors and windows. In a house like that it is hard to tell where indoors ends and outdoors begins. Another less modest house I admire, this one in Beverly Hills, California, has a formal indoor dining room for cold or rainy days. But just beyond its glass doors is a roofed-over dining terrace, with floodlit banks of flowers that make it a charming place for evening meals. The terrace borders a sunny swimming pool, where the lady of the house often has lunch under a flowering jacaranda tree. Her teen-age children give parties on the terrace, alternately splashing and eating.

Westerners are view lovers, and many of their houses perch on steep hillsides with roads winding up like corkscrews. The terrace or patio is generally placed wherever the view is best; it may, in fact, be supported on steel girders over a rocky slope, or hang there cantilevered. And somehow, a soaring view of sea or mountains turns a meal that may be no more than competent into a treasure to be remembered.

Outdoor eating makes it easy to entertain many more guests than a house has room for. At a recent garden party in La Jolla, California, 100 guests came nowhere near crowding Mrs. David Casey's two-and-a-half-acre garden, which clambers over a hillside with a view of the Pacific. Each course was served at a different "station." The hors d'oeuvre—Mexican *tostaditas (Recipe Index)* with a hot, spicy dip—were served near the house at the front patio, where trellises of jasmine and baskets of red fuchsias competed for attention with a fish pond. After the guests had sampled the hors d'oeuvre and tasted the wine (Korbel champagne and white wine cassis made with Charles Krug Chablis), they followed arrows to a higher terrace for the fish course: a whole stuffed salmon, chunks of king crab and large fresh-water cultivated prawns flown in from Hawaii. Accompanying this course were two wines, Robert Mondavi Chardonnay 1968 and Souverain Johannisberger Riesling 1969. At the third station, an exposed terrace commanding a magnificent Pacific view, the sun was setting gorgeously over the ocean as the guests gathered. Here they munched tender vegetables in lieu of salad, dipping them into curry or *aïoli* sauce, and sipped Buena Vista Gewürztraminer 1968 and Wente Brothers Sauvignon Blanc 1965. Then they strolled down a

After whetting their appetites with vegetables on the Caseys' terrace *(page 158),* guests move on to a luxuriantly planted garden for a meat course of glazed ham with orange and cranberry sauce, *vitello tonnato* (boneless shoulder of veal prepared with anchovies, tuna and vegetables) and a beef fondue with Béarnaise sauce. The six courses offered at the party were served at six different locations on the grounds of the Casey residence.

lamplit path to the fourth station for beef fondue, *vitello tonnato* (cold veal with a tuna sauce) and glacéed ham in a chafing dish with orange and cranberry sauce. The wines: Beaulieu Cabernet Sauvignon Private Reserve 1965 and Louis M. Martini Mountain Pinot Noir 1962. Fruit, cheese and dessert were served indoors by candlelight, with Mirassou Petite Sirah, Ficklin port and Almadén brandy.

The food could hardly have been better, and the wines were chosen from California's best. But much of the party's charm came from the spectacular setting and the guests' freedom to wander, glass in hand, along winding paths bordered with flaming flowers.

Few parties are as elegant as the Caseys', even in affluent La Jolla, but the West has outdoor dining pleasures for everyone. In Southwestern backyards, where anyone who takes a little trouble can have year-round flowers, even simple meals are enhanced by the outdoors. For daytime parties the sun almost always shines, and at night the stars sparkle like diamonds against the velvet-black sky. I remember a dinner with Arizona friends on a terrace that was carefully screened from light except for the yellow glow of a single candle. When my eyes adjusted to it, this weak illumination proved plenty to eat by, and when I looked up at the sky I saw the full splendor of the heavens. The big stars glared like beacons, some of them in colors—red, ice-blue or yellow—and between them were dustings of little stars that cannot be seen at all where the air is not so clear. What I ate that night was modest enough—as I remember, there were meat loaf and mashed potatoes—but the meal was touched with glory; I enjoyed it as much as the most lavish and sophisticated feast.

The spectrum of outdoor eating shades from elegance into various kinds of "roughing it," which many Westerners do with delight whenever they get a chance. From the Rio Grande to the Grand Canyon, from California beaches to the plains of Texas, they roam like nomads, eating any number of strange and wonderful foods—including some that are very modern indeed. A backpacker on a mountain trail may have in his knapsack packages of dried foods that range from a humble beef stew to a subtle chicken Tetrazzini. By a motorized camper down in the desert a family may pitch a tent for a dinner of their own stew, cooked at home and put up in jars—then enrich the dish with dumplings made on the spot. Anglers in the Rockies dine on trout that is fresher and better tasting than any they will ever get elsewhere; in national parks and forests, campers rejoice in charcoal-grilled steaks under the stars. Wherever they may go, these Western wanderers find in outdoor eating a new rapport with their land and their traditions.

Part of the Western passion for chronic nomadism probably stems from one of the most picturesque of these traditions. The early cowboys, those hero figures of the Great West, were seminomads who spent a good part of their lives in the open, riding the range, rounding up their herds or driving them to market. In this roving outdoor life, all the cowboys needed for the preparation of their food was a chuck wagon equipped for rough-and-ready cooking.

The first chuck wagons were two- or four-wheeled vehicles drawn by oxen, mules or horses and with their contents stowed conveniently and covered with hides or tarpaulins. Out of these prototypes developed the classic chuck wagon—chuck, like "grub," is a Western synonym for food —built specially to serve as the nucleus of a camp on the move. Its key device was a large compartmented box (the chuck box) set at the wagon's rear with a back that swung down like a tailgate to form a working surface for the cook. It is said to have been invented about 1866 by Charles Goodnight, a famous Texas cattleman who also distinguished himself in his nineties by siring a son.

A whole library of books has been written about chuck wagons and about the pleasantly barbaric life that centered around them, a life now vanished in the past and scarcely remembered. Open-range roundups and the long cattle drives to market are things of yesterday. The range is fenced in now; the ranches are smaller and largely motorized. Cowboys on horses are still needed for some harder tasks than posing for cigarette ads, but they usually get back to the ranch house at night, if not for the midday meal. When hot food is wanted at a distant camp, it can either be sent out from a central cookhouse or cooked on a truck equipped with a refrigerator and propane stove.

Chuck wagons are still around, however, as sentimental relics. There are occasional chuck-wagon races at rodeos, and some dude ranches maintain these lumbering vehicles to give their hardier guests a taste of life as it was lived in the storied old days. I once went on a camping trip in Arizona with a mule-powered chuck wagon, rode 20 miles a day among sculptured mountains, slept in a sleeping bag, listened to coyotes singing and watched the moon rise out of the desert. That was years ago, but I still remember the food from that wagon as little short of miraculous: steaks fried over an open fire; delicious stews of mysterious composition; long-cooked beans, with and without chili powder; hot sourdough bread and hearty pies filled with stewed dried fruit. We may, I suppose, have eaten better than the cattlemen did a generation before us, but it was the same satisfying style of food.

The pleasures of that trip led me to look up some accounts of how the old-time chuck wagons did their difficult job. The cook, called "cookie" or "coosie" (from the Spanish *cocinero*), was often an aging cowboy—but he was paid more than the other hands because the smooth functioning of the camp depended largely on him. He was absolute boss of the wagon and all that pertained to it, and was often famous for his flaming temper and bad language. No cowboy could help himself to food or even touch any cooking utensil without cookie's permission. If he did, he might catch a skillet behind the ear.

The cooking was done on open fires, normally set in a trench, to help the coals hold their heat. Getting fuel was simple in forested country, where wood could be gathered, but much of the Southwest has only small shrubs or grass. In such places the cook fell back on cow manure, or "prairie coal," which burns well when dry. The cowboys were expected to watch for this fuel; when one of them brought in a sackful, cookie might reward him with a delicacy.

The basic cooking utensil was the Dutch oven, that ancient all-purpose pot. It is a deep cast-iron vessel, perched on three legs that raise its bot-

tom a little way above a bed of coals. Its heavy, tight-fitting cover has a rim designed to hold more coals. When it is used skillfully, which is by no means easy, the coals below delicately brown the bottoms of biscuits while their tops are browned by the coals on the cover. A Dutch oven can also be used to bake pies, simmer pot roasts or stews, cook puddings and fry steaks. In the old days a proper chuck wagon had several Dutch ovens, sets of kettles and skillets, and a huge coffeepot that hung over the fire on an iron rod.

The staple chuck-wagon foods were biscuits, beans and beef. (Though beans were popular, a stingy outfit was known by the high proportion of beans to meat in its meals.) Biscuits were baked three times a day in one or more of the Dutch ovens. Some books imply that only sourdough biscuits were baked, but I have my doubts. I know an elderly man named S. L. Gonzales, now living in Fort Stockton in West Texas, who was a chuck-wagon cook years ago. He says that the only bread he ever baked was made with baking powder and that the boys of his outfit much preferred it. (Mr. Gonzales' bread, incidentally, was never baked in the form of biscuits, but as a single disk covering the bottom of the Dutch oven.)

Sourdough is more romantic, and a good many modern Westerners (not only San Franciscans, who are by far the most devoted) make a mystique of it. Traditionally, its preparation began in a crock or large keg filled with a medium-thick batter of flour and warm water. The batter was left covered in a warm place until yeast organisms and bacteria in the flour interacted with the flour and water, making the batter ferment and bubble. (A little sugar, molasses, potato water or vinegar was sometimes

Wranglers from two Western ranches, the YL and the Upside-Down T Two Bar, meet for lunch, as recorded in this picture made in the 1890s by the pioneer Western photographer A. A. Forbes. For cowboys like these, a meal from a chuck wagon *(rear)* was no picnic. Sometimes the food consisted of little more than lukewarm beans or tough stew, served with sourdough biscuits and bitter black coffee; to make matters worse, the cooks were usually despots whose general cussedness inspired a saying of the day: "Only a fool argues with a skunk, a mule, or a cook."

163

added to hasten the process.) When added to fresh dough or batter, the fermenting batter—called starter—would act as a leavening and flavoring agent. But the success of a starter was unpredictable, for it depended on many factors: the type of flour, the amounts and types of yeast and bacteria and their proper blend, the temperature and the humidity. Theoretically, a good batch of starter could be kept going as long as each portion that was used was replaced by an equal amount of flour and water, and chuck-wagon cooks prided themselves on how long they had kept a keg of starter going.

To make biscuits, the cook put flour in a large pan, made a hole in the center and poured into it the proper amount of bubbly sourdough batter. He added shortening, salt and a little baking soda to the mixture, and worked the ingredients together. Then he kneaded the dough smooth, adding either water or flour to get the desired consistency. To make biscuits, the dough was pinched off in balls, dipped in a layer of melted fat at the bottom of the Dutch oven, and packed tightly together. Before baking, the oven was put in a warm place for about half an hour to give the dough a chance to rise.

Making sourdough bread or biscuits in the open in a Dutch oven is no easy matter. There is no thermometer to tell you the temperature inside the oven, no thermostat to keep that temperature steady. The bottoms of the biscuits are invisible, and it is all too easy to burn them before the tops are presentably browned. The only dependable guide is experience, but one good policy is to use only a few hot coals under the oven and a good many on the cover, which should be preheated in the fire. You can take the cover off to peek. When the tops of the biscuits are properly browned the bottoms will usually be done too. If they pass this minimum test the biscuits will have a flavor and texture that are hard to duplicate in an indoor oven with a spoil-sport thermostat. You may even reach the state of accuracy and bliss recorded by Arthur Chapman in his book of verse, *Out Where the West Begins:*

> *The old Dutch oven never failed to cook the things just right.*
> *'T was covered o'er with red-hot coals, and when we fetched her out,*
> *The biscuits there were of the sort no epicure would flout.*

Other departments of traditional chuck-wagon cooking were less chancy. Beans, usually called by their Mexican name, *frijoles,* were searched for tooth-breaking pebbles, washed to remove dirt, soaked overnight, and put with salt pork and plenty of water in a pot over a slow fire. Alternatively, they could be buried in a covered kettle in a hole full of coals. They had to cook many hours, especially at high altitude where boiling temperature is low, to bring them to a desirable condition, soft but not mushy. Even then they may have tasted rather tame—but modern camp cooks, who have a wide choice of such flavorings as molasses, chilies or tomatoes, should have little trouble in producing creditable beans.

Beef was something the oldtime range cooks had in quantity, for it was generally running around loose within easy reach. A substantial part of a yearling went into steaks, which were tenderized by pounding with a mallet, then dredged with flour, salted and fried in a Dutch oven with an inch or so of melted tallow from the same animal. The rest of the animal served for such dishes as pot roast or stew (which was sometimes cooked with dumplings). Long-simmered short ribs were considered a delicacy.

The biggest treat, endearingly called son-of-a-bitch stew, took four or five hours to prepare. It was based upon the variety meats of a calf—not all of them, just the liver (or part of it), heart, tongue, brains, sweetbreads and the marrow gut, which is the connection between two of the four compartments of a calf's stomach. For a really good S.O.B. stew, marrow gut was considered essential.

To start the stew, the heart—the toughest ingredient, taking longest to cook—was cut into small pieces and sautéed in suet in the pot. Then came the skinned, diced tongue, later the sweetbreads, marrow gut, liver and a little water. Some of the tenderloin was generally included. The brains were cooked separately, sometimes with flour, and they served as the stew's thickening. The seasoning was salt and pepper and sometimes a "skunk egg," as an onion was called in chuck-wagon days. If the boys liked hot stuff, as they generally did near the Mexican border, chili powder was added to the pot.

I have often been assured that son-of-a-bitch stew was utterly delicious, and however that may be, it certainly figures prominently in the chuck-wagon legend. The origin of the name (which is sometimes daintily reduced to "son-of-a-gun stew") is much discussed, but I have never heard a convincing explanation. I do know that the famous stew was used as a subtle vehicle for insult. If a cookie in Wink, Texas, say, had an enemy in nearby Monahans, he might call his stew "the gentleman from Monahans" as an indirect way of expressing his opinion of his foe.

In the chuck-wagon era pies were a treat not served every day—and in fact not any day if the boss of the outfit was thrifty. Those that were made generally consisted of stewed dried peaches, apricots or apples sandwiched between two layers of biscuit dough and baked in the Dutch oven. Such hearty pies taste much better than they may sound—especially when they are eaten outdoors. My friend Mr. Gonzales, the retired chuck-wagon cook, told me he used to make a popular pudding out of day-old bread, canned tomatoes and sugar. Some canned goods were carried on the fancier wagons, and canned tomatoes were said to be the greatest prize of all, for the cowboys carried them out on the range to slake their burning thirst during the long day's work. They surely tasted far better than the water from the wagon's barrels, which was often stale, alkaline and wiggling with wildlife.

To feed 10 or 20 wolfish appetites out of a chuck wagon was a strenuous job. The cook crawled out of his bedroll long before sunup, fixed the fire and started a batch of bread. Breakfast was likely to be coffee, biscuits and beans. Mr. Gonzales told me that the boys in his outfit often ate breakfast in the saddle—after a night of sleeping on the hard ground, they felt more comfortable that way. The midday meal was hasty—there was too much work to do—but again the cook baked some biscuits, boiled beans and fried steaks or dished out stew. Supper was the big meal; the boys had time to enjoy it, and ate enormously. If there was whiskey as well as food—and there sometimes was—they had their own rough-and-ready toasts, like this one:

"Cooking under Difficulties" was the title supplied by photographer George Fiske for this 1891 picture of a rain-soaked picnic in California's Yosemite region. Despite the downpour, however, the picnickers persisted with their preparations, using an outdoor stove and a portable larder *(far right)*. With such adventurers blazing a trail, cooking in an unspoiled setting became a national cult soon after the turn of the century.

      Up to my lips and over my gums;
      Look out, guts, here she comes.
There might even be a grace of sorts, perhaps said by cookie himself:
      Thar's the bread, thar's the meat;
      Now, by Joe, let's eat.
And then the boys fell to, washing down every few bites with the inevitable black coffee, always hot and plentiful. Long after they were snug in their bedrolls, cookie was still awake and busy, cleaning up and preparing for another day.

Not many Westerners try to do unmodified chuck-wagon cooking nowadays, but quite a few scorn the luxuries of modern equipment and produce good food with Dutch ovens and campfires. These enthusiasts claim that their biscuits, beans, stews or pot roasts are better than anything that will ever come from a modern dream kitchen, and I know just how they feel, having had the sensation of good camp food on a mountain or desert trail. For a hefty price it is possible to acquire a camper truck or trailer with a comforts-of-home kitchen: a freezer-refrigerator, electrical outlets, a sink with hot and cold running water and a gas range. People who want home comforts in the wild—and the highways are full of those who do—can have them, but they lose the feeling of closeness to nature that is the great joy of camping.

Much better in my opinion is a judicious compromise. There is room in a station wagon or even the trunk of a car for a butane stove, a Dutch oven, double boiler, a well-made grill, a skillet, a large kettle for heating water and a pan for washing up. For a short trip a full supply of paper plates is a blessing for all hands. Canned foods, used in moderation, need not give the impression of "eating out of cans." If the cook feels that he or she cannot cope with baking outdoors in a Dutch oven, then pancakes can take the place of biscuits.

The next best thing to camp cooking is cooking outdoors on a charcoal grill. This is done, of course, in all parts of the United States except the stony hearts of cities, but it is nowhere so popular as in the West. There, nearly every family has a grill in frequent use, not just tucked away in a corner of the garage. To be sure, not all of these outdoor cooks show much enterprise or imagination. A San Diegan told me that all his neighbors used grills, "but all they cook on them is steaks, steaks and more steaks." Charcoal-grilled steaks are fine food—it seems almost un-American to question them—but even they get tiresome with too much repetition. One of the virtues of outdoor cooking is that it makes possible a variety of other delicacies, based on techniques that are difficult to employ in an indoor kitchen.

For one thing, the meat is accessible all the time and thus is easy to baste with a sauce that dries and browns on its surface to form a delectable crust. A simple baste, especially good for chicken, is lemon juice mixed with melted butter, herbs and salt. An elaborate and excellent Oriental version consists of honey, soy sauce, wine vinegar, oil, ginger and garlic. Once I watched a dedicated and skillful outdoor cook anoint an array of chicken breasts and thighs with this mixture. He turned them carefully for almost an hour over a very slow charcoal fire, building up a thick layer of brown, tangy crust. Inside, the chicken was tender, moist and hauntingly flavored.

The grill-cooked meal that I recall with most pleasure, though, featured *teriyaki* steak as cooked by Phillips Ruffalo of Tustin, California, on his patio. Mr. Ruffalo started with two slabs of top round steak cut two inches thick. He punctured their surfaces on both sides with a fork and left them swimming for six hours in a marinade of water, soy sauce, brown sugar, sherry, dry mustard, ginger and minced garlic. Then he lighted his charcoal grill and waited for the coals to become covered with gray ash. He shook the grill to settle the ash down under the coals and grilled the steaks about 12 minutes on each side, basting them periodically with the marinade in which they had soaked. They came out medium rare on the inside and covered with a crunchy brown crust—much better, to my taste, than grilled steak *au naturel*.

Smoke cooking is another technique that is best used outdoors. You can buy elaborate apparatus for it, and many enthusiasts (particularly in California, where the Oriental influence on cooking is strong) have Japanese smoke ovens, which are massive earthenware affairs as big as barrels. These ovens are decorative and also economical, for they will operate efficiently with only a few charcoal briquettes in the bottom, but they are not really necessary. All that is needed for effective smoke cooking is a device that will hold hot smoke in contact with the meat; a simple covered grill is adequate, and even an old-fashioned dishpan over an open grill will do for a starter.

Smoke cooking gives any kind of meat, fowl or seafood a variety of interesting flavors derived from the smoke. You can settle for the natural smoke that rises when grease drips onto the hot coals, or you can add dampened hardwood chips, shavings or sawdust; grapevine prunings; mesquite or desert sage; or even aromatic leaves. My favorite in the last category is tea-smoked duck, a Chinese specialty cooked slowly in relatively cool smoke from damp tea leaves. I cannot say that it tastes like tea; it has in fact an indescribable flavor that is neither ordinary duck nor ordinary smoke—but when properly done, it is a triumph.

In parts of the West, some of the best cooking outdoors or in is done on dude ranches. These popular institutions started as far back as the 1880s, but in those days they were ordinary cattle ranches that took a few paying guests and treated them as kinfolk. The food they served was simple but plentiful, and the "dudes" could join—if they chose, and were up to it—in the rugged life of the cowboys. A few such places can still be found, but they are neither as rough nor as remote as they used to be, and they are getting fewer as guests demand more comfort and attention. The modern fashion is for ranch resorts, which are now scattered all over the Southwestern states, especially in the mountain regions, where breathtaking scenery, clean air and proximity to virgin wilderness are crucial attractions. Some of these new-style ranches still run cattle commercially. The guests can watch the roundup or tag along on fence-mending expeditions. But many ranches have abandoned cattle or reduced them to token numbers to decorate the landscape. As one ex-cattleman expressed it, "I just run dudes now."

The ranch resorts are nevertheless delightful and lively places. Lazy guests can sit around admiring the scenery, soaking up sun and mountain air and eating their heads off. More active ones go out on short horseback rides or on pack trips lasting several days. Many of them fish in the clear mountain streams and lakes. Guides are available to take them to the best fishing and, if they stay out long enough, to help them cook their catches in the open. The simplest method, probably as old as man's knowledge of fire, is to impale the trout lengthwise on a slender stick and toast it over a campfire. It often gets slightly smoked and has an interesting woodsy aroma. Personally I find pan-fried trout *(Recipe Index)* in butter or bacon fat a better dish. A nice variation is to shake the trout in a paper bag with a little seasoned cornmeal and then fry it. Whatever the method, the freshness of the trout is what makes the meal. When you first eat trout cooked in the open beside a rushing mountain stream, you feel no food could be better for men or for gods.

On the fancier dude ranches, indoor food is remarkably good too, in spite of remoteness and wild surroundings. The kitchens are not primitive, and neither are the chefs; and the better-known ranches compete with one another in food, taking pride in both its quality and inexhaustible quantity. The recipes commonly call for twice as much per portion as is allowed in city restaurants. There would be trouble if they did not. On dude ranches slender girls eat more than men do in New York, and the men eat accordingly.

At my favorite dude ranch, the C Lazy U (in cattle brands a "lazy U" is a U lying on its side) at Granby, Colorado, a good deal of the food is

 Continued on page 173

The Care and Feeding of Pampered Dudes

Dude ranching has come a long way since vacationing city folk first began to sample the rough-and-tumble of the Wild West. Originally, the visiting dudes were paying guests at hard-working cattle ranches, and a few outfits of that kind still take in rugged vacationers, but only as a sideline. Most of today's dude ranches, however, are scenic retreats where a passion for the outdoor life and a nostalgia for the Old West can be simultaneously gratified in solid comfort—or even downright luxury. Among the best of these ranches is Katie Schoenberger's C Lazy U, some 100 miles northwest of Denver.

Mrs. Schoenberger and a staff of some 65 employees unabashedly pamper their guests. Along with such citified facilities as a sauna bath and a heated swimming pool, some 120 well-heeled dudes enjoy a notable variety of gourmet meals. Prime meats, home-grown greens and herbs, and homemade baked goods are prepared in an expansive Western style with subtle French and Italian touches. A Sunday lunch may feature charcoal-roasted turkey or Cornish game hens with wild rice and mushrooms. The main course at dinner may range from a rustic wagon-wheel stew to a sophisticated beef Stroganov, and the meal may end in a superb dessert of flaming crêpes suzette.

A day at the C Lazy U begins with an hour-long ride across part of the ranch's 6,000 acres to a spot for an outdoor breakfast *(overleaf)*. For their rides on the vast upland domain, guests can take their pick of 135 fine saddle horses. The ranch also offers its guests a skeet-shooting range, tennis courts and, in winter, facilities for ice skating, skiing, sledding and snowmobiling.

After a brisk horseback ride at 6:30 a.m., guests and wranglers gather at a favorite spot near the C Lazy U for a Western breakfast *(left)* designed to satisfy the most voracious appetite. Buttermilk griddle cakes, scrambled eggs, strip steak, bacon, hashed brown potatoes, fresh-baked sweet rolls and coffee—any or all are swiftly dished out by a staff made up in part of genuine cowboys and in part of college girls on working vacations. The meal is at tables or log seats *(background)* affording a spectacular view of Willow Creek Reservoir. An added attraction at the C Lazy U consists of delicious little doughnuts, a specialty of the ranch's pastry cook. At right, a batch of the cinnamon-and-sugar-covered confections is sampled by five-year-old Todd Wilson, the son of one of the ranch managers.

171

simple and familiar: such universal favorites as trout fried in butter and thick grilled Colorado steak. An American dish served at the ranch, and one that everyone seems to like, is called wagon-wheel stew. The "stew" starts with sirloin chunks browned and simmered until tender. The meat is arranged on a large platter and surrounded by radiating spokes of vegetables in contrasting colors—perhaps carrots (orange), onions (white), peas (green) and new potatoes (white again). These vegetables are boiled separately, so that each retains its own color and flavor, and the stew is served with a beef-and-onion gravy. When I first saw wagon-wheel stew in Colorado, I welcomed it as a delightful inland counterpart of an old coastal friend: the colorful New England boiled dinner, which has corned beef or sometimes salt codfish as its centerpiece, surrounded by bright, contrasting rings of vegetables.

The C Lazy U's Japanese chef, Koji Wada, is at home in all styles of cooking. I was once privileged to hang around his kitchen and watch him cook six fat ducks. Koji pricked their skins to let out the excess fat and rubbed them with salt, pepper, paprika and a little monosodium glutamate; then he put them on racks to roast for two and a half hours at 350° (at a mile and a half above sea level, a duck roasts slowly). He poured off the melted fat every now and then, and an hour before the birds were done he rubbed a tablespoon of grated orange peel on the breast and back of each one, putting some of it in the cavity. Fifteen minutes before the finish, he repeated the treatment with a quarter cup of orange juice per bird. On taking them out of the oven, he anointed each duck with a tablespoon of Cointreau and chopped it in six pieces with a cleaver. When he made the gravy, he added an entire cup of Cointreau. Each piece was superb, with crisp, greaseless skin and a wonderful orangey taste. I asked Koji whether the dish wasn't a kind of duck *à l'orange*. He replied that "it used to be, but now it's duck *à la* C Lazy U."

Not all of Koji's inventions are that splendid or elaborate. One of the most attractive dishes at the C Lazy U is a glorified version of hot dogs. Katie Schoenberger, the ranch proprietor, originally supplied hot dogs for her teen-age guests, but Koji "made them so good that the grown-ups wanted them too." This new demand encouraged Koji to make them even better. Now they are called "stuffed hot dogs," and are a favorite item on the regular menu.

Koji starts with top-quality hot dogs. He cuts them in two lengthwise, and puts a long, thin slice of sharp Cheddar cheese between the halves. The "sandwich" is then wrapped in one or more slices of bacon that has been cooked enough to lose much of its grease but not enough to get crisp. The bacon-clad dogs are baked long enough to make the bacon good and crisp, cook the dogs and melt the cheese. They are good in themselves, simply as a light luncheon dish, but they are touched with glory when served on Koji's fresh homemade hot-dog rolls. I refuse to say how many I ate, but I remember watching one charming young woman, who had just come in from a riding trip, tuck away no fewer than six. Here at the C Lazy U the humble frankfurter that, despite its German antecedents, has become as American as pumpkin pie, gets royal treatment—and appropriate appreciation.

With a wall of mountains marking the Continental Divide in the background, an early-morning fisherman at the C Lazy U Ranch casts for trout in Willow Creek, a dammed tributary of the upper Colorado River. Both the creek and the reservoir in the background are stocked by the ranch with brook and rainbow trout. Any trout that are not eaten immediately will be frozen and kept until the following Friday, when all hands at the ranch join in an outdoor lunch of pan-fried fish served with Spanish rice, a salad of fresh fruit and cottage cheese, cornmeal muffins and coffee.

Pan-fried Trout

Wash the trout briefly under cold running water and pat them completely dry inside and out with paper towels. Sprinkle the cavities and skins of the fish evenly with the salt and pepper. Mix the cornmeal and flour together in a large bowl.

In a heavy 12-inch skillet, melt the butter with the oil over moderate heat. When the foam begins to subside, roll each trout over in the cornmeal-and-flour mixture, shake off the excess coating, and place the fish in the skillet. Fry them for 4 to 5 minutes on each side, or until they are golden brown and crisp, and feel firm when prodded gently with a finger.

Arrange the trout attractively on a heated platter and serve them at once, accompanied by the lemon wedges.

Stuffed Baked Potatoes with Cheese

Preheat the oven to 350°. With a pastry brush, spread 2 tablespoons of the softened butter evenly over the skins of the potatoes. Bake the potatoes on a rack set in the middle of the oven for about 45 minutes. The potatoes are fully baked if they feel soft when squeezed gently between your thumb and forefinger.

Cut a ¼-inch-thick lengthwise slice from each baked potato. With a spoon, scoop the potato pulp into a bowl, leaving a boatlike shell about ¼ inch thick. Set the potato shells aside.

Mash the pulp to a smooth purée with the back of a fork, or force the pulp through a ricer or food mill into a deep bowl. Add 3 cups of the grated cheese and mix well. Then beat in the sour cream and, when it is completely incorporated, add the 4 tablespoons of butter bits, the salt and the pepper. Taste for seasoning.

Spoon the potato mixture into a large pastry bag fitted with a No. 5B decorative tip and pipe it into the reserved potato shells. Or spoon the mixture directly into the potato shells, dividing it equally among them and mounding it slightly in the center of each one. Brush a jelly-roll pan evenly with the remaining tablespoon of softened butter and arrange the stuffed potato shells side by side in the pan.

If you wish to serve the potatoes at once, preheat the broiler to its highest setting. Sprinkle the remaining ¾ cup of grated cheese evenly over the potatoes, then slide them under the broiler for a minute or two to melt the topping.

If you prefer, the stuffed potatoes may be arranged on the buttered pan, draped with wax paper and kept at room temperature for 2 or 3 hours before serving.

In that event, preheat the oven to 400°, sprinkle the ¾ cup of grated cheese over the potatoes, and bake the potatoes in the middle of the oven for 15 to 20 minutes, or until they are heated through and the tops are golden brown and crusty. Serve them at once.

To serve 4

Four 8- to 10-ounce rainbow, lake or mountain trout, cleaned but with heads and tails left on and thoroughly defrosted if frozen
2 teaspoons salt
¼ teaspoon freshly ground black pepper
½ cup yellow cornmeal
½ cup flour
3 tablespoons butter
6 tablespoons vegetable oil
1 lemon, cut into 4 or 8 wedges

To serve 6

3 tablespoons butter, softened, plus 4 tablespoons butter, cut into ¼-inch bits and softened
6 eight-ounce baking potatoes, each about 4 inches long, thoroughly scrubbed and patted dry with paper towels
3¾ cups (about 1 pound) freshly grated sharp Cheddar cheese
½ cup sour cream
1 teaspoon salt
½ teaspoon ground white pepper

Rolled in a cornmeal coating *(right)* and pan-fried, rainbow trout becomes an epicurean treat and a fitting climax to the pleasures of angling.

To serve 8

6 tablespoons butter
1 cup finely chopped onions
1 cup coarsely chopped celery
2 medium-sized carrots, scraped and
    sliced into ⅛-inch-thick rounds
2 one-pound cans tomatoes, drained
    and chopped, with all liquid
    reserved
2 large boiling potatoes, peeled and
    cut into ½-inch cubes
1 small fresh cauliflower, trimmed
    and separated into flowerets
2 quarts chicken stock, fresh or
    canned
2 teaspoons salt
Freshly ground black pepper
A large bunch of fresh dill leaves,
    tied together with string
½ pound fresh green string beans,
    trimmed and cut into 2-inch
    lengths
1 pound fresh green peas, shelled,
    or one 10-ounce package frozen
    peas, thoroughly defrosted
Fresh dill sprigs for garnish

To make about 1½ dozen 4-inch
    round buns

2 cups lukewarm water (110° to
    115°)
2 packages active dry yeast
2 teaspoons plus ¼ cup sugar
5 to 6 cups unsifted flour
1 cup wheat germ
⅔ cup dry milk solids
4 teaspoons salt
2 eggs
8 tablespoons butter, cut into
    ½-inch bits and softened, plus
    2 tablespoons butter, softened
1 egg lightly beaten with
    1 tablespoon milk
3 tablespoons sesame seeds

Dill Soup

In a heavy 5- to 6-quart pot, melt the butter over moderate heat. When the foam begins to subside, add the onions, celery and carrots, and stir frequently for about 5 minutes, or until the vegetables are soft but not brown. Stir in the tomatoes and their liquid, the potatoes, cauliflower, stock, salt and a liberal grinding of pepper. Bring to a boil over high heat, reduce the heat to low and simmer partially covered for 30 minutes.

Add the dill, string beans and peas, and simmer partially covered for 15 minutes longer, or until all the vegetables are tender but still intact. Pick out and discard the dill and taste the soup for seasoning. Ladle the soup into a heated tureen or individual heated soup plates, garnish with sprigs of fresh dill, and serve at once.

Wheat-Germ Hamburger Buns

Pour ½ cup of the lukewarm water into a small bowl and sprinkle the yeast and 2 teaspoons of the sugar over it. Let the yeast and sugar rest for 2 or 3 minutes, then mix well. Set in a warm, draft-free place (such as an unlighted oven) for about 10 minutes, or until the yeast bubbles up and the mixture almost doubles in volume.

Place 5 cups of the flour, the remaining ¼ cup of sugar, the wheat germ, dry milk solids and salt in a deep mixing bowl and make a well in the center. Add the yeast mixture, the remaining 1½ cups of lukewarm water, the eggs and the 8 tablespoons of butter bits and, with a large spoon, gradually incorporate the dry ingredients into the liquid ones. Stir until the mixture can be gathered into a medium-soft ball.

Transfer the ball to a lightly floured surface and knead, pushing the dough down with the heels of your hands, pressing it forward and folding it back on itself. Incorporate up to 1 cup more flour by the tablespoonful as you knead, adding only enough to make a nonsticky dough. Continue kneading for 10 minutes, until the dough is smooth and elastic.

With a pastry brush, spread 1 tablespoon of the softened butter inside a large bowl. Place the dough in the bowl and turn the ball to butter the entire surface. Drape the bowl with a kitchen towel and set it in the draft-free place for 1½ hours, or until the dough doubles in volume.

Brush the remaining tablespoon of softened butter evenly over two large baking sheets. Punch the dough down with a blow of your fist, set it on a lightly floured surface and, with your hands, roll it into a cylinder about 18 inches long and 4 inches in diameter. Cut the cylinder into 1-inch-thick rounds and shape each round into a bun about 3 inches in diameter and 1½ inches thick. Arrange the buns 1½ inches apart on the buttered baking sheets and drape them with towels. Set the buns in the draft-free place to rise for about 45 minutes, or until doubled in volume.

Preheat the oven to 400°. Brush the buns with the egg-and-milk mixture and sprinkle each one with ½ teaspoon of the sesame seeds. Bake in the middle of the oven for 15 minutes, or until the hamburger buns are golden brown. Slide the buns onto wire racks to cool before serving.

Dill soup offers a colorful kettleful of onions, celery, carrots, tomatoes, potatoes, cauliflower, string beans and peas, simmered in chicken stock and enlivened with a fragrant bunch of fresh dill sprigs.

To serve 4 to 6

A 3½- to 4-pound T-bone or
porterhouse steak, cut 2 inches
thick
Salt
Freshly ground black pepper

To serve 4

1½ pounds lean boneless pork,
trimmed of excess fat and cut into
1-inch cubes
3 tablespoons lard
2 cups fresh red chili sauce *(below)*
3 cups freshly cooked rice

To make 2 to 3 cups

½ pound fresh hot red chilies,
stemmed, seeded and coarsely
chopped *(caution: see note, page
20)*
1 cup boiling water
½ cup coarsely chopped onions
¼ cup vegetable oil
2 tablespoons coarsely chopped
garlic
2 teaspoons dried oregano
2 teaspoons salt

To serve 4

Four 10- to 12-ounce trout, cleaned
but with heads and tails left on,
thoroughly defrosted if frozen
2 teaspoons salt
Freshly ground black pepper
1 cup unsifted flour
1 cup yellow cornmeal
2 eggs
1 cup vegetable oil
8 tablespoons butter, cut into bits
¼ cup strained fresh lime juice
2 tablespoons finely cut fresh chives
2 tablespoons finely chopped fresh
parsley

Charcoal-broiled T-Bone or Porterhouse Steak

Light a 1- to 2-inch-thick layer of briquettes in a charcoal grill and let the coals burn until white ash appears on the surface.

Broil the steak about 4 inches from the heat until it is done to suit your taste, turning it once with heavy tongs or with a kitchen fork inserted into the outer rim of fat. Broil it about 7 to 8 minutes on each side for rare steak, 9 to 10 minutes for medium, and 11 to 12 minutes on each side for well done.

Transfer the steak to a heated platter, season it lightly with salt and a few grindings of pepper, and serve at once.

Red Pork Chili

Pat the pork cubes dry with paper towels. In a heavy 12-inch skillet, melt the lard over moderate heat until it is very hot but not smoking. Brown the pork in the hot fat, turning the cubes frequently with tongs and regulating the heat so that they color deeply and evenly without burning.

Stir in the red chili sauce and bring to a boil over high heat. Then reduce the heat to low and simmer partially covered for 35 to 40 minutes, or until the pork shows no resistance when pierced deeply with the point of a small sharp knife. Transfer the pork chili to a heated bowl and serve at once, accompanied by the rice.

Fresh Red Chili Sauce

Combine the chilies and boiling water in a bowl and let them steep for about 10 minutes. Transfer the mixture to an electric blender and blend at high speed for 30 seconds. Turn off the machine, scrape down the sides of the jar with a rubber spatula, and add the onions, oil, garlic, oregano and salt. Blend until the chili sauce is reduced to a smooth purée, then taste for seasoning.

Fresh red chili sauce may be used as the base for red pork chili *(above)* or served as an accompaniment to tacos and enchiladas *(Recipe Index)*.

San Francisco Fried Trout

Wash the trout under cold running water, pat them dry and season them inside and out with the salt and a few grindings of pepper. Spread the flour on one piece of wax paper and the cornmeal on a separate piece; break the eggs into a shallow bowl and beat them to a froth with a fork.

In a heavy 12-inch skillet, heat the oil over moderate heat until a light haze forms above it. Roll each trout in the flour, immerse it in the egg and then turn it about in the cornmeal to coat it evenly. Fry the trout in the hot oil, two at a time, for 4 to 5 minutes on each side, or until they are golden brown. Drain the trout briefly on paper towels, then place them on a heated platter.

Melt the butter over moderate heat in a separate skillet, stirring so that the bits melt without browning. Remove the pan from the heat, stir in the lime juice, chives and parsley, and taste for seasoning. Pour over the trout and serve at once.

A fireside dinner at the C Lazy U Ranch features roast beef, stuffed baked potatoes with cheese *(Recipe Index)* and salad.

Chuletas de Carnero con Piñones
LAMB CHOPS WITH PINE NUTS

To serve 4

Place the pine nuts in a small ungreased skillet and, stirring frequently, toast them over moderate heat for 5 to 10 minutes, or until they are golden brown. Transfer ¼ cup of the nuts to a large mortar or small heavy bowl and set the rest aside.

With a pestle or the back of a spoon, pulverize the ¼ cup of pine nuts. Add the garlic, chilies and salt and pound the mixture to a smooth paste. Stir in the vinegar and sugar, then add the tomato paste and, when it is well incorporated, beat in ¾ cup of the olive oil, 2 tablespoons at a time. Set the tomato sauce aside.

Set the broiler pan and rack 4 inches from the heat and preheat the broiler to its highest setting. With a pastry brush, spread the remaining tablespoon of olive oil over the broiler pan rack. Place the lamb chops on the rack and brush each one with a heaping tablespoon of the sauce. Broil the chops for 5 to 6 minutes, turn them over, and coat the top of each one with another heaping tablespoon of sauce. Broil for 5 to 6 minutes longer, or until the lamb chops are done to your taste.

Arrange the lamb chops attractively on a heated platter and scatter the reserved whole pine nuts over them. Warm the tomato sauce briefly over low heat and present it separately in a small bowl.

½ cup pine nuts *(pignolia)*
3 large garlic cloves, peeled and
 coarsely chopped
2 dried hot red chilies, each about
 1 inch long, stemmed, seeded and
 coarsely crumbled *(caution: see
 note, page 20)*
½ teaspoon salt
2 tablespoons distilled white
 vinegar
1 teaspoon sugar
A 6-ounce can tomato paste
¾ cup plus 1 tablespoon olive oil
4 lean shoulder lamb chops, each
 cut about 1 inch thick

179

VIII

New Life in an Old Wine Country

At the Heitz vineyard in California's Napa Valley, the September harvest of Cabernet Sauvignon grapes, the variety that produces most of the great red wines of Bordeaux, lies ready for pressing. California grapes yield more than 70 per cent of the wines consumed in the United States.

Makers of alcoholic beverages are apt to be genial hosts. They offer free samples and go into genuine ecstasies about the delights of their products. I have enjoyed their hospitality in Spain, where one major sherry company at Jerez de la Frontera employs a former bullfighter to show guests around, as well as in Chile, Japan and other places.

The California wine makers beat them all. Part of their success as hosts stems from the expansive California spirit, part from the beauty of the countryside where their wine grapes grow. Equally important is the quality of the wines themselves. California produces some indifferent varieties (as do all wine-growing areas), but its good wines are very good, and its best ones are marvelous, with no end of improvement in sight. The last time I visited the wineries of the Napa Valley, the great wine-producing district north of San Francisco Bay, I had to curb my enthusiasm. I took sips instead of satisfying swallows, skipped many inviting gateways and kept repeating to myself, "Remember, you're driving."

But there is, in fact, nothing more agreeable than touring the wineries. Some of these are unpretentious buildings on a half dozen acres of vineyard; many others are large-scale enterprises housed in a complex of spacious, beautifully landscaped structures, with grapevines reaching into the distance in all directions. But large or small, most of California's 237 wineries open their doors to visitors. One of the largest plays host to some 400,000 people a year.

A modest winery's tasting room for the public may be merely a humble shed where a smiling woman fills paper cups with the establishment's

181

only kind of wine, poured from a pitcher. A bigger winery may have an elaborate hospitality room with tables and a bar offering samples of a dozen wines ranging from red and white table wines to champagnes and so-called dessert wines such as sherry and port. The large Robert Mondavi winery in the Napa Valley, which roguishly calls itself "the navel of Bacchus," has several tasting rooms that are especially memorable. Situated in a building whose austerely handsome architecture recalls an old California mission, the rooms are floored with Spanish tiles and lighted by copies of early California wrought-iron oil lamps. The tables for visitors have raw walnut tops supported by wrought-iron legs, and other picturesque furnishings include such antiques as a 17th Century butcher's bench and massive Spanish-oak doors that date from a century earlier. Some wineries, such as Buena Vista, also have picnic areas on the grounds where a box luncheon can be an unusually gala affair when accompanied by a refreshing bottle of wine bought at the winery's store. Often, in such settings, there are great, shaggy eucalyptus trees, whose penetrating scent, I suspect, has some head-clearing effect on the wine drinker.

Beyond the convivial tasting room, a tour of a typical well-equipped winery leads through buildings that are a maze of pipes, tanks, valves and pumps. These are the buildings where the wine is made, and they are clean, fragrant with the heady, agreeably musty aroma of fermenting wine, and usually soundless. There may be a distant clatter from bottling machinery, but the biological miracle that turns grape juice into wine takes place in rooms that are as hushed as churches. In other quiet rooms are great aging vats, made of concrete or stainless steel, that may hold up to 50,000 gallons apiece, and stacks of oak barrels or redwood vats containing wine that requires added aging to acquire added character. A few men make the rounds, checking and recording temperatures, taking samples, occasionally turning a valve or moving a barrel. But over all there is a sense of unhurried peace, as if the wine were smiling in its sleep.

Perhaps the most tranquil—and certainly the most charming—of the wineries I have visited is that of Paul Masson Vineyards, high in the foothills above the Santa Clara Valley at the end of a twisting mountain road. The Masson company makes most of its wine in more modern plants elsewhere, and the mountain winery is now used mainly for aging wine in casks. Its façade is a 12th Century Romanesque church front brought around Cape Horn from Spain for a Roman Catholic church in nearby San Jose. When the church was wrecked in the great earthquake of 1906, Paul Masson, the winery's founder, bought the ruins, had the stones of the façade carried up the mountain and set them up again at his vineyard.

The old winery is now a California Historical Landmark and the scene of concerts by outstanding soloists and chamber groups, but I shall always think of it as an enchanted place for winetasting. Around it on steep hillsides grow the vines, some of them with trunks as gnarled as old olive trees. In the distance lie the southern reaches of San Francisco Bay. The air is clear, the sun is bright, and colorful semitropical plants bloom with gorgeous abandon. Whenever and wherever I sip a California wine, my mind harks back to scenes like this, and with each sparkling drop I relish some of their beauty all over again.

The wines of California are made from varieties of *Vitis vinifera,* a species of grape imported from Europe, where it has been the source of the best wine for many centuries. California has the ideal climates for this venerable grape, some as ideal as the balmy Mediterranean climate of Italy, the world's greatest wine producer by volume. They are better for grapes than the climate in parts of France, where wet and cloudy summers frequently keep the fruit from ripening properly. And certainly the elements in California are kinder to grapes than in Germany, where vines need special protection in winter to prevent them from being killed by cold. California summers are almost rainless and cloudless, and the winters are mild. It would be stretching the truth to say that every year is good, but the bad wine years are not very bad. That is why most California wineries until recently did not print vintage dates on their bottles. The annual variation, they say, is usually slight.

Vitis vinifera and the art of wine making arrived in California with the Spaniards via Mexico. Tradition says that the first vines were part of the baggage of the Franciscan padre Junípero Serra and were planted at the mission he founded at San Diego around 1769. Nearly all of the wine made at the early missions was for sacramental use, but by 1830 a number of laymen had established vineyards and wineries, mainly near Los Angeles, and were producing secular wine in respectable quantities. A discriminating Frenchman named Auguste Bernard Duhaut Cilly visited Los Angeles about that time; he admired the wine makers' enterprise but turned up his nose at their product. He wrote that the "wine and brandy . . . are very inferior to the exquisite quality of the grape used for it." A decade or so later, however, after the arrival of settlers from such celebrated wine centers as Bordeaux in France, Southern California wine was showing improvement. One contemporary expert did not hesitate to judge certain vintages as "fine," some even as "choice."

Meanwhile, nonmissionaries had begun planting wine-yielding vineyards to the north, around San Francisco Bay. The first to produce quality wine there was the *commandante general* of the Mexican army in California, Mariano Guadalupe Vallejo, headquartered at Sonoma. Vallejo, who remained at Sonoma after Mexican rule ended in California in 1846, encouraged others to grow wine grapes, but he met no serious rival until the appearance of Colonel Agoston Haraszthy, often referred to as "the father of California viticulture." The friendly but keen competition between the two men to produce the better wine was the spur that eventually turned California wine making into large-scale business.

Haraszthy was an expatriate Hungarian nobleman and an unusually colorful and energetic figure in an era abounding in such individuals. Fleeing his homeland presumably for political reasons, he settled first in the Territory of Wisconsin, where he was co-founder of Sauk City, and went on to California by ox team during the Gold Rush of 1849. After serving as sheriff and city marshal of San Diego and in the California legislature, he moved north to Sonoma in 1857.

At that time practically all the grapes grown in that part of the state were the kind that the Franciscan fathers had brought from Mexico nearly a century before. Haraszthy, as he later wrote, was convinced that all

The Happy Harvest of a Grape-growing Grandee

Wine making in California, which had spread slowly during the 18th and early 19th Centuries, received a great boost in 1836 from a Mexican general, Mariano Guadalupe Vallejo *(right)* of Northern California's Sonoma Valley. In that year Don Mariano took over a small mission vineyard, and in 1851 built an estate nearby named Lachryma Montis (Tear of the Mountain), after a spring on the property. He built a lavish home *(above, left)* and installed a wine press in an outbuilding (both structures are now museums). Vallejo's success attracted other winegrowers to the area; in 1856 Agoston Haraszthy *(page 186)* settled nearby, and the two men vied with each other in the quality and volume of their wines. This amiable rivalry ended with the founding of a wine-making dynasty in 1863, when two of Vallejo's daughters married Haraszthy's sons in a double ceremony.

Mariano Vallejo *(above)* traced the lineage of his wine grapes to vines imported by Spanish missionaries in the 18th Century. Similar vines still thrive at his Sonoma Valley home *(opposite)*.

Agoston Haraszthy, "the father of California viticulture," was a rakish Hungarian who arrived in California in 1849. Sent back to Europe by the state to study Continental wine-making methods, the self-styled "Count" returned with 100,000 European vines he had bought at his own expense for replanting in California soil.

Opposite: Valley quail, California's state bird, comes to the table at its succulent best after careful braising. The quail are browned in butter and oil, braised in a white stock based on a Napa Valley white wine, and served with a sauce containing the pan liquid, thick cream and blanched lemon-peel strips. Lemon slices ringed with parsley decorate the platter; and a full-bodied Pinot Chardonnay complements the dish.

California needed "to produce generous and noble wine is the varieties of grapes from which the most celebrated wines are made, and the same care and science in its manufacture." He began to import large quantities of superior varieties from Europe, and the products of his winery soon bore him out. Sensing a bright and profitable future for California wines, the governor of the state sent Haraszthy abroad in 1861—at Haraszthy's own expense—to gather information about the most up-to-date wine-making methods. He returned not only with this, but also with 100,000 meticulously packed cuttings collected in France, Germany, Switzerland, Italy and Spain, representing some 300 varieties of *Vitis vinifera.*

Meanwhile the Civil War had broken out, and partly because of Haraszthy's Confederate sympathies, the state refused to foot the bill for the cuttings. Left holding this rather large bag, he distributed the 100,000 plants throughout the state on his own and did this so effectively that by 1869, when he died, California wine production had risen from about 58,000 gallons a year in 1849 to around three million gallons.

Robert Louis Stevenson and his American bride honeymooned near San Francisco in 1880, and the Scottish writer recorded some of his California impressions in *The Silverado Squatters.* Well acquainted with fine French wines through earlier travels, Stevenson found that California wines compared favorably. He wrote of an afternoon he had spent sampling some of them in the cavernous cellar of a mountain winery near St. Helena, owned by a Mr. Schram, ". . . who followed every sip and read my face with proud anxiety. I tasted all. I tasted every variety and shade of Schramberger, red and white Schramberger, Burgundy Schramberger, Schramberger Hock, Schramberger Golden Chasselas, the latter with a notable bouquet, and I fear to think how many more. . . . In this wild spot I did not feel the sacredness of ancient cultivation. It was still raw . . . yet the stirring sunlight, and the growing vines, and the vats and bottles in the cavern, made a pleasant music for the mind."

Four decades later the California wine industry, by then vastly expanded, was laid low by Prohibition. By the time the Volstead Act was repealed in 1933, the wine-making equipment had disappeared or deteriorated; the skilled vintners had died or found other occupations; and most of the vineyards had been abandoned or given over to raisin grapes or to inferior varieties whose tough skins could stand shipment to kitchen wine makers in distant parts of the United States. Some of the first legal post-Prohibition wine made in California was poor and earned a bad reputation, but gradually the old skills were revived and new methods developed. Vineyards planted to the finest grape varieties came into bearing. New areas were discovered that would grow superlative grapes. The agricultural branch of the University of California at Davis, near Sacramento, taught grape growing and wine making so successfully that it attracted students from every wine-producing country in the world, including France. The wines themselves got better, then good, then very good indeed. Today 73 per cent of all the wine consumed in the United States, domestic and otherwise, flows from California's booming wineries, and California wines have won high honors in international competitions. Even some Frenchmen admire them and go so far as to say so.

A blanket of the white-wine grapes called Chardonnay covers a gentle slope at the Stony Hill vineyard in Napa Valley. Stony Hill makes all its wines from grapes grown in its own vineyards, but many California vintners supplement their own crops and add variety to their lines of wines by pressing grapes purchased from contract growers.

All this latter-day sophistication would have flabbergasted the old Franciscan padres and most early California grape growers, for their wine was made by the crudest of methods. Their basic equipment might be no more than a raw cowhide fastened hair down between four posts and allowed to sag in the middle. The grapes were poured in, and an Indian laborer mashed the fruit with his bare feet. When this "must" (crushed grapes and their juice) was left alone in a tub or vat for several weeks, it fermented. Yeast cells on the skins or floating in the air multiplied in the juice and turned its sugar into carbon dioxide gas and alcohol. When fermentation subsided, the resulting liquid was wine.

This fermenting process, which originated centuries ago, is still in use, with few changes. Unless special precautions are taken, lots of things can go wrong with it. Uninvited microorganisms may turn the wine to vinegar, give it a "mousy" taste or damage its flavor in dozens of other ways. Skilled vintners using primitive methods and equipment may avoid such disasters and produce fine wine, but they do not succeed every time, and may never get the best out of their grapes.

A few small California wineries still follow time-honored procedures as faithfully as they can, and dedicated connoisseurs keep close watch on them, tasting their wine as it comes along. When an expert wine lover spots what he considers a superlative vintage, he tells his friends or fellow members of a wine club, and they may gather at the winery for a private tasting party. I attended one such party where judgment was to be passed on a limited vintage that showed real promise, and learned that this was something not lightly undertaken. When the ruby-red wine was poured into their glasses, the experts first held it up to the light and remarked on its admirable color and brilliant clarity. Next they swirled the wine about in the glasses for a moment or two to release its full fragrance and then sniffed its rich, fruity bouquet. Satisfied that they were faced with an exceptional wine, they finally got around to the actual tasting, not in mouthfuls but in delicate sips that they rolled among their taste buds, savoring every subtlety of flavor. The unanimous verdict was that the wine was superb—and a volley of orders quickly exhausted the small winery's offering. Such happy events contribute to the pleasure of living in California but do not put much wine on the national market.

The larger, highly mechanized wineries that produce wine in great quantities cannot afford to use hit-or-miss methods and are geared to take full advantage of scientific advances. Some of these produce mostly popular-priced wine. Part of their output is inexpensive sherry, port, muscatel and other fortified wines, so called because their natural alcoholic content, about 12 per cent, has been increased to 20 per cent by the addition of alcohol. These do not help the reputation of California's better fortified wines, some of which are excellent. I have a bottle of tawny-colored California port that would be hard to surpass even in Portugal. It was made from the choicest of all Portuguese grapes transplanted to California soil and aged in an oak cask to a mellow perfection.

However, any damage done to California's image as a wine producer by less-than-ordinary wines is more than atoned for by the fine natural table wines that come from the lovely valleys near San Francisco Bay, where the climate is moderated by cooling winds from the Pacific. The most famous is the Napa Valley, that narrow, north-south strip of gentle country between two rugged ranges of hills. Everywhere are vineyards, nearly 12,000 acres of them. On the flatland near the Napa River the vines march in long straight rows. On the hills the rows curve gracefully around the contours. The grapes themselves, generally hidden by the broad leaves, are firm, tight clusters of green and golden-yellow fruit whose ancestral vines flourished in Alsace or the Rhineland; deep blue or purple grapes first developed in the vineyards of Bordeaux or in the Italian Tyrol; and many other varieties with a distinguished heritage. The first time I picked and tasted a ripe grape, still warm from the California sun, I got a surprise. Unlike an eating grape whose juice is flavorsome and usually only moderately sweet, the wine grape was cloyingly sweet, with hardly any distinctive flavor. I wondered how such saccharine stuff could be transformed into lively, zesty wine. The answer is that much of a red wine's flavor is released not from the juice but from the grapeskins, or is developed during fermentation. For a sweet table wine, fermentation is halted when much but not all of the sugar has been converted into carbon dioxide gas and alcohol. In making a dry, or nonsweet, wine, fermentation goes on until the sugar is almost completely converted.

A recent triumph of the Northern California wine districts is champagne that threatens the long-held supremacy of France on this score. Bubbling champagne, the most festive wine of all, is also the trickiest to make. To produce the finest quality by the traditional French method,

At the Heitz vineyard in Napa Valley, amateur winetasters sniff and sip samples of Cabernet Sauvignon, one of 14 wines made by owner Joe Heitz. Like many California vintners, Heitz often arranges special tastings and vineyard tours for groups applying well in advance; the wine lovers shown here came from Santa Clara, about a hundred miles away.

Overleaf: So-called "vineyard" leg of lamb *(Recipe Index)* is studded with garlic, marinated in brandy before roasting, then basted with white wine and sherry while in the oven. The finished dish, crisp and chestnut-colored outside, pink and tender within, is accompanied by potato shells stuffed with a blend of potato purée, sour cream, butter and egg yolks *(Recipe Index)*.

part of the fermentation must take place in strong, tightly corked bottles, where the carbon dioxide builds up a pressure of about 60 pounds per square inch and creates the joyous bubbles. The bottles are then stacked away on their sides for a year or more to give the wine time to ripen. Meanwhile a thin layer of yeast forms inside the glass and acts on the wine to give it the distinctive champagne taste.

The yeast and other natural sediment must then be removed without losing the bubbles. The French champagne masters accomplish this by twisting the bottles every day and gradually tilting them neck down so that the sediment settles on the cork. When the neck is plunged into a freezing brine solution, a plug of ice forms and pops out as the bottle is uncorked, carrying the sediments with it. Then a *dosage*—a syrup generally made of white wine, sugar and brandy to give the desired degree of sweetness—is added and the bottle is securely recorked.

This traditional process consumes an enormous amount of highly skilled labor and is therefore impractical in the United States, where labor costs more. But when shortcuts are attempted, such as fermenting the wine in large pressure tanks instead of in individual bottles, they do not produce the true "fermented in the bottle" champagne flavor.

The makers of the best California champagne have solved this problem by combining respect for tradition and mechanical inventiveness. They ferment and ripen their wine in bottles, just as the French do, to let the yeast create the flavor that makes champagne so delightfully different from all other wines. Then the bottles are fed to a complex machine that uncorks them, pours out the wine, filters it free of sediments, puts it in sterilized bottles, adds the *dosage,* inserts the corks and wires them on. All this is done under pressure so the bubbles are not lost. The result is wonderful—an elegant wine full of sparkling life and gaiety.

California vintners are especially pleasant people, but they are deadly serious in striving to produce wines equal to or better than the "great" wines of France. They do not agree, however, on how to accomplish this feat. Some follow the lead of the scientists at the University of California's Davis branch, who are studying every aspect of grape growing and wine making. At Davis they analyze grapes and wine to learn more about the chemical reactions and microorganisms responsible for good or bad flavors. They test the effects of new practices and apparatus. A recent innovation, a mechanical grape picker, promises to revolutionize harvesting. This machine selects only those grapes that are at their peak of readiness. Some vineyards are crushing the newly picked grapes right in the field with portable crushers to capture the absolute freshness of the fruit.

Other vintners have reservations about the role of science. They agree that scientific research can help to produce good wines, but feel that some almost mystic quality plays a part in producing truly great ones. They point out that in the Burgundy and Bordeaux regions, which yield the most aristocratic French wines, not all vineyards are equally good even when their growing conditions seem identical. Some famous wines come from a few acres in a large vineyard, while nearby vines beyond some mysterious boundary yield inferior wine. No one knows why—it may be some subtlety of soil, drainage or exposure to the sun. Surely, say the less scientific vintners, these enchanted spots must have their parallels in California. Some of the wine makers who seek these ideal spots think they will be found in marginal climates where frost strikes early, as it does on the Rhine, or among rugged hills like those of eastern France. My own feeling is that California will indeed succeed in producing greater wines through the joint efforts of the Davis scientists and the romantics who search for magical patches of soil.

Some general guidelines may prove useful in selecting California wines. Most California table wines are either *generic* (named after some well-known European wine that they resemble, such as Burgundy, Chablis or Chianti) or *varietal* (named after a particular variety of grape that gives the wine its distinctive taste, aroma or some other characteristic). Generic wines can be made from any kind of suitable grape and without long aging or other special attention. They are usually inexpensive, and most of them compare with the *vin ordinaire* of France, the unpretentious wine that is commonly drunk there at every meal.

Usually better and often not much more expensive are varietal wines that bear the names of grape varieties such as Cabernet Sauvignon, the grape from which the finest red Bordeaux wines are made. California law requires that varietal wines include at least 51 per cent of the juice of the variety specified on the label. Most of them contain much more of it, if not 100 per cent.

The chances of getting a superior wine are considerably increased when a varietal name is coupled with that of a reputable California producer. I do not know all of these and would be sure to omit some worthy wineries if I attempted to list them. But it is safe to say that a winery that has devoted years to earning an honorable name is not likely to risk it by marketing a poor wine, although it may offer cheaper ones of average quality. So, if you have enjoyed a table wine from a certain winery, it is a good gamble to try another wine of the same brand. A dependable brand name also carries considerable weight in selecting a California fortified apéritif or dessert wine.

I believe that the best guide to wine is personal preference, educated or otherwise. Wine is one of life's great joys: it makes any kind of food taste better and adds warmth to social occasions, from picnics in the country to formal banquets. It should be drunk for simple pleasure, not to conform to any taste except one's own.

Californians, who not unexpectedly drink twice as much wine per capita as the rest of the United States, usually have this relaxed attitude. They have their favorite wines and are loud in their praise. But even those who have studied wine with devout attention respect the less demanding tastes of other drinkers, as I have learned from personal experience. I once told the president of a California wine company that I liked white wine better than red. Knowing that this sweeping statement might sound naïve to a wine expert, I persisted and asked the Californian whether it proved anything about my character. He pondered this for a moment. "Yes," he said at last, "it does. It proves you like white wine better than red." Then he smiled. "Drink any damn wine you please. If you like it, it's the best for you. Just be sure it's California-made."

To serve 4 to 6

A 3-pound chicken, cut into 6 or
    8 serving pieces
½ teaspoon salt
¼ teaspoon ground white pepper
4 tablespoons butter
2 tablespoons finely chopped
    shallots
¼ cup brandy
½ cup chicken stock, fresh or
    canned
½ cup dry white wine
2 fresh parsley sprigs and
    ½ teaspoon dried tarragon,
    wrapped together in cheesecloth
1½ cups heavy cream
2 tablespoons dry sherry
3 egg yolks

Chicken Raphael Weill

*Chicken Raphael Weill is named after a San Francisco businessman who
was an inspired amateur chef.*

Pat the pieces of chicken dry with paper towels and season them on all
sides with the salt and white pepper. In a heavy 12-inch skillet, melt the
butter over moderate heat. Add the shallots and stir for 2 or 3 minutes,
until they are soft but not brown. Add the chicken and turn the pieces
with tongs until they become opaque and firm, and are a pale golden
color. Regulate the heat if necessary so that the chicken does not brown.

Warm the brandy in a small pan, ignite it and, as it flames, pour it
over the chicken. Slide the skillet back and forth gently until the flames
die, then add the stock, the wine and the cheesecloth bag of parsley and
tarragon. Bring to a boil over high heat and reduce the heat to low.
Simmer partially covered for 25 to 30 minutes, or until the chicken is
tender and shows no resistance when pierced deeply with the point of a
small sharp knife. With tongs, transfer the chicken to a plate.

Pick the wrapped herbs out of the skillet and discard them, and add
the cream and sherry. Stirring constantly, bring to a boil over high heat
and cook briskly, uncovered, until the mixture has been reduced to about
2 cups. Reduce the heat to its lowest setting.

Beat the egg yolks lightly with a wire whisk, ladle about ½ cup of the
cream mixture into the yolks and mix well. Stirring constantly with the
whisk, pour the yolk mixture into the skillet in a slow, thin stream and
cook for 2 or 3 minutes, until the sauce thickens heavily and is smooth.
Do not let the sauce come anywhere near a boil or the yolks will curdle.
Taste for seasoning, then return the chicken to the skillet. Turning the
pieces frequently, simmer for a minute to heat the chicken through.

Arrange the pieces of chicken attractively on a heated platter, pour the
sauce over them and serve at once.

To serve 4

2 tablespoons butter, softened, plus
    1 tablespoon butter, cut into
    ¼-inch bits
¼ cup finely chopped shallots
4 four-ounce skinned fillets of rex
    sole, or substitute any other
    4-ounce skinned sole or flounder
    fillets
¼ teaspoon crumbled dried
    rosemary
½ teaspoon salt
⅛ teaspoon ground white pepper
½ cup dry white wine
1 cup water
½ cup heavy cream
2 egg yolks

Fillet of Rex Sole Santa Monica

Preheat the oven to 350°. Brush the 2 tablespoons of softened butter
over the bottom of a shallow baking dish large enough to hold the fillets
comfortably and spread the shallots in the bottom of the dish.

Season the fillets on both sides with the rosemary, salt and pepper, and
arrange them in one layer in the baking dish. Pour in the wine and water,
and dot the top with the butter bits. Cover the dish with buttered wax
paper, then poach the sole in the middle of the oven for 10 minutes, or
until the fillets feel firm when prodded gently with a finger. Using a
slotted spatula, transfer the fillets to a heated platter and drape the wax
paper over them to keep them warm while you prepare the sauce.

Strain the poaching liquid through a fine sieve into a 1- to 1½-quart
enameled or stainless-steel saucepan, pressing down hard on the shallots
with the back of a spoon to extract all their juices before discarding
them. Bring the liquid to a boil over high heat and cook briskly, un-

covered, until it is reduced to about 1 cup. Add the cream and stir over high heat until the mixture thickens slightly. Then reduce the heat to low.

Beat the egg yolks lightly with a wire whisk, pour in about ½ cup of the cream mixture and whisk together thoroughly. Stirring the remaining cream mixture constantly with the whisk, pour in the yolk mixture in a slow, thin stream, then cook for 2 or 3 minutes, until the sauce thickens heavily. Do not let the sauce come near a boil or the yolks will curdle.

Taste the sauce for seasoning, pour it over the fish and serve at once.

Olive Beef Stew

Preheat the oven to 350°. Pat the cubes of beef dry with paper towels and season them with the salt and pepper. Roll the cubes in the flour to coat all sides evenly, then vigorously shake off the excess flour.

In a heavy 4- or 5-quart casserole, heat the olive oil over moderate heat until a light haze forms above it. Brown the beef in the hot oil, 5 or 6 cubes at a time, turning them frequently with tongs and regulating the heat so that they color deeply and evenly without burning. As they brown, transfer the cubes to a plate. Add the onions and garlic to the fat remaining in the casserole and, stirring frequently, cook them for about 5 minutes, until they are soft and translucent but not brown. Pour in the vermouth and water and bring to a boil over high heat, meanwhile scraping in the brown particles that cling to the bottom and sides of the pot.

Stir in the beef and the liquid that has accumulated around it, cover the casserole tightly, and braise in the middle of the oven for about 2 hours, or until the beef shows no resistance when pierced deeply with the point of a small sharp knife. (Check the beef from time to time and regulate the oven heat as necessary to keep the liquid at a gentle simmer.)

Meanwhile, drop the olives into enough boiling water to cover them completely and cook briskly for 2 or 3 minutes. Drain the olives in a sieve or colander and, with a small sharp knife, cut them from their pits in spiral strips. Discard the pits.

When the beef has cooked its allotted time, gently stir in the olives and simmer the stew over low heat for a few minutes to heat them through. Taste for seasoning and serve at once, directly from the casserole or from a heated bowl.

Guacamole with Chilies
AVOCADO DIP

Cut the avocados in half. With the tip of a small knife, loosen the seeds and lift them out. Remove any brown tissuelike fibers that cling to the flesh. Strip off the skins with your fingers or the knife, starting at the narrow or stem end. Chop the avocados coarsely; then, in a deep bowl, mash them to a rough purée. Add the tomato, half of the chopped eggs, the onions, chilies, lime juice and salt, and mix them together gently but thoroughly. Taste for seasoning.

Mound the *guacamole* in a serving bowl, scatter the remaining chopped eggs over it and, if you are using it, sprinkle the coriander on top. Serve at once, accompanied by the *tostaditas*.

To serve 6 to 8

3 pounds lean beef chuck, trimmed of excess fat and cut into 1½-inch cubes
2 teaspoons salt
1 teaspoon freshly ground black pepper
1 cup flour
½ cup olive oil
2 large onions, peeled and sliced crosswise into ¼-inch-thick rounds
1 tablespoon finely chopped garlic
1 cup dry vermouth
2 cups water
2 dozen large green olives

To make about 2 cups

2 large ripe avocados
1 large firm ripe tomato, peeled, seeded and finely chopped (*see chile con queso, page 20*)
2 hard-cooked eggs, finely chopped
½ cup finely chopped onions
2 canned green chilies (not the *jalapeño* variety), drained, seeded and finely chopped
1 tablespoon strained fresh lime juice
2 teaspoons salt
1 tablespoon finely chopped fresh coriander (optional)

Tostaditas (Recipe Booklet)

Vineyard Leg of Lamb

This method of roasting lamb is a fairly complicated one. The surface of the finished roast, however, takes on an unusually rich chestnut-brown color and is well worth the extra effort.

To serve 6 to 8

A 5- to 6-pound leg of lamb, trimmed of excess fat and with the fell (the parchmentlike covering) removed
2 medium-sized garlic cloves, peeled and cut lengthwise into paper-thin slivers
1 cup brandy
1 teaspoon ground cumin
1½ tablespoons salt
2 teaspoons freshly ground black pepper
¼ cup dry sherry
¼ cup dry white wine
Sprigs of watercress for garnish

With the point of a small sharp knife, cut a dozen or more 1-inch-deep slits all over the surface of the leg of lamb and insert a sliver of garlic into each slit. Cut a double thickness of cheesecloth about 16 inches wide and 18 to 20 inches long and drench it thoroughly with ½ cup of the brandy. Wrap the cheesecloth around the leg of lamb and cover it tightly with plastic wrap to prevent the brandy from evaporating. Set the lamb aside to marinate at room temperature for about 2 hours.

Preheat the oven to 450°. Mix the cumin, salt and pepper together in a small bowl, and combine the sherry and white wine in another bowl. Unwrap the lamb and place the leg, fat side up, on a rack in a shallow roasting pan. Press the cumin mixture into the surface of the lamb, coating the meat with the spices as evenly as possible. For the most predictable results, insert a meat thermometer 2 inches into the thickest part of the leg, being careful not to touch the bone.

Roast the lamb in the middle of the oven for 20 minutes. Then reduce the heat to 350° and baste with a tablespoon or so of the wine mixture. Continue to roast 40 to 60 minutes longer, or until the leg is cooked to your taste, basting two or three more times with the remaining wine mixture. A meat thermometer will register 130° when the lamb is rare, 140° when medium and 150° when well done.

Transfer the lamb to a heated platter and let the roast rest for 15 minutes for easier carving. Just before serving, warm the remaining ½ cup of brandy in a small saucepan. Ignite the brandy with a match and pour it flaming over the lamb. When the flame dies, garnish the platter with sprigs of watercress and serve at once.

Glazed Oranges

To serve 6

6 navel or Temple oranges
1 cup dry white wine
2 tablespoons red wine vinegar
¾ cup sugar
A 2-inch cinnamon stick and 10 whole cloves, wrapped together in cheesecloth
2 tablespoons Grand Marnier or other orange liqueur (optional)

With a small sharp knife, remove the skin from two of the oranges without cutting into the bitter white pith beneath it. Cut the peel into strips about ⅛ inch wide, drop them into enough boiling water to cover them completely and cook briskly for about 2 minutes. With a slotted spoon, transfer the strips to paper towels to drain.

Cut the white outer pith and membrane from the two skinned oranges, using short sawing motions. Then cut away and discard the peel, pith and all the white outside membrane from the remaining four oranges.

Combine the wine, vinegar, sugar, and the cheesecloth-wrapped cinnamon and cloves in a 3- to 4-quart enameled or stainless-steel saucepan and bring to a boil over high heat, stirring until the sugar dissolves. Add the oranges and the strips of orange peel, and turn them about with a spoon to coat them evenly with the syrup. Reduce the heat to low, then simmer uncovered for 15 minutes, turning the oranges over frequently.

With a slotted spoon, transfer the oranges and peel to a deep bowl. Pick out and discard the cheesecloth bag of spices and taste the syrup for sweetness. If you like, you may add 1 or 2 tablespoons of orange liqueur to the syrup. Pour the syrup over the oranges and cool to room temperature. Cover the bowl tightly with foil or plastic wrap and refrigerate the oranges for at least 2 hours to chill them thoroughly before serving.

Quail in Lemon-Wine Sauce

With a small sharp knife, remove the skin from two of the lemons without cutting into the bitter white pith beneath it. Cut the peel into strips about ⅛ inch wide, drop the strips into enough boiling water to cover them completely and boil briskly for 2 minutes. With a slotted spoon, transfer the strips of lemon peel to paper towels to drain. Cut the remaining lemon crosswise into four or six rounds and set aside.

Wash the quail under cold running water and pat them dry with paper towels. Season them inside and out with salt and pepper, twist the wings behind the backs and truss the birds securely. Roll one at a time in the flour to coat it evenly and vigorously shake off the excess flour.

In a heavy casserole large enough to hold the quail in one layer, melt the butter with the oil over moderate heat. When the foam begins to subside, brown the birds in the hot fat, two or three at a time. Turn them frequently with tongs and regulate the heat so that they color richly and evenly without burning. As they brown, transfer them to a plate.

Add the onions to the fat remaining in the casserole and cook for about 5 minutes, stirring frequently until they are soft and translucent but not brown. Pour in the wine and water, and bring to a boil, meanwhile scraping in the brown particles that cling to the bottom and sides of the pan. Return the quail and the liquid that has accumulated around them to the casserole, cover tightly and simmer over low heat for 30 to 40 minutes. To test for doneness, pierce a thigh with the point of a small sharp knife. The juice that trickles out should be pale yellow; if it is still tinged with pink, braise the quail for another 5 to 10 minutes. Transfer the birds to a heated platter and drape them loosely with foil to keep them warm while you prepare the sauce.

Strain the braising liquid through a fine sieve set over a small heavy saucepan, pressing down hard on the onions with the back of a spoon to extract all their juices before discarding the pulp. Add the cream and, stirring frequently, cook the sauce over moderate heat until it thickens slightly and is reduced to about 1 cup. Stir in the reserved strips of lemon peel and taste for seasoning. Pour the sauce over the quail, then sprinkle the parsley in a ring around the outside edge of each lemon slice. Arrange the slices attractively on the platter and serve the quail at once.

NOTE: Where doves are available, they may be substituted for quail.

Crab-Olive Spread

Combine the mayonnaise, parsley, lemon juice, Worcestershire sauce and horseradish in a deep bowl and mix well. Stir in the chopped eggs and olives and, when they are thoroughly incorporated, gently fold in the crabmeat. Serve at once as a spread for crackers, or cover the bowl with plastic wrap and refrigerate until ready to serve. Tightly covered, the crab-olive spread can safely be kept in the refrigerator for a day.

To serve 6

3 large lemons
6 four-ounce oven-ready quail, thoroughly defrosted if frozen
1 teaspoon salt
½ teaspoon freshly ground black pepper
½ cup flour
3 tablespoons butter
1 tablespoon vegetable oil
½ cup finely chopped onions
½ cup dry white wine
½ cup water
½ cup heavy cream
2 tablespoons finely chopped fresh parsley

To make about 2½ cups

½ cup homemade mayonnaise (Recipe Booklet), or substitute ½ cup unsweetened bottled mayonnaise
2 tablespoons finely chopped fresh parsley
2 teaspoons strained fresh lemon juice
2 teaspoons Worcestershire sauce
1 teaspoon bottled horseradish
2 hard-cooked eggs, finely chopped
½ cup finely chopped ripe olives
1 cup freshly cooked, canned or defrosted frozen crabmeat, drained and picked over to remove all bits of shell and cartilage

A Guide to California Wines   by Robert Lawrence Balzer

Magnificent wines from California are now a part of the American heritage. Over a period of two centuries, the tendrils of California vines have survived disease, drought, economic perils and marketing crises, the disaster of national Prohibition and, within the past decade, the confiscating menace of urban encroachment upon treasured vineyard land. California vintners have triumphed over this last threat in two ways: by the discovery of superb new wine lands in Monterey County, and by state laws that have established certain grape-growing areas, such as the Napa Valley, as worthy of "agricultural preserve." The present is prosperous; the future, brilliant.

Production figures for last year approached a record 196 million gallons, but statistics matter little to anyone who is simply in search of the pleasures of wine. To provide him with the kind that can suit his particular thirst, California produces wines that can be classified in three categories: *good, fine* and *outstanding.* There will always be an ample supply of good, or ordinary, wine; there will always be a shortage of fine and outstanding wines. Yet with elementary guidance, even a novice oenophile can find his way to the bottles that will best satisfy his purse, the occasion and, most important, his taste.

The evolution of one's taste in wine follows a predictable curve. At first one tends to prefer unobtrusive, fragrant white wines of a definite but delicate sweetness. (Many of tomorrow's connoisseurs are not yet that advanced; they are drinking sweet "pop" wines today, with names like Ripple, Zapple, Waikiki Duck, Boone's Farm Apple Wine, Annie Green Springs, Spañada, I, Love and You.) These sweet wines lead one on to semidry white wines, and then to an awareness of the highly complex charms

Robert Lawrence Balzer, author of *Adventures in Wine,* writes a column on wine and food for the *Los Angeles Times* Sunday edition. He teaches a course in winetasting at UCLA, and issues a widely read monthly newsletter, *Robert Lawrence Balzer's Private Guide to Wine and Food.*

of dry red wines and their undeniable harmonies with food. California wines include the whole range, with something for everyone, including mass-produced champagnes for $1.99, and bottle-fermented champagnes for not much more than $6—a distinct economic edge over European competition.

Both the *varietal* wines of California (named for the dominant grape varieties from which they are made) and the *generic* wines (with titles bearing geographic identifications, such as Burgundy, Rhine and Chablis) have familiar European counterparts. Pinot Chardonnay (sometimes labeled simply Chardonnay) is the principal white grape of Burgundy and Chablis; in California it produces a wine that is wholly dry and, in superior wine making, reminiscent of sun-ripened pears. Sémillon, the principal grape of French Sauternes, produces a tart, dry wine from the Napa Valley vineyards, and a range of pleasing, softer tastes, both dry and sweet, from the vineyards at Livermore. Chenin Blanc, prized in the valley of the Loire for its gentleness, has become increasingly popular in California. Widely grown in many parts of the state, it is invariably flowery, often with a touch of sweetness —an ideal wine to serve with poultry. White Riesling (also called Johannisberg Riesling) is improved in California by cool, controlled fermentation that gives this aristocratic Rhine wine a crisp, fruit-acid, dry perfection, with an assertive fragrance in premium bottlings. Red wines made from the Cabernet Sauvignon grape of Bordeaux and the Pinot Noir of Burgundy can be rated on a par with many of the best bottles from their native regions; they are, in fact, the two best red wines of California.

California has one unique red wine, Zinfandel, with no European counterpart. While it varies from wine maker to wine maker and from region to region, it is always fruity, fragrant, deep-colored and dry, berrylike when young, more mellow with age, and with the authority of a noble Burgundy or claret.

California offers a wide variety of rosés, nearly all of them delightful, each different, made not only from the traditional French Gamay and Grenache grapes, but also from Zinfandel, Cabernet Sauvignon, Petite Sirah, Grignolino and even Pinot Noir.

Finally, there is a host of varietal grape

labels: Emerald Riesling, Gewürztraminer, Sauvignon Blanc, Flora, Green Hungarian, Folle Blanche, French Colombard, Sylvaner, Barbera, Pinot St.-George, Pinot Blanc, Ruby Cabernet, Gamay Beaujolais, Merlot, Grignolino, and Royalty. Each is an invitation to adventure at a modest cost.

While there is a trend toward vintage-dating California wines, the date serves only as a point of identification. (All years are good, say the vintners, but some are better.) Some wineries deliberately blend wines of different years in the belief that more consistent quality can be ensured. This is often true. Vintage-dated lots from a single winery will have subtle differences. Such terms as *Cask, Lot, Limited Edition* or *Private Reserve* indicate that a wine comes from a limited supply, probably separately aged. These wines will always command premium prices. Read the labels carefully. They are the words of the wine maker addressed to you, describing his product. Some labels even carry the full legend of bottling date and amount of the harvest. If the label reads "Estate-Bottled," the wine has been made from grapes grown and bottled on the winery's own land. The term puts the proprietor's prestige on the line, elevating the rank—and the price—of the wine. "Produced and Bottled by . . ." in small print on the front label is similar assurance of justifiable pride of production from the vineyard to the bottle.

The terms large and small, as applied to a winery, have little meaning in today's wine market. A small winery does not necessarily produce outstanding wine, nor a large winery an ordinary product. Today only the larger wineries can afford the expensive stainless-steel, water-jacketed fermentation facilities necessary for scientific quality control, but both large and small wineries must bow to nature and the selective bounty of vineyard slopes. Beyond science, there is the factor of time. Some wines, particularly white wines, are better in their youth; mellowness in red wines comes from aging, in oak and in bottles. Proper cool storage is essential for the ultimate mature perfection of all table wines. In buying, seek the wine merchant who stores his wines properly; that is, lying on their sides in a cool place. Attend his counsel, for you are likely to be rewarded with pleasing selections.

A Selection of California Wines

Some fine California wines are easier to find than others, and many outstanding wines are never sold outside the state. This table of wineries with their acreages (when the figure is available) is coded for types of distribution: in the first half of the table, (N) indicates national distribution, (L) limited. A star (★) denotes an outstanding selection; taken together, the starred wines comprise a list of 50 outstanding wines of California. The list does not presume to be complete or comprehensive, but it should offer a dependable guide to contemporary California wines.

WINES IN NATIONAL AND LIMITED DISTRIBUTION

ALMADÉN VINEYARDS (N) 8,136 acres
★ Blanc de Blancs Champagne
Le Domaine Extra Dry Champagne
Le Domaine Cold Duck
★ Solera Cocktail Sherry
Pinot Chardonnay
Johannisberg Riesling
Gewürztraminer
★ Sauvignon Blanc
Grenache Rosé
Cabernet Sauvignon

BEAULIEU VINEYARDS (N) 745 acres
★ Private Reserve Champagne Brut
Beaufort Pinot Chardonnay
Beauclair Johannisberg Riesling
Château Beaulieu (Sauvignon Blanc)
★ Private Reserve Cabernet Sauvignon
★ Beaumont Pinot Noir

BERINGER BROS. (L) 800 acres
Barenblut
Zinfandel

BUENA VISTA HARASZTHY CELLARS (L) 320 acres
Sparkling Sonoma Cabernet Rosé
Cabernet Sauvignon
Pinot Noir—Cask Bottling
Haraszthy Zinfandel—Cask Bottling
★ Rosebrook (Cabernet Sauvignon Rosé)
★ Gewürztraminer—Cabinetwine

THE CHRISTIAN BROTHERS (N) 2,000 acres
★ Meloso Cream Sherry
Château La Salle
Pineau de la Loire (Chenin Blanc)
★ Cabernet Sauvignon
Gamay Noir

CONCANNON VINEYARD (L) 350 acres
Johannisberg Riesling
★ Petite Sirah
Zinfandel Rosé

ERNEST & JULIO GALLO (N)
Gallo Champagne
Old Decanter Very Dry Sherry
Old Decanter Livingstone Cream Sherry
Pink Chablis
★ Hearty Burgundy

INGLENOOK VINEYARDS (N)
Inglenook Brut Champagne
Traminer—Estate Bottled
Pinot Chardonnay—Limited Vintage
★ Cabernet Sauvignon-Cask—Limited Vintage
★ Zinfandel—Estate Bottled

KORBEL & BROS. INC. (N) 700 acres
★ Korbel Natural Champagne
Korbel Champagne Rosé
Chenin Blanc
Pinot Noir

HANNS KORNELL CHAMPAGNE CELLARS (L)
Third Generation Brut Champagne

CHARLES KRUG WINERY (L) 600 acres
★ Chenin Blanc
Johannisberg Riesling
★ Pinot Noir

LOUIS M. MARTINI (N) 850 acres
★ Moscato Amabile
★ Pinot Chardonnay
Gewürztraminer
Johannisberg Riesling
Folle Blanche
Cabernet Sauvignon
Pinot Noir
★ Zinfandel

PAUL MASSON VINEYARDS (N) 3,000 acres
★ Blanc de Pinot Champagne
Extra Dry Champagne
Rare Dry Sherry
★ Rare Souzão Port
Madeira
★ Emerald Dry
Rhine Castle
Johannisberg Riesling
Sylvaner
Cabernet Sauvignon
Pinot Noir

MIRASSOU VINEYARDS (L) 1,125 acres
Pinot Chardonnay—Limited Bottling

Gewürztraminer—Limited Bottling
Petite Rosé
Cabernet Sauvignon—Limited Bottling
★ Zinfandel

ROBERT MONDAVI WINERY (L) 300 acres
★ Fumé Blanc (Sauvignon Blanc)
Chardonnay
★ Gamay
Cabernet Sauvignon
Pinot Noir

SAMUELE SEBASTIANI (L)
★ Gamay Beaujolais—Special Bin
Zinfandel

WEIBEL CHAMPAGNE VINEYARDS (L) 100 acres
★ Champagne Chardonnay Brut
★ Dry Bin Sherry
Green Hungarian
Gamay Beaujolais
Cabernet Sauvignon

WENTE BROTHERS (N) 1,100 acres
★ Le Blanc de Blancs (Ugni Blanc and Chenin Blanc)
★ Pinot Chardonnay
Sauvignon Blanc (Dry)
Sémillon (Dry and Sweet)
★ Château Wente (Sweet Sauterne)

WINES AVAILABLE LOCALLY IN CALIFORNIA

The wines listed below, of limited production from small wineries, are often available only at the winery, or in choice restaurants and wine shops, or by mail order.

DAVID BRUCE, Los Gatos, 37 acres
★ Chardonnay—Cask Bottling

CHALONE VINEYARD, Soledad, 50 acres
★ Pinot Blanc—Limited Bottling
Chenin Blanc—Limited Bottling
Chardonnay—Limited Bottling
Pinot Noir

CHAPPELLET WINERY, St. Helena, 136 acres
★ Johannisberg Riesling
Chenin Blanc

FETZER VINEYARD, Redwood Valley, 100 acres
★ Zinfandel
Cabernet Sauvignon

FICKLIN VINEYARDS, Madera
★ Tinta Port

FREEMARK ABBEY, St. Helena
★ Johannisberg Riesling
Pinot Chardonnay

HANZELL VINEYARDS, Sonoma, 16 acres
Chardonnay
★ Pinot Noir

HEITZ WINE CELLARS, St. Helena, 30 acres
★ Chardonnay
Pinot Noir

LLORDS & ELWOOD WINERY, Fremont, 125 acres
Superb Extra Dry Champagne
★ Castle Magic Johannisberg Riesling
Velvet Hill Pinot Noir

MAYACAMAS VINEYARDS, Napa, 40 acres
★ Pinot Chardonnay
Zinfandel Rosé

NOVITIATE OF LOS GATOS, Los Gatos, 625 acres
★ Black Muscat

MARTIN RAY, Saratoga, 100 acres
Blanc de Noir Champagne
Chardonnay

RIDGE VINEYARDS, Cupertino, 45 acres
★ Zinfandel (Geyserville)

SAN MARTIN VINEYARDS, San Martin, 1,096 acres
Aprivette
Marsala D'Oro
Malvasia Bianca

SCHRAMSBERG VINEYARDS, Calistoga, 35 acres
★ Blanc de Noir Champagne
Blanc de Blancs Champagne

SOUVERAIN CELLARS, St. Helena, 30 acres
Flora
★ Pineau Souverain (Chenin Blanc)
Burgundy
Zinfandel

SPRING MOUNTAIN VINEYARDS, St. Helena, 109 acres
Cabernet Sauvignon
Pinot Chardonnay

STERLING VINEYARDS, Calistoga, 350 acres
★ Merlot

STONY HILL VINEYARD, St. Helena, 35 acres
★ Chardonnay
Gewürz Traminer

WINDSOR VINEYARDS, Windsor, 1,100 acres
★ Chardonnay
★ Sauvignon Blanc

Recipe Index

NOTE: An R preceding a page refers to the Recipe Booklet. Size, weight and material are specified for pans in the recipes because they affect cooking results. A pan should be just large enough to hold its contents comfortably. Heavy pans heat slowly and cook food at a constant rate. Aluminum and cast iron conduct heat well but may discolor foods that are made with egg yolks, wine, vinegar or lemon. Enamelware is a fairly poor conductor of heat. Many recipes recommend stainless steel or enameled cast iron, which do not have these faults.

Mail-Order Sources for Foods and Utensils

Mexican-American Supplies

Taco fryers, tortilla presses, dried hot peppers, canned green and red chilies, canned *jalapeño* chilies, canned *tomatitos, masa harina, chorizo* sausage and frozen tortillas can be obtained from a number of sources, listed by state and city. Because policies differ and managements change, check with the store nearest you to determine what it has in stock, the current prices, and how best to order the items that interest you. Not all stores have every item.

TACO FRYER (RECIPE BOOKLET):
Casa Molina Mfg. Co.
6225 East Speedway Blvd.
Tucson, Arizona 85716

The foods mentioned above can be obtained from the following sources. Stores marked with an asterisk also carry tortilla presses.

Arizona
El Molino
117 South 22nd St.
Phoenix 85034

Sasabe Store
P.O. Box 7
Sasabe 85633

Best Supermarket
55555 East 5th St.
Tucson 85711

Bullards*
7113 North Oracle Rd.
Tucson 85704

Santa Cruz Chili and Spice Co.
P.O. Box 177
Tumacacori 85640

California
Mercado La Tepiquena
2030 Del Paso Blvd.
North Sacramento 95815

La Victoria Foods, Inc.
9200 West Whitmore St.
Rosemead 91770

Casa Lucas Market*
2934-24th St.
San Francisco 94110

Florida
Alamo Tortilla Factory
Kirk Plaza
Suite 9-B
Titusville 32780

Iowa
Nelson's Meat Market
3201 1st Ave., SE
Cedar Rapids 52403

Swiss Colony*
Lindale Plaza
Cedar Rapids 52403

Michigan
La Paloma
2620 Bagley St.
Detroit 48216

Minnesota
La Casa Coronado Restaurant*
23 North 6th St.
Minneapolis 55403

Missouri
Heidi's Around the World Food
  Shop
1149 South Brentwood
St. Louis 63117

New York
Casa Moneo Spanish Imports*
210 West 14th St.
New York 10011

Pennsylvania
Kaufmann's Department Store
Epicure Shop
5th Ave. & Smithfield St.
Pittsburgh 15219

Stamcolis Bros. Grocery
2020 Penn Ave.
Pittsburgh 15222

Texas
Adobe House*
127 Payne St.
Dallas 75207

Simon David Grocery Store
711 Inwood Rd.
Dallas 75209

Ashley's, Inc.
6590 Montana Ave.
El Paso 79925

Gebhardt Mexican Foods Co.
P.O. Box 7130, Station A
San Antonio 78207

Los Cocos Products*
202 Produce Row
San Antonio 78207

Washington
El Ranchito*
P.O. Box 717
Zillah 98953

Bread and Baking Supplies

DRIED SOURDOUGH STARTER:
Sourdough Jack's Kitchen
2901 Clement St.
San Francisco, Calif. 94121

UNBLEACHED HARD-WHEAT FLOUR:
El Molino Mills
P.O. Box 2025
Alameda, Calif. 91803

Carolyn Foods, Inc.
P.O. Box 311
Ithaca, N.Y. 14850

Great Valley Mills
Quakertown, Pa. 18951

BAKING AND PROOFING TRAYS:
Argonaut House
2901 Clement St.
San Francisco, Calif. 94121

ROSE TUBES AND FLOWER NAILS:
Mail Order Sales
Wilton Enterprises, Inc.
933 West 115th St.
Chicago, Ill. 60643

General Index

Numerals in italics indicate a photograph or drawing of the subject mentioned.

Credits and Acknowledgments

The sources for the illustrations that appear in this book are shown below. Credits for the pictures from left to right are separated by commas, from top to bottom by dashes.

Photographs by Mark Kauffman—Cover, pages 9, bottom 14, 18, 19, 22, 25, 32, 33, 48, 50, 51, 53, left 56, top 62, 63, 78, 79, 88, bottom 102, bottom 103, top left 103, 109, 111, 112, 114, 115, 146, 147, 153, 154, 156, 157, 187, 190, 191. Photographs by Richard Meek—pages 54, 81, 83, 85, 95, 140, 149, 150, 151, 158, 160, 169, 170, 171, 172, 174, 175, 177, 179. Photographs by Ted Streshinsky—pages 96, 97, 98, 99, 121, 122, 123, 124, 125, 126, 127, 128, 129, 130, 131, 142, 143, 180, 188, 189. Other photographs by—page 4 —Richard Henry except top left Walter Daran, bottom right Ted Streshinsky. 6—Map by Gloria duBouchet and Lothar Roth. 13 —Paul Slaughter. 14—top Paul Jensen. 15—Grey Villet for LIFE —Fred Lyon from Rapho Guillumette. 26, 29—Brian Seed from Black Star Publishing Co. 35 through 46—Brian Seed from Black Star Publishing Co. 56—right Paul Jensen. 59—Paul Jensen. 60, 61 —Fred Schnell. 62—bottom Fred Schnell. 65 through 75—Paul Slaughter. 86—Fred Schnell. 87—Paul Slaughter. 90—California Museum of Science and Industry. 92, 93—Paul Slaughter. 100 —Robert A. Isaacs. 102—top Paul Slaughter. 103—top Paul Slaughter except left. 104—Stuart Muller. 105—Map by Gloria duBouchet and Lothar Roth. 106—Fred Lyon from Rapho Guillumette. 116—Ken Kay. 132—Paul Slaughter. 134—William Perrin, National Marine Fisheries Service. 135—U.S. Department of Commerce, National Oceanic and Atmospheric Administration, National Marine Fisheries Service. 138, 139—Stuart Muller. 163 —Los Angeles County Museum of Natural History. 166—courtesy Bancroft Library, University of California, Berkeley, California. 184 —courtesy Bancroft Library, University of California, Berkeley, California—Wine Institute. 185—Jon Brenneis. 186—Wine Institute. 198—Elson-Alexandre.

For assistance and advice in the production of this book, the editors and staff extend their thanks to the following: *in Arizona:* Ben Avery, *The Arizona Republic;* Tom Bahti; Mr. and Mrs. Lee S. Bradley; Joseph Chretin, Chretin's Mexican Food Restaurant; Mrs. Ruth Cox; Mrs. Gene England, Santa Cruz Chili and Spice Co.; Mrs. Howard Gwynn; Mrs. Tirzah Honanie; Alma Hunt; Mrs. Leila Jennings; Fred and Mike Kabotie, Hopi Arts and Crafts Guild; David Kimball; Joseph I. Knapp, Montezuma Castle National Monument; Charles J. Merchant; Leonard Monti, Casa Vieja Restaurant; Mrs. Yndia Smalley Moore; E. E. Newcomer, *The Arizona Republic;* Jim Parker, Heard Museum; Mrs. Luisa Rojas; Carlos E. Ronstadt; Mr. and Mrs. Sam Swisher; Mrs. Rosemary Taylor; Ken Windsor, Pinnacle Peak Patio Restaurant; *in California:* Izadore Barrett, National Marine Fisheries Service; Jackson Beatty; Don R. Birrell, The Nut Tree; Clifford Brignall; Mr. and Mrs. Philip Brown; Lee Burtis, California Historical Society; Frieda Caplan; Thomas E. Cara; Mrs. Earl Carpenter; Mr. and Mrs. David Casey; Ward Cheadel, Sunset Growers; Charles Clegg; Harold Clemens, California Department of Fish and Game; Miss Jean Cox, California Museum of Science and Industry; James Ducote; William Duflock, El Centro Chamber of Commerce; Pierre Dupart, Marrakesh Restaurant; Joyce Goldstein; Roger Green, National Marine Fisheries Service; Edward Greenhood, California Department of Fish and Game; Mr. and Mrs. Joseph Heitz; Sybil Henderson; Dr. C. O. Hesse, University of California at Davis; Leslie Hubbard, Council of California Growers; Robert Ilse,

Consolidated Olive Growers; Judd S. Ingram; Ron Klamm, California Fig Institute; George Kraus; Al Kuehl, Calavo; Marilyn Kiser and Hood Littlefield, California Honey Advisory Board; Oswaldo Llorens, Señor Pico's restaurant; Mr. and Mrs. Eanna J. MacGeraghty; Mr. and Mrs. Frederick H. Macrae; Morley Mason, La Purísima Concepción Mission; Mrs. Alice Mohs; Mr. and Mrs. Neil Morgan; Mr. and Mrs. Edward J. Muzzy; Simon Nathenson, California Department of Agriculture; Mr. and Mrs. Fred Nolan; Daniel O'Brien; John Olguin, Cabrillo Beach Museum; Leo Pearlstein; Mr. and Mrs. Edmund Pilz; Miss Doris Robinson, National Marine Fisheries Service; Mr. and Mrs. Sol Rosner; Mr. and Mrs. Phillips Ruffalo; Shirley Sarvis; Chuck Sites, Sites' Abalone and Shell Shop; Robert L. Smith, U.S. Department of Agriculture; Mrs. Alice Stalk; Ward Stanger, University of California at Davis; Nick S. Trani; Mrs. Sylvia Vaughn Thompson; Pierce Thompson; John Barr Tompkins, The Bancroft Library; Lillian L. Vlymen, National Marine Fisheries Service; Jeanne Voltz, Los Angeles Times; Ernest Weil, Fantasia; Wine Institute; Woo Chee Chong; Hillman Yowell, California Date Growers' Association; in Colorado: Sam Arnold, The Fort restaurant; Mrs. Dana Crawford; Jim Davis; Donna Hamilton; Mrs. Marian Miller; Ken Monfort, Monfort of Colorado; Mrs. Beverly Nemiro; Miss Marion Palmer; Gail Pitts; Floyd E. Rolf, Colorado Crop and Livestock Reporting Service; Mrs. Katherine Schoenberger, C Lazy U Ranch; Mrs. Dorothy Schomburg; Koji Wada; Mr. and Mrs. Bill Wilson; The Wine Press Ltd.; H. H. Zietz Jr., Buckhorn Pioneer Lodge; in Connecticut: Mr. and Mrs. Anthony Anable; in Nevada: Gerry Appleby; Dick and Helen Chappell; Ray Chesson; Ruth Curtis; John and Grace Juansaras; Donald Keating; Sheriff Ralph Lamb; in New Mexico: Mrs. Santana Antonio; Mr. and Mrs. Anthony Bryan; Mrs. Pauline P. Cable; Mrs. Ann Clark; Lucy Delgado; Arturo Jaramillo, Rancho de Chimayó; Jean Mayer, St. Bernard Hotel; Senator and Mrs. Joseph M. Montoya; Mrs. Joann C. Murphy; Nambé Ware Inc.; Ortega's Weaving Shop; José Sanchez, Jack Sitton, The New Mexican; John Stebbins; in New York: Dr. Paul Buck, Cornell University; Dr. Robert L. Carneiro, Museum of Natural History; Dr. Frederick Dockstader, Museum of the American Indian Heye Foundation; Mr. and Mrs. Joe Flaherty; Jean O'Connor Fuller; Earl Huntington; Elizabeth Ortiz; Larry Pardue, New York Botanical Garden; in Oklahoma: Jack Haley, University of Oklahoma; in Texas: Joe Arcidiacono; Harley H. Berg; Mrs. Robert Blount; Sam Campanello; Fidel G. Chamberlain Jr.; Helen Corbitt; Orman Farley, U.S. Department of Commerce; Mrs. Wanda Ford; Wick Fowler; S. L. Gonzales; Mrs. Ilo Hiller, Texas Game and Fish; The Houston Club; Mrs. Mary Faulk Koock; William Kuykendall; Terrence Leary, Texas Game and Fish; Mrs. B. Lee Lipshutz; Oscar Longnecker, Texas Shrimp Association; John Mahos, Liberty Fish and Oyster Co.; W. W. McAllister, Mayor of San Antonio; Holland McCombs; Mrs. W. D. McNeel; Leonard McNeill, Lenox Barbecue and Catering Co.; Mrs. V. H. McNutt; Allan Marburger, Texas Crop Reporting Board; Matt Martinez; Guy Matherne, Gulf King Shrimp Co.; Walter Mathis; Mrs. Alfred Walter Negley; Mr. and Mrs. Frank Oltorf; Mr. and Mrs. Jack Owen; Mrs. E. C. Parker; Miss Andrew Peyton; Miss Sallie Peyton; Mr. and Mrs. Carson Pryor; Felix Real; Mrs. Ben H. Rice Jr.; Mrs. Jayne Robinson; William Schaaf; Mr. and Mrs. D. J. Sibley; Mrs. Roberta Smith; Mrs. Rodolf Smith; Roger Stallings, Institute of Texas Culture; Mrs. Marshall Steves; The Gallagher Ranch; The Greenhouse; Mrs. Lewis Tucker; Trigg Twichell; Mrs. A. L. Williams Jr.; Mrs. Ruth Wolfe; Gus Wortham, Nine-Bar Ranch;

Mrs. Agnes Young; in Utah: Kate B. Carter; Jean Dunn; Ray Huntington; Winifred Jardine; Mrs. Donna Lou Morgan; Helen Thackery.

The following shops and firms supplied antiques, tableware and other objects used in the studio photography in this book: in New Jersey: The Millstone Shop Antiques; in New York City: Arras Gallery Ltd.; Caronia and Corless Flowers Inc.; Country Floors Inc.; Decorative Resale Inc.; Fortunoff; Fred Leighton Imports Ltd.; Gilbert Pelham; Hammacher Schlemmer; Mary Page Antiques; Norsk, Inc.; Obelisk; Paulette's Place; Pearl Design Center; Raphaelian Rug Co.; Rees and Orr Inc.; Tablerie; The American Indian Arts Center; The Phoenix; The Pottery Barn; Trident Antiques; U.S. Plywood; Walker Mineral Co.; screen by Russ Elliott courtesy Isobel Worsley Inc.

Sources consulted in the production of this book include: Come 'N Get It, Ramon Adams; Wine, An Introduction for Americans, M. A. Amerine and V. L. Singleton; Fryingpans West, and Food and Drink of the Early West, Sam Arnold; The Standard Cyclopedia of Horticulture, L. H. Bailey; Western Expansion, Ray Allen Billington; Helen Brown's West Coast Cook Book; How to Fish the Pacific Coast, Ray Cannon; Story of the American Nation, Mabel B. Casner and Ralph H. Gabriel; Modern Fruit Science, Norman F. Childers; American Guide Series: Arizona, California, Colorado, Nevada, New Mexico, Oklahoma, San Francisco, Texas, Utah, Federal Writers' Project; Golden Tapestry of California, Sydney Clark; "The Authentic Haraszthy Story," Wines and Vines, Paul Fredericksen; The Life and Times of Junipero Serra, Maynard Geiger, O.F.M.; "Olives," Gourmet; Economic Botany, Albert F. Hill; The Southwest, Old and New, W. Eugene Hollon; Great River, The Rio Grande in American History, Paul Horgan; Montezuma Castle Archeology, Earl Jackson and Sallie Pierce Van Valkenburgh; The American Heritage Book of Indians, ed. Alvin M. Josephy Jr.; Indian Heritage of North America, Alvin M. Josephy Jr., Metates and Manos, Museum of New Mexico Press; The Texas Cook Book, Mary Faulk Koock; "Early California Wine Growers," "The Oldest Names in California Winegrowing," and "Vallejo, Pioneer Sonoma Wine Grower," California-Magazine of the Pacific, Irving McKee; McLane's Standard Fishing Encyclopedia; "The Purse Seine Revolution in Tuna Fishing," Richard L. McNeely; A Guide to California Wines, John Melville; The Romance of North America, ed. Hardwick Moseley; Tour of San Francisco, Doris Muscantine; The World in Your Garden, National Geographic Society; The Complete Book of Mexican Cooking, Elizabeth Ortiz; Pacific Fisherman's Canned Fish Hand-i-Book, Edition III; Everyman's Eden, Ralph Roske; Crab and Abalone: West Coast Ways with Fish and Shellfish, Shirley Sarvis; Encyclopedia of Wine, Frank Schoonmaker; "A Potential New Crop for California," Robert L. Smith; California Ocean Fisheries Resources to 1960, State of California Department of Fish and Game; From Scotland to Silverado, Robert Louis Stevenson; Beachcombers' Guide, Mexican Cookbook, Seafood Cookbook, The California Missions, California Wine Country, Sunset Books; The Shrimp Fishery in Texas, 1970, Texas Parks and Wildlife Department; A Bowl of Red, F. X. Tolbert; "The Story of California Figs," John G. Tyler; Pueblo Crafts, Ruth Underhill; American Wines and Wine-Making, Philip M. Wagner; "A Guide to the Grunion," Boyd W. Walker; Book of the Hopi, Frank Waters; Ethnobotany of the Hopi, Alfred F. Whiting; The Course of Empire, Bernard De Voto; "Kiwi, the Ugly Visitor from Down Under," Western Fruit Grower.